A SILVER TAPESTRY

THE BEST OF 25 YEARS OF CRITICAL WRITING FROM THE BRITISH HAIKU SOCIETY

Edited by Graham High

Published 2015 by The British Haiku Society
2, Clifton Lawns, Ramsgate,
Kent CT11 9PB
www.britishhaikusociety.org.uk
www.anotherkindofpoetry.org.uk

BRITISH HAIKU SOCIETY

ISBN 978-1-906333-03-4

Edited by Graham High

Design, lay-out and typesetting by Graham High with Jim Kacian
(Jim Kacian courtesy of *Red Moon Press)*
Cover design by Graham High

Printed by Bookpress.eu

ACKNOWLEDGEMENTS

The BHS wishes to express its gratitude to The Sakaguchi Literary Studies fund which has provided a dedicated fund in financial support of the BHS in the production of special publications.

In addition, special thanks must go to Akiko Sakaguchi herself for her personal donation in respect of this particular publication.

The Society wishes to thank the selectors, Jon Baldwin and Margery Newlove, for taking on the difficult task of selection. This was a labour of love which required the reading and re-reading of every single essay, feature, and article which has appeared in 100 issues of *Blithe Spirit.*

Thanks also are due to all the past editors of *Blithe Spirit* which, during the 25 years of the Journal's life so far, has provided the source for this selection. Without the editors' skill and encouragement and the high standing in which the Journal is held, some of these essays may have turned elsewhere for first publication.

Finally the BHS wishes to thank the authors themselves. The republication of a chosen selection of features and essays in celebration of the Society's 25th anniversary is a consolidation of all the passion, scholarship and originality of the members that has been the enduring character of the Society since 1990.

FOREWORD FROM THE SELECTORS

There are pure and acute moments of life in which no poetic form or composition is superior to that of haiku. Therefore it was an honour to be invited to make a selection of critical writings from *Blithe Spirit* on this twenty-fifth anniversary. Such a considerable array of rich material ensured that choices and decision were difficult. The reading, selection, discussion and finalisation were conducted over a period of eighteen months. Selectors were provided with a full collection of the journal. There are four issues per year and approximately three or four articles in each issue. A rough estimate would suggest that selectors considered three to four hundred pieces. It is fair to say that the exegetical, critical and creative activity in the journal over the decades has helped shape, inform, prompt, challenge and broaden the view of the community of the British Haiku Society and had wider appeal.

It was agreed early on in the process that we should not consider articles that had been published elsewhere prior to *Blithe Spirit*. We further decided that we would not consider the smaller sections - no less valuable to the journal - such as the editorial, correspondence, book reviews, 'favourite haiku', award discussions, or reports from group meetings. Initially, we found that some authors' work had been proposed for inclusion by more than one essay so for reasons of variety, balance and equality we felt it beneficial to select only one essay per contributor. Whilst haiku is the dominant focus of the journal there are also quality discussions of associated forms such as tanka, renga, haibun, and haiga. We felt that having an eye on including contributions on these matters would allow the anthology to reflect the interests of the journal and the society as a whole.

With these qualifications in mind, the criterion for selection was quality and the best that the journal offered. After due consideration and reflection each selector produced a substantial long-list of articles. There was a certain overlap and unanimous agreement on a number of the articles now in your hands. Long-lists were then whittled down by considering how best to represent the journal's diverse concerns. As the reader will notice, essays can happily range from discussion of Nobel Prize winning haiku poets to teaching haiku to children; from metaphysical meditations on the 'haiku moment' to the role of the internet; from mindfulness, simplicity, and healing to wordplay, puns, and sport; from metaphor, form, and intertextuality to Shinto and Zen; from Beat poets, glances abroad, and historical accounts to individual reflections upon process, ideas, and trends. The final selection, then, was constructed with the aim of reflecting the wide scope of the journal.

As a physical object, it was remarkable to see the growth of the journal over the years from a relatively slim volume to the contemporary thickness of eighty pages, and with various changes in paper-stock, layout, typesetting, design, tactile sensation, and binding. Visually, the move in cover art was quite striking: from early simple, monochromatic, copyright-free, generic 'clip-art' to the members' art that creatively adorns the cover in more recent times.

In terms of critical approach and appreciation, it was fascinating to see continuity and change, fashions and trends, ebb and flow. One can find courteous contestation, occasional throat-clearing, definitions clarified, points raised and rebutted, avenues explored, and certain debates considered closed - often only to blossom open years later with ever new beginnings. Upon reflection, the practice of selection often felt like a form of floristry – a blend between an English Garden and Ikebana arrangement. Perhaps with poetic contemplation and life in mind, the great Matsuo Bashō wrote, "To talk casually about an iris flower is one of the pleasures of the wandering journey." May these selections be further pleasures on your journey.

Jon Baldwin and Margery Newlove

INTRODUCTION

This is the Silver Anniversary of the British Haiku Society. The twenty five years of its existence have seen a great many changes both to the Society itself and to the way that haiku, and related Japanese literary forms, have impressed themselves on the consciousness of the world at large. The BHS has, from its inception, published a quarterly journal, *Blithe Spirit,* now up to issue 100. The content of *Blithe Spirit* was wide reaching from the outset and has, over the years, managed the almost impossible task of meeting a variety of demands. It has consistently steered a course between two main duties. On the one hand it has represented the work and aspirations of new members, fresh to the experience of haiku, without succumbing to any suggestion of common denominator 'dumbing down'. On the other hand it has attracted scholarly articles from all around the world whilst avoiding the whiff of academic elitism or over-specialisation. In doing so it has acquired the status of a respected journal whilst never losing touch with its grass roots, the subscribers that form the membership of the Society.

Back in 1990 the two founding instigators of the (pre-society) 'haiku interest group', Dee Evetts and David Cobb, sent out a call to see if there were many others interested in haiku. To their surprise there were quite a few. These were people who may have come to haiku from a variety of starting positions. Some valued haiku as an accessible and unusual form of poetic expression; others adopted haiku as an awareness-based writing practice as part of a search for spiritual discipline; others were searching for a brief and concrete way to express the immediate impressions of the senses - what it feels like to be alive and existentially aware. For some others haiku had value as a focused way of intensifying their appreciation of the natural world. And others again wished to increase their knowledge of a Japanese culture that was already important to them in their life's experience.

Twenty five years on the membership of the BHS has changed but this variety of starting points remains. This diversity of interest is a testament to the cultural complexity embedded in the provenance and history of haiku, both in Japan and in its manifestations in places where it has been adopted – which is almost world-wide. The search to increase our understanding of haiku's past, and of its present and future possibilities goes on.

The essays and studies that comprise this anthology reflect the talent, enthusiasm and committed study and enquiry that the writers have dedicated to their subject. The variety and depth of the resulting articles yield insights and original ideas that together advance the interest in, and understanding of, the writing of haiku as well as other forms of Japanese inspired writing practices. Twenty five years is a long time and, sadly, a small number of the contributing writers have died during that time. A fact which gives added poignancy to this publication as a historical document as well as a perenially relevant collection of essays.

The 50 essays chosen, (averaging two for every year of the BHS) were taken from the large list of published material – features, critical essays, papers on technique or on the history of haiku; articles concerned with haibun, tanka, renku, - a vast body of accumulated wisdoms and experience from a range of British Haiku Society members both past and present. These include some voices already well known and others new to committing their ideas to print; some writers who are international in perspective: others very intimate and particular. All are highly engaging and illuminating. I hope this book reaches a wide readership and will take its place as a vital witness to the development and concerns surrounding English language haiku over the last 25 years.

Graham High
Editor, president of the British Haiku Society

CONTENTS

A SILVER TAPESTRY

David Cobb

Between Moments

Some of us have a feeling that the purest "haiku moments" are the ones that just occur, unprovoked. The signal is picked up in a flash by one or more of our senses and relayed to some mysteriously deep part of our brain (some will call it 'intuition', some 'inspiration', others 'intellect'), and then expressed instantly in a statement which has the succinct brevity and maybe even the exact form of haiku.

We are fortunate if "moments" of this peerless quality come to us, as almost involuntary receivers, very often. Between such moments it is only human, and to my mind no error, to feel "in the mood for haiku", and to wish to stimulate one's receptivity. "Ask, and ye shall find". But how does one "ask"?
I was once on a writing course and one afternoon our tutor told us to take a long walk, meanwhile "surrendering" ourselves, i.e. tuning in our consciousness, to our surroundings. Each of us drew from a hat a different phrase which would help us to focus our non-thoughts. Mine was "the space between".

In half-an-hour I was able to scribble down about a dozen haiku or proto-haiku, of which two (more or less as I wrote them down originally) have survived the "test of time", i.e. I'm still glad to have been the medium by which they came into the world.

These two are:

between the cow's legs
grazing the hill crest
snips of blue sky

stepping stones:
in the middle of next stride
a wasp at rest

Though I have been brought up to try to please teachers, I didn't allow myself to include any of my previously-written "between" haiku, though I recollected several, e.g.

between shrew and cat
set to time the moment
a dandelion clock

a moment between
lighthouse flashes
cold smell of fish

But later, a quick check through my "extant works" revealed how many contained this, or some other preposition, usually as a key word in the whole. (23 of the 140 haiku in my book "A Leap in the Light" have "strong" prepositions, i.e. prepositions which have a real sense of movement or position: above 2, against 2, below 1, beneath 1, beside 1, between 5, outside 2, over 1, past 1, round 2, through 2, under 2, within 1. I exclude from the count the prepositions in, on, at, to, from, with, which generally have a much weaker effect. I notice the conjunction of time, before, is also prominent.)

Prepositions seem therefore to be at the heart of haiku creativity. Perhaps I may recommend them to you as a focussing device.

Brian Tasker

Haiku as a Homecoming

English language haiku developed in America. Maybe it was easier for them; without the rigid Victorian values and the flowery Victorian poetry that we still seem to find traces of, they do have a looser way with words. But it's not true to think that Americans have a harder eye; or an edge on reality that we lack. Rock music began in the U S; we imported it, created our own version and have been exporting it back to them ever since. These two forms of rock music merge without losing their separate identities.

We owe a debt of gratitude; firstly, of course, to the Japanese, but also to the American poets who have developed the form of haiku in English. Yet nobody owns the franchise on haiku, its province is in the vastness and the microcosm of the present moment. If we have decided that we do want to write haiku; then we should try and get our heads around the concept. We need to put aside our reluctance to speak foreign languages and write some poetry in a foreign way, but with a 'British' accent.

In haiku we are not just writing about something, in the way of telling somebody that the raindrops are like diamonds. We need to find our depth in the concrete fact that raindrops are just raindrops. In haiku we enter into something and for that moment we merge with it. To then describe it by comparing it with something else is not being honest to the experience.

It has been said that all words are metaphors. In a subjective sense they are; they can spark all kinds of associations and implied, if not stated, meanings. For example:

> at the doorway
> pausing for a moment;
> the autumn rain

Autumn rain is a statement of fact: it also becomes a metaphor or a symbol.

Autumn rain brings with it the passing of summer and the turning year, the onset of colder weather, a confrontation with our own mortality, the dying down of nature and the unrelenting cycle of change. All these things we can perceive in a moment, whether knowingly or not. In haiku we tell it like it is: as plainly as we can…

In haiku, we need to call a spade a spade; if we call it by any other name the spade will lose its meaning. To be 'in haiku' is to be in momentary connection with things just as they are, it is to be on the edge of unfolding.

R H Blyth described haiku as a temporary enlightenment. The moment of haiku becomes the agent of enlightenment: the moment not the poem. The poem is a valid expression of nostalgia for that which we cannot grasp. The creative energy that informs haiku doesn't have quite the same desperate need for fulfilment as other forms of creative writing.

It's still a good idea to carry a notebook and jot down strands of experience. It is possible to reconstruct haiku from strands of experience; but they never feel quite as rounded out as haiku gathered from the instant. Quite often, we are unable to frame the moment in the right way to create a worthwhile poem. When, in fact, just to be a silent witness can be enough, to pay attention and observe: to let a duck skim the surface of the lake without trying to contain it within the ego's grasping, is just to let it go. To imprison the duck in a bad poem is not being kind to the duck. The action of the duck is poetry in itself and fulfils itself.

This can teach us not to cling: to both the 'deliciousness' of the moment and the urge to record it. To be freed of writing is to be free to write. The very best haiku have an organic nature that can't be contrived or made up. They manifest themselves out of emptiness or 'unpreparedness'. It's not that everything happens at the right time: but that we are available as a witness without any investment in distorting the facts.

Haiku arise out of a true spontaneity. In that sense; haiku move beyond the usual parameters of poetry to a space just beyond. To be in haiku is to be dispossessed: of the past and of the future and all that we project onto the present with our minds, yet at the same time to connect with ourselves. Before we can approach selflessness, we must approach self. A kind of circular understanding is needed It is forgetfulness of ourselves and a momentary freedom from ourselves, it is just to come home. As Zen would have it: to abide in non-abiding.

Haiku have the sadness of truth within them - the momentary realisation that all our striving has come to nothing, and yet, despite that, we have arrived anyway.

Will Morris

The Importance of the Moment

Jack Kornfield in *Seeking the Heart of Wisdom* writes: "We begin to see that our whole being and our entire physical and mental universe is made up of moments... It is only by being fully in the moment that the fundamental questions of the heart can be answered; it is only in the timeless moment that we can come to that intuitive silent knowing of the truth..."

There is in fact only the present moment, but the trap is that we think of this as being part of the continuum from past to future, whereas it is a unique totality. Everything happens now, nothing happens outside it. The past has already happened, the future hasn't yet emerged - that is why Kornfield refers to it as timeless. Being a Buddhist he has no difficulty in seeing moments as discrete entities like the stills which make up a moving film, each one of which can be retained and reviewed in its dynamic entirety.

We are so dominated by clock time, Newton's measured time, that we are unaware that we experience time differently and yet every day we grumble about the elasticity of time. How slowly it goes when we are clockwatching, how quickly when we are busy, how dramatically things happen in slow motion when we are involved in a life threatening situation. "'We then see that 'existence' time is always entire time. Existing things, existing phenomena are all times; all existence and the entire world are embraced within the time of every single moment." (Dogen in *Impermanence is Buddha-nature* by Joan Stambaugh)

This is the moment that is touched with haiku; it is the sudden awareness that everyday seemingly unimportant happenings are IT in all its fullness, utterly complete.

We usually think of ourselves as an object, separate from other objects, whereas Heidegger, a Western Existentialist philosopher, pointed out that humans are not subjects, spectators, observers, separated by a glass window from the world of objects, but are part and parcel of it all, in amongst it all. He saw the world as already 'articulated' with everything already laid out and humans functioning or 'discoursing' within this context, what is referred to by modern Zen practitioners as 'going with the flow'.

This sudden realisation that in seeing one thing you see it all, that the part can contain the whole, can be demonstrated now by the hologram from which the whole can be reproduced from any fragment. William Blake saw this clearly when he wrote:

> To see the world in a Grain of Sand
> And Heaven in a Wild Flower,
> Hold Infinity in the palm of your hand
> And Eternity for an Hour.

William J Higginson

A Sense of the Language

Perhaps because of the difficulties of translating, especially from Japanese to European languages, certain habits have crept into English-language haiku. Those who try to adhere to a syllable-count form usually pad their work with words that add no meaning ('the cold winter wind', for example). However, the impression that seventeen syllables in English equals seventeen of the 'sounds' *(on, onji,* or *bunji)* that Japanese poets count has faded considerably from being an exotic fad among American school teachers who know nothing about either the Japanese language or English poetry (or American) in the 1950s.

But as a shorter haiku in English has gained ground, the opposite extreme brings with it 'telegraphese' that hardly resembles normal speech or writing. Such a phrase as 'sit on warm bench' would grate on the ear much less with a strategically placed 'the'. Absence of necessary articles makes awfully large number of haiku claiming to be "in English" seem to have been written by beginning student of English with no access to native speakers. Note that only three were omitted from that last sentence of thirty-one words, but their minute absence gives it a very strange ring.

Translating brings up another problem that seems endemic in our haiku today. The desire to pack as much as possible into the fewest words tends to result in dangling particles, mainly the '-ing' kind. Sometimes this results from a desire to omit a person - especially the writer - from the poem. In the Japanese language such words as I/me /my rarely occur, so translators have often resorted to leaving them out of the English translations of haiku and using just the '-ing' form of the verb, creating dangling particles in the process.

Most English words ending in the '-ing' are either nouns or partial verbs, called 'present participles'. Such nouns seem relatively rare in haiku, as they usually suggest an abstract level of thinking. The last word of that sentence is a good example of the '-ing' form as noun; grammarians call it a 'gerund'. When a gerund does show up in a haiku, it had better have an article in front to prevent it from being understood as a verb:

evening fog ...
whispering of mothers
quiets the children

Can't you just hear the fog going around whispering about mothers? Simply putting 'the' before 'whispering' would eliminate the problem. (See what telegraphese does to haiku"). A present participle can get a haiku into trouble. The worst are participles without grammatical subjects (and therefore 'Jangling'). Since participles can appear before - and change the meaning of - nouns, one lacking a subject normally refers to what follows. A penchant for omitting subjects often yields ludicrous results, of which the modest author may be quite unaware:

choking, coughing,
the moon shining over
the quiet lake

Heard the moon cough lately? Much better to give the action to a third person, and put the verbs in the plain present tense:

he chokes and coughs...
the moon shines over
the quiet lake

In many haiku participles show up without the 'helping verb' needed to make a complete sentence. This does not usually result in great confusion, but can create an awkwardness that gets in the way of taking in the meaning on first reading. How much better to simply use the present-tense verb. Then ambiguities, unconscious or intended, become clearer to the writer, and might lead to further improvement. Compare:

the dusty corral
a breeze wafting gently
the hum of bees

the dusty corral
a breeze wafts gently
the hum of bees

Ah, now I see that 'the hum of bees' can - and perhaps should - be the object of 'wafts'. Also, 'breeze' and 'wafts' and 'gently' all contain the idea of 'gentle', a redundancy to be avoided in haiku. How about:

the dusty corral—
on a midday breeze comes
the hum of a bee

Note also that in this instance removing the redundancy allows the addition of more visual information, and making it one bee eliminates the thumping rhyme while bringing the experience a little closer to the reader.

There will, of course, be times when one wants the sense of continuing action which only the present participle can provide. Some poems will sound better without adding the auxiliary verb that would make a complete sentence. But generally it is better to avoid using the present participle in haiku, especially without a clear grammatical subject. Whatever else a haiku in English might do, it will find a more appreciative audience if it indeed sounds like English. 'Poetic licence' need not extend to redundancy, padding, telegraphese or dangling participles.

James W Hackett

Haiku and Spiritual Penetration

Early in our correspondence I posed the following question to my mentor R.H.Blyth:

There in this world of NOW
That I worship with wonder
Is the ANCIENT ALONENESS
Of my only moment
Undreamed?

Though Blyth never offered a direct answer, in time I resolved this spiritual question through further study and Zen meditation. Key to this understanding was *interpenetration,* a Zen principle that Blyth subsequently emphasised in his foreword to my first book of haiku poetry. I came to realize that interpenetration exemplifies the spiritual Oneness that is not only at the heart of Zen, but is the mystical basis of every major religion. As it turned out, Blyth did indeed finally answer my question, albeit elliptically. He knew I had to grow into the understanding that the interpenetration he discerned in my haiku was an intuitive, existential realization of the Zen dictum: 'Samsara is Nirvana - Nirvana is Samsara'. This is how I finally became conscious of the Oneness that can profoundly influence poetry and life.

All true haiku correctly reflect the *concrete,* categorical world of myriad separate things, that is, Samsara. But through an intuitive interpenetration of poet and subject some haiku can also, quite mysteriously, intimate Samsara's metaphysical counterpart Nirvana: the ultimate spiritual identity we all share. However, in haiku poetry the concrete Suchness of the thing-in-itself must prevail, or the haiku ceases to be worthy of the name. The point is that haiku demand not only a centred consciousness, but an all-compassionate heart as well. To spiritually interpenetrate - to become one with things - to find our self in union with all things - is to live the Way of Zen. And in so far as this spirit is manifest in syllables, it can become a way of haiku.

Spiritual interpenetration is an ontological state in which a transcendent sense of identity is intuited between what we usually think of as ourselves and other things. In haiku this interpenetration results when a compassionate and intuitive identification (most often unconsciously realized) exists between the poet and the subject of the moment.

Left by the tide
  within a shall owing pool:
    a frantic minnow.

A bitter morning:
  sparrows sitting together
    without any necks.

Interpenetration in haiku is however a formidable quality, as Blyth recognises: 'To attain this ability to express the immediate sensation, to pour all of oneself into the thing, and let the thing penetrate every part of one's self, needs much travail of mind and body.' (Blyth in Hackett) And, being a state of spirit, interpenetration is essentially transcendental and difficult to impart through words. However, Blyth's following descriptions of Zen apply as well to interpenetration, and show the mystical essence they share:

In Zen, the soul must 'become the thing it contemplates' ... it means that state ... in which we are not separated from other things, are indeed identical with them, and yet retain our own individuality and personal peculiarities ... The aim of Zen, the aim of the poetical life, is to reach and remain in that undifferentiated state where subject and object are one... (Blyth)

Now centred upon
  the flavor of an old bone
    the mind of my dog.

In her book *The Haiku Form*, Joan Giroux states that spiritual identification in haiku is not merely "cute anthropomorphism" but is ' ... an instant in which man becomes united to an object, virtually becomes the object, and realizes the eternal, universal truth contained in being ...' (Giroux)

Each kelp in the tide
comes at last to rest, beside
its anchor of rock.

When an intuited sense of identity takes place between poet and subject, it is an important part of the haiku moment, and should be manifest in the finished haiku poem. But again, I stress that such interpenetration, when it does occur, is often achieved unconsciously. In any case, the sense of, compassionate empathy *intuitively* felt by the poet must be a true feeling from our heart of hearts. Spiritual interpenetration must *not* be mistaken for anthropomorphism; such an attribution of strictly human characteristics to things is merely egocentric. Genuine examples of interpenetration between poet and subject testify to nothing less than a spiritual union. That interpenetration was a cardinal principle to Basho is borne out by his advocacy of 'entering into the object, perceiving its delicate life, and feeling its feelings, whereupon a poem speaks for itself.' (BHS Consensus) And again, from Basho: ' ... you must leave your subjective preoccupation with yourself. Your poetry issues of its own accord when you and the object have become one ... However well-phrased your poetry may be, if the object and yourself are separate - then your poetry is not true poetry but a semblance of the real thing.' (Yuasa)

Now free in the world
the old parakeet just perches:
his loneliness!

The scriptural basis for discerning Oneness in some haiku is found in the 'perennial philosophy' of various religions:

This entire Earth - is it not myself? ... a great loving heart transforms this earthly world into one of splendor and mutual fusion, and this is where the Buddha is always abiding. (D.T.Suzuki)

He is One, the lord and innermost Self of all; of one form, he makes of himself many forms... He became all things whatsoever...

(Prabhavananda/Upanishads)

D. T. Suzuki suggests that interpenetration can intimate something cosmic, quite beyond the spiritual union between the poet and things '... an infinite fusion or penetration of all things, each with its individuality yet with something universal in it.' (Suzuki)

Chopping kindling from
 a knotty block...in each stick
  a part of its shape

A spider crouches
 at the centre of this empty web,
  trusting his design.

Spiritual interpenetration with all things is not confined to the sages of Eastern philosophy, as the medieval Christian theologian Meister Eckhart makes clear: ' ... God is in all things ... Every single creature is full of God ... all creatures are interdependent ... We must learn to break through things (through interpenetration) if we are to grasp God in them.' (Fox/Eckhart)

Look at this fly
 that long since met eternity,
  his kneeling remains.

The mystical scriptures of India provide vivid examples of how spiritual interpenetration has influenced the culture of Asia. There, the 'all-compassionate heart' is commonly to be seen to embrace not only humans, but animals, insects and the whole ecological kingdom of life. For, as revealed in the Upanishads: 'The lord is the one life shining forth from every creature ... Whatever... creatures are, whether a lion or a tiger, or a boar, or a worm or a gnat, or a mosquito ... All these have their self in him alone. He is the truth ... THAT ART THOU.' (Prabhavananda/Upanishads)

Hardy ant, even
 heavily burdened you climb
  the sheer mountain wall.

Spiritual interpenetration is repeated throughout the Upanishads, whose very song - the spiritual Oneness of all things - is 'That Art Thou'. So brief a statement, yet how very profound it is. For encapsulated here is a spiritual vision of cosmic proportions: a sacred Ghandian view of *Oneness* that is all too rare in this world - namely that the true disciple knows another's woes as his own. The same view of Oneness and compassion is echoed by the Christian mystic, Meister Eckhart: 'What happens to another, be it bad or good, pain or joy, ought to be as if it happened to you ... To find God you must become One ...' (Fox/Eckhart). A transcendental sense of identity clearly recognised by Blyth: '... the Indian (and the Ancient Taoist) view of the world is mutually interpenetrative, each thing containing all things, all things concentrating itself into each thing.' (Blyth) And from Lao Tsu himself: 'Be at one with the dust of the earth. This is primal union. This is the highest state of man.' (Lao Tsu)

Gusts of ocean wind
wander this deserted beach
drifting all...to one.

Miraculously, some haiku poems can be seen as veritable mirrors of the universal Spirit, in which the 'King of Emptiness' recognises its Self in all things. For, as Zen masters well know, '... the Buddha-eye is everywhere, seeing itself.' (Blyth) And Nyogen Senzaki notes that: 'It is the inherent nature of the Buddha-body that it individualizes itself in myriad manifestations in the phenomenal world. It does not stand outside particular existences, but abides in them, animates them, and makes them move freely ... Its essence is infinite, but its manifestations are finite and limited.' (Senzaki)

Bug lights on the leaf,
takes a wild ride through the rapids,
then flies away.

In summary, spiritual interpenetration creates the sense of Oneness extolled in the 'perennial philosophy' by the mystics of every religion. Although a profound quality in haiku and one well known to Bashō as we have seen, such identification is all too commonly overlooked by poets and commentators alike. Interpenetration in haiku exemplifies the Vedantic theme of That Art Thou. Such a union between poet and subject is ultimately nothing less than an intuitive recognition of the One within All that abides in becoming. Incredible as it may seem, the *haiku moment* then becomes a mirror of the universal Spirit: the illusory veil of multiplicity (or Maya) is seen through and our *true* identity recognizes it's cosmic Self in all things, every moment.

I submit that the living and writing of haiku can become, for some, a spiritual Way, a Way of living awareness, as well as a Way of poetry. A Way that leads to a reverence for life, and when combined with mind-centring meditation, to, possibly, even a realization of the infinite Spirit _ the Ancient One whom we all *really* are. For, as mystics know from experience: 'This Ancient One is unborn, eternal, imperishable ... ' and 'THAT ART THOU.' (Prabhavananda/Upanishads)

his blessed present
Wherever I look I see
nothing - but the Lord. (Buddha)

(All haiku in this essay are by the author)

Susan Rowley

A Personal and Partial Account of Life with Haiku

A cursory glance back through the pages of possible haiku, proto-haiku, hardlia-haiku, halfa-haiku, neverahopeofa-haiku and all the other members of the family of scribblings assembled in what I hopefully dub Haiku '92, Haiku '93 etc just goes to show that

> haiku
> is evolutionary:
> time tells

(That, by the way, is an apology for what I call a Meta-haiku. Metalanguage is the form we use to talk about language itself so ... I find they creep in sometimes when I'm playing with improving on a previous idea.)

My own stabs at haiku until two years ago were trying to teach it in a primary classroom or three from a particularly uninformative paragraph in a 1952 English textbook. I knew, of course, that it had to have the hallowed 5-7-5 form but, apart from that, it seemed, anything went:

> stuck, my poem stops;
> I hold up my begging bowl
> A word falls in – plop

(The children, bless them, wrote some lovely poems in spite of me.)
Once with a friend I remember standing on a tube station platform producing, at our better moments, what were probably closer to the hardlia-senryu form. Then came **Blithe Spirit** and the **BHS**. Aha! Counting endlessly on my fingers, beating out that rhythm anywhere and everywhere I launched into a new era of glazed and faraway 'moments'.

> Andirons takes three.
> Poke the fire and watch the sparks
> hoping for a star.

This was followed by hours of compiling all my efforts from scrappy bits of paper, backs of envelopes (where, as we all know, all truly great poetry is scrawled - other than on beermats and menus, that is) and my hopefully named 'haiku notebooks'. These were a series of spiral-bound shorthand books, inevitably also home to the odd recipe, sketch for a new craft idea, half-written letters and shopping lists. I could get side-tracked for hours reworking haiku when I was really looking for the kitchen window measurements.

pen poised
waiting for inspiration;
the kettle boils

I confess I do something which part of me frowns upon: I type all my efforts on to computer disc. So unnatural, but so easy to rewrite, reorder, try out. I'd really love to have each one hand-inscribed on hand-made paper but I simply don't have the time. I'd rather use any seconds I can grab to myself at the chalk face, hacking away at another nugget. (YOU may not find nuggets in chalk - I keep hoping!) Of course the hi-tech approach can have its drawbacks:

forgotten haiku
gone to computer heaven;
libation to the gods

I avidly read the articles in **BS** and tried to follow all available advice. **The Haiku Handbook** was sheer bliss. I stopped writing so many telegrams. "Anything on haiku?" I asked at the local library. Back came three weeks' silence, followed by a copy of the Manyoshii with a note: "Will this do?" They did later come up with two tomes of Blyth's translations - after which I appear to have moved on to writing in a form of pidgin English.

I read more. And reached the point of having no idea at all of what a haiku was and no confidence in myself to write one. I was rejecting anything which didn't magically bring together two disparate images. Too clever by half. Great when it happens but even Bashō et al didn't expect that all the time:

the indecision
(which what yes no perhaps - damn)
of a final draft

Back to nature and the 'suchness', the 'treeness of a tree', the 'oneness' and all the other-nesses which we, the lay people of haiku (who don't happen to subscribe to one or the other set of jargon, but have a happy eclecticism and do, as a matter of fact, experience exactly what the rest are talking about) bumble along without. I've always loved the religion and hated the dogma, as it were, in many things. Although learning different labels for something is interesting and sometimes downright useful if it gives expression to the hitherto unexpressed, you can tell more from the haiku people write. 'By their deeds shall you know them' (and know their deeds/moments) or something like.

clean page and no thoughts
but emptiness and whiteness
- this is the poem

As in all creative activities, we don't run on high all the time. Like many people I expect, I go from a dozen or more attempts in one session to one in three weeks if I'm lucky. I find that change and bereavement have left big gaps in my writing, apart from a few almost therapeutic outpourings and then, even months later, something has sparked off another spate of work, I've been surprised, too, by haiku moments coming back from what I'd thought of as lost time.

wakeful night
turning and turning
a single word

Well, I now allow myself to forgo the strict 5-7-5 and have been known to knock out a two- or four-liner, - a one liner still seems very outré, but you never know: watch this space, as they say.

Recently, I've gulped down large and very satisfying helpings of the Blyth Genius (known locally as 'Essex man goes East'), James Hackett and, probably more significantly freeing than the others, James Kirkup. Now I feel more able to just write and experiment. A more natural approach. All that reading and struggling has helped. Maybe even slightly more important than writing haiku is just that we can write. To me, writing something that is haiku in the moonlight on the lake – 'frosting on cakes' doesn't happen to be my idea of a treat.

Towards a Consensus (a Society essay on the BHS website suggesting some attitudes and guidelines) has been good to have on hand and I love the bit about not cutting up a sentence 'like some poor worm'. (I've found a few, luckily one or two still wriggling and saveable, in looking back over my work.) Much has and could be written about the way we revise our haiku. It's a fascinating process.

On re-reading my *Blithe Spirits* I now find advice on many of the things I've struggled for there all along. I think there's probably a Reading-Readiness effect somewhere here! There could be a place for a 'selected essays from ...' for people new to haiku and I definitely recommend a regular dip into past copies.

Although some of my haiku arrive complete and fairly set, things do evolve and seem to need a settling time. The mind goes on subconsciously musing over the more recalcitrant efforts, I find. It's often easier to improve them or throw them out when there's a space between the first impulse and the drafting(s). Trouble is, I think I'll still be changing some of them in ten years' time. Well, they're mine, I'm allowed!

sleepless - kept up again
by the two o'clock haiku

Of course the main reason we write haiku is that it's a form in which we want to communicate or express something. It has a discipline all its own, whether we want to stick to counting or not. It has a 'feel' to it and that's what we're aiming for. The Rules, Guidelines, Towardses are signposts which do help, but basically they're in a foreign language. So much of the process is intuitive. It's a tuning in. It's holistic. Go on, grab the Gestalt!

When we get it right someone says, "Oh, yes!". When we get it spot on, many people do. When it's just pretty good, it makes a memory for ourselves and that's worth keeping it for; a haiku collection can be like a diary ... It can probably also be like a fish - but I've said enough. Happy Haikuing!

looking up from the keyboard
- the sky is dark!

Barry Atkinson

Haiku in the Western World

The world of modern western haiku presents a conundrum difficult to solve: Japan gave us rules that we of the west would like to follow but within which we are inclined to flounder. We might have ideas that empathise with Bashō and Issa, but much of our understanding and our environment is completely different. Nothing can change that. However, we try. We battle with syllables and Zen content - fair enough; it never does any writer or philosopher harm to grapple with their chosen path. Yet, through this intellectual fight, where does the truth stand? Does it matter, for example, even in the international world of today, that many of us have a basically Christian background when the ‹big four› of haiku were Buddhist? How much that is worthwhile has had to be discarded for the sake of accepted form?

It is a dilemma, especially if you accept that haiku is a matter of philosophy combined with poetical expression. After all, we have been born to a poetical process of some length. Personally, I have nearly always found this process flawed by verbosity and I was attracted by haiku›s succinctness. My thinking leads me to experiment whilst keeping the original concepts in mind. That sounds obvious and, of course, incorporates the cause of the controversy that surrounds us. It means, I believe, that we should have an open mind. Here are three of my experimental haiku:

The shadow / of the aeroplane / disintegrating / as we climb
(First published in RAW NerVZ HAIKU Canada)

Oranges ripen alongside my life
(Published in 'l-orizzot' Malta and RAW NerVZ)

Wildness of the sea
keeping my ferry in port *(First published in Azami, Japan)*

Mel McClellan

Some Thoughts on the Haiku Process

I encountered haiku for the first time early in 1995 and was immediately drawn to its paradoxically condensed yet infinitely expressive form. I liked the idea that haiku can have moods and textures, be like watercolours, or oil paintings or precise pen-and-ink drawings. As haiku's an art of enhancing a single image poetically, and I'm interested in the visual enhancement of poetic texts, it seemed the ideal genre for experimentation with multimedia (my day job) to explore Pound's statement from *Vorticism* that "The one image poem is a form of super-position; that is to say it is one idea set on top of another."

This seemed an interesting basis for on-screen poetry with visual and aural enhancement; dynamically intensifying the single image with pictures, music, symbols, ideograms; creating dreamy mindscapes or rapid image sequences superimposed one on top of another; a texture of mood created by computer graphics and hypertypography - multi-dimensional, interactive textwork ...

However, this is something for later: first I needed to read and research and begin to learn what haiku was all about and find my own path within it. Primarily, I needed to be writing, and writing about what's informing my development at this point in my life - which happens to be computers and information technology. Technology, against all odds, is a creative stimulant, an endlessly fascinating resource, and probably the single most influential factor on my creative production at the moment is the Internet.

The Internet

Deciding to use the Internet for research and feedback was a turning point. Choosing at random one of the many searchable indexes supplied by the World Wide Web (the graphical, user-friendly major highway of the 'Net') and typing in the keyword 'haiku' turned up 109 matching responses within two minutes. Following up several that looked promising, within minutes I'd located some excellent haiku 'sites', and found a body of people around the world writing haiku, corresponding with each other about haiku, composing renga-on-the-fly and generally having a good time in an artform they love.

Suddenly, the texts I'd been reading and struggling to make sense of came alive. Instantly, I had access to a body of current, contemporary work (a month, a week, a day old) as well as recourse to archival material from all ages and locations. Haiku publications, discussion groups, individuals' pages and mailing lists, all encouraging submissions in the form of original work, critiques, discussions and short articles. I half expected that the anarchic, unregulated nature of the internet would necessitate wading through much bad work to find something worth reading, but instead most sites functioning in the best way as nurseries for new talent, with good editorial control, erudite argument and positive, supportive criticism.

I find this very exciting. Far from being the isolating, dehumanizing monster its detractors babble about, the Internet is a nurturing environment, a communication technology turned mass medium. a global meeting-place for like minds. Things are changing at lightning speed: reality has taken on the shape of a William Gibson or Bruce Sterling novel.

This opens up all sorts of new possibilities regarding audience/readership: a writer no longer has to 'arrive' in the poetry world to get published: authoring a 'Web' page affords self-publication with little overheads. With a little research and effort, it's possible to reach a large, real-time audience keen to read one's work even contribute to it. Games of *maekuzuke* ('joining to a previous verse') may be played, where *maeku* ('previous verses') are thrown to the winds of hyperspace and *tsukeku* ('joined verses') added by others perhaps the same day, certainly within the week.

A new poetic backwater exists in cyberspace, peopled by a virtual community of writers and critics who inhabit this curious hybrid world of man and machine, With the internationalization of haiku, the geographical, religious and cultural associations that function to make a haiku are subject to multicultural conversions: the influence of the Japanese masters is becoming diluted, This is what Bashō wished for. He always encouraged his students to cultivate their individual talents rather than follow him with blind faith. Informed by the eclectic exchange of ideas fostered by the Internet, the art of haiku can only grow and benefit.

Form and Process

The first material I read about haiku dealt only with the Japanese traditional form - the necessary inclusion of a *kigo* (season word), the strict form of 3 lines of 17 syllables, arranged 5-7-5. Being drawn to tradition and feeling that more intellectual rigour would obtain in adhering to those rules, I made my first haiku conform accordingly, It didn't work, and resulted in first attempts that were too ambiguous, metaphorical, not concise enough, because I was trying to make them fit the pattern. Once I'd done some research via the Internet and other sources, I came to understand that the Japanese and English languages have inherent differences, that the best haiku in English tend *not* to be 5-7-5, that there are many schools and styles of haiku, and that the debate goes on, The British Haiku Society's statement that "it proves elusive to reach a description of haiku which all those fascinated by the genre can accept without reservation" sums it up neatly!

It seems to me that the Japanese view of life may be so foreign to the westerner that it's difficult for us - maybe impossible - to write 'true' haiku. I'm comfortable with the idea that the non-negotiable criteria of haiku apply to spirit and content and not to form; that an unwaivable syllable count is less important than good syntax, lineation and rhythm.

It's been said (on the Net, and probably elsewhere) that most haiku beginners, both western and Japanese, start with good form (ie 5-7-5) and poor content. In the west, they then find the content and shed the form, while Japanese poets find the content and keep the form. I'd like to achieve both, with the proviso that if HAIKU (the international kind) works best within some other form better suited to the characteristics of the English language (Blyth thought the English equivalent is 2 stressed syllables plus 3 stressed syllables plus 2 stressed syllables), then that should be aimed for, rather than 5-7-5. As far as I can see at the moment, the 'organic' style, where form is reinvented for each new poem/experience, seems best for haiku, enabling form and content to reflect each other. I want to learn from the richness of Japanese haiku, ground myself firmly in the tradition, but, with respect and knowledge thus gained, find an equally valid approach appropriate to the culture I live in.

Worrying at first that I didn't have time for the relaxed mind required of the haijin, I realised eventually that it can be induced. In the West, we haven't the Japanese mind-set, the Zen orientation of meditation and contemplation, by nature, but we can observe, concentrate anywhere in our hectic urban lives and create the necessary conditions. We have no idea when the haiku moment will find us but can be prepared for it. As someone said "Carry a notebook with you at all times, but forget why you have it"! The voice of nature is everywhere - in the city we just have to listen for different things. Instead of wolves howling or frogs croaking, there's the roar of traffic or the sound of the TV.

After April rain
- in puddles of oil
city rainbows. (author unknown)

In cyberspace, there's no sound but that which one creates oneself - a limitless reality.

Audience

Using the Internet had various profound effects, not least being the discovery of a new type of audience. The relationship between writing and readership becomes much more immediate, much more personal, much more interactive, when publishing takes place on-line. If a haiku publication were to be printed in the usual way, it would probably be read by a small constituency of poets and haiku enthusiasts in its country of origin. With an Internet presence, it would be accessible to a large international readership with direct communication with the author (if s/he so desired). Using this medium for renga etc. provides an immediacy often lost by the intervention of postal delays. Constructive feedback and discourse, thus generated, enables new ideas and revisions - and because Net-published material can be changed, updated at a moment's notice without need for prohibitively expensive reprints, a constant flow of energy is possible.

This conduit for rapid interchange generates an intensely fecund arena for poetry. It also, of course, undermines copyright protection and renders intellectual property free to all with access, but many authors and artists are already embracing the Internet spirit of freedom of information by publishing on the Net; these issues are being dealt with and creative ways forward will be found.

For the writer of the nineties, the Internet is becoming one of the sharpest tools in the shed. The Net provides access to other writers, editors and readers through e-mail critique groups, USENET newsgroups and newsletters about writing. Writers can enjoy access to countless small-press publications, literary journals and a chaotic and eclectic mix of electronic magazines. These markets can prove more receptive to unpublished writers than the major markets and there are many interesting on-line haiku sites, most with more links connecting to other haiku sites.

[Editor's note: Mel records that in 1996 a search of the WWW with typing in the keyword 'haiku' turned up 109 matching responses. When Mel repeated the exercise in July 2015 by googling 'haiku' the return was 21,000,000 hits in 0.23 seconds. It would seem that global haiku awareness has gone viral!]

Bill Wyatt

Bashō - Cultivating Simplicity

No one notices it
springtime- on the mirror's back
an apricot scene (Bashō)

Most of us go through life not noticing anything that does not come from within our own sphere of existence, all is taken for granted. Spring comes and goes, and before we are aware of it, the blossoms fall. Bashō had the type of mind that took everything in. Even the old mirror with apricots carved on the back, blends in with the spring scenery. One of Bashō's favourite writers, the Chinese philosopher Chuang-tzu had written, "In uncarved simplicity the people attain their true nature." I feel sure that this philosophy was one of the bases for Bashō's theory of *karumi,* or lightness.

The birds and fishes
can we ever know their hearts?
our year end party

Of course Bashō did not know everything. He empathised with the birds and fishes, but in the end, he admitted he could never know their true feelings. He nevertheless envied them their freedom. In his younger days, Bashō wrote from the prospect of birds, flowers, etc. What we would term anthropomorphism, that dreaded word which we are encouraged not to emulate. Earlier he had written:

Bush clover lies down
so good looking - with her
flowery face

and

Late autumn shower-
looking displeased the pine
waiting for the snow

Are these anthropomorphic? I suspect it only appears that way if we examine the haiku through our blinkered Western concepts. Being a Buddhist, Bashō was at least aware of impermanence: that nothing lasts forever. Issa's and Ryokan's poetry are imbedded from this point of view. As a result they sympathised and empathised with birds, animals and plants. If they didn't they would have become as Bashō described, no better than beasts. Buddhism well before the modern era had humanised animals and all sentient beings which are all so many potential or actual Buddhas. The inchworm possesses an inch-long Buddha nature.

From the fragrant earth
one branch of apricot blossoms
on which a wren sings

Bashō must have delved deeply into Chuang-tzu's writing, as many of his haiku reflect that philosophy, - more so than Buddhism or Zen. The "uncarved simplicity", from the Chinese word 'pu', translated as "original simplicity", "natural integrity", "uncarved block", is a recurring theme in the *Tao Te Ching,* where Lao Tzu writes, "Display natural simplicity and cling to artlessness". During Bashō's last years his goal in haiku was 'lightness' *(karumi),* whereby a poet living in this topsy-turvy world could still gain a sense of equilibrium, like the Zen monk sweeping snow:

Sweeping the garden
forgetting all about the snow -
my besom broom

Bashō did not write a great deal about the actual art of composing haiku. What we do have are those sayings recorded by his disciples, especially those of Doho, who recorded his master's "The haiku must be composed by the force of inspiration. If you get a flash of insight into an object, record it before it fades in your mind". Haiku should be done "like felling a massive tree, like leaping at a formidable enemy, like cutting a watermelon, or like biting at a pear".

Chrysanthemum flowers
in bloom - between stones where
the stone mason lives

Jackie Hardy

Simile, Metaphor and Anthropomorphism in Modern Japanese Haiku

Most English readers of Japanese haiku will be more familiar with the work of Bashō than with any of the modern Japanese haiku writers. With 800 or so haiku clubs active in Japan today, this is not because of a dearth of modern Japanese haiku but must, in some part, be the result of few available English translations.

A Hidden Pond - Anthology of Modern Haiku edited by Koko Kato and translated by the editor and David Burleigh, is to be welcomed because it offers an opportunity to the English reader to experience 218 modern Japanese haiku. This edition contributes a new wide-open window on the haiku-writing way and at the same time reveals recurrent arguments.

The British Haiku Society in its *Towards a Consensus...* has been unequivocal in its attitude towards simile, metaphor and anthropomorphism. Professor Arima Akito in his Foreword to *A Hidden Pond,* tells us that haiku are 'symbolic and objective'. Koko Kato states that 'The haiku poet presents him or her [the reader] with some fresh experience or observation that is conveyed directly'.

When a simile is introduced it can be recognised by the words 'as' or 'like'. It has been said if something is like something, it is never itself. What simile does is evoke a world that exists alongside that which is being described. Can it then be considered to be 'conveyed directly'?

Here are some examples:

Like a Mozart
sonata - the sea
on a morning in spring *Hoshino Bakkyujin*

The thinnest ice
retreats like cherry blossoms
deep in the mountains — *Fujita Shōshi*

in spring sunlight
the rows of tea bushes
ripple like waves — *Morita Tōge*

As sharp and piercing
as a sudden flash of light -
winter withering — *Kurahashi Yoson*

Metaphor can be recognised in a text by the use of the word 'is' or the implication that something is something else. In haiku, with its often incomplete syntax, the verb is frequently implied. A metaphor's function is not to express the otherwise inexpressible, rather, what a metaphor does is express the way in which, seen in a certain light, two very different things can be essentially similar. A haiku moment.

Some examples:

Spinning the light rays
from my hometown into yarn
this pussy willow — *Shimada Maki*

Daybreak in spring -
the waves drape silk gauze around
the skirts of an island — *Hara Kajō*

Through fire on the sea
a single line of warriors
goes marching past — *Kawano Ryōsō*

A transparent fish
is flying in the dark sky-
autumn at night — *Fukuhara Keiichi*

Bashō's advice was to observe directly from the natural world with an open heart. The following poets have taken that advice. If anthropomorphism is in tune with what Bashō was saying then these must qualify as haiku:

White peonies
flushed ever so slightly
with carnal desire *Hinoki Kivo*

Fireflies in love
where the sound of two rivers
flow together as one *Shihashi Seisui*

Right in the heart
of a waterlily plays
a dewdrop child *Asakura Kazue*

Inside my closed eyes
the white soul of each snowflake
just passes away *Akao Ei*

These haiku from *A Hidden Pond* illustrate clearly that simile, metaphor and anthropomorphism are all alive and well in modern Japanese haiku. The case against simile I find unchanged. As for metaphor and anthropomorphism when they appear in English haiku and are placed in the pans of the editor's scale, they will continue to receive a considered balance; the weight of judgement will not necessarily go against them.

David Hart

Why I Don't Write Haiku

Haiku seems to me either the easiest or the hardest kind of poetry to make. I like to think I can knock off a haiku at will and imagine, if I get it right, that I shall have said all there is to say in a nutshell: Which must make it difficult beyond measure.

But here is a Journal containing a great many haiku, and in the next issue there will be a great many more. So are they, far from the great summation, merely petals that fall and are blown away in the wind?

If I myself am a character type amenable to being summed up: I rather think it's a manic-depressive person that I am. I gave up alcohol some ten or more years ago and I am glad I did; I might have drunk myself to death by now. Not that I thought of myself as alcoholic - but it may have been a close thing - rather, that when I'd drunk a bit, I would make notes or write little poems and feel I'd caught the essence. I hadn't of course, but my attraction to haiku seemed to be of a similar kind: the manic belief that I had summed up the whole of an experience in a few choice words.

Manic sounds crazy, but there is a quiet version of it that still wants to believe that an experience, or the sum of what we are, can be given brief and accurate verbal form, Maybe this is true, or maybe it's a delusion that we are better off without. The answer might be, yes, the haiku can do that summarising job and doesn't have to be labelled manic or anything else as a put-down; that, on the contrary, it's the sanest, wisest, unblemished way to put experience into words.

My experience of haiku has been that once I start to make poems in this formI am stuck with the habit. It's the same with puns - once I get into that groove I can't think of anything else. This comes to seem sterile and then no longer interests me. The habit becomes an end in itself - it isn't leading anywhere, even if it carries the illusion that it is.

On the other hand I recall with pleasure and something like smiling veneration a small book of poems by Bashō I had some thirty years ago. Recently I was staying with friends and read some photocopied haiku of Issa in the room in which I was sleeping. I found myself awake in the middle of the night with those images provoking me to write a poem of my own. I recall with gratitude Dom Sylvester Houedard's enigmatic and playful presence, in person and in his poems and other writings. The haiku that in his version goes:

frog

pond

plop

has been a kind of touchstone. So perhaps there's more to haiku for me than I am willing to admit. Perhaps on my death bed I will be playful enough to leave a haiku as my final poem, but in my present everyday life I don't yet know how to measure the great unknown of experience, to be quiet enough, to be patient and detached enough; I don't yet trust the brief summing up that a haiku seems to be. The poems I feel I need to write will have to get busier yet, with their sleeves rolled up in experience, keeping a record, letting the rag bag of my imagination throw up what it will. Distillation through haiku might one day be the blessing I have arrived at.

But still I hear myself saying that haiku is a delusion, a simplistic escape from the harder perceptions. I wonder if what I feel in the High Street most days can be given the haiku treatment:

Crossing between the cars
the child in the buggy
breathes in the bad news

I have heard myself say that one of the paradoxes of poetry is that pain can be transformed into something beautiful, but even to say it now as a principle shames me. Whose pain? Does a haiku about the poisoning of a child's lungs in any way make recompense? What use is beauty here? So should we keep off the hard subjects, the painful perceptions, the bad news and make pretty haiku about our neutral or easy perceptions of beauty?

Speaking for myself in my own poems I can shape my pain and confusion, my uncertainties and fragmentary discoveries, I can let the mystery of poetry speak for me if it will. I can shape my pleasure, too, and if whatever I write meets anyone else where they are, thank the gods for that. Perhaps one day I shall arrive at haiku as a kind of spiritual fulfilment; it won't be a pretence for me then, but a true expression.

For there is a sense in which I aspire to that: or I would like it - the haiku essence - to allow itself to me. It will be the playfulness, perhaps, that I shall understand properly then. Our Western spirituality has been heavy in comparison: I know myself as the inheritor of Shakespeare, Nietzsche, Kafka, Dostoevsky, Samuel Beckett and much as I find Wordsworth and even Keats and Shelley rather wordy, I cannot escape their type of engagement with experience. And then, of course, there is the inheritance of the Bible and the Book of Common Prayer, both heavy with being here, however much they speak of self-sacrifice and the hereafter. I am happy in principle to sit more lightly to attachment to experience, to take the Zen path; non-being has long been where I know I am - or where I am not. And surely - I argue back to myself - a haiku at best can do more than suggest that, it can open a window on to it and fly through. But perhaps it is the flocking of the birds of haiku that has made me not want to join that club:

> So many elegant birds
> free wheeling in blue
> no blue is to be seen

Such poems are a pleasure to me for a while, but then seem to have been too easy; they carry no weight beyond the illusory moment. There's a simple pleasure in doing it, but no real sense of purpose. The poems I write that do matter to me seem to have come out of a greater struggle. Rarely do they have such an obviously satisfying form and when published in newspapers have met with the response from some people that they have no form at all.

But they wouldn't satisfy me unless they had form of some kind and if I have any sense at all of what poetry is, it is radically different from everyday talk or from the kind of prose I am writing now. Perhaps in relation to haiku I am still earthbound, not yet ready to fly. Or, as I am inclined to say, the haiku is only a pretence at flight and I'm still after the real thing.

Nobuyuki Yuasa

The Englishness of English Haiku and the Japaneseness of Japanese Haiku

What is English haiku and what is Japanese haiku are two questions about which, perhaps, no two persons can reach an agreement. What follows, then, is a somewhat wild attempt to define the qualities of English and Japanese haiku, as I see them from my biased point of view. This kind of attempt, however, is worth trying because it enables us to see the essential elements of haiku and variations within the limits of those elements both in English and Japanese haiku. This is, perhaps, what Basho had in mind when he preached about *fueki* and *ryuko,* permanence and change. I think there are some basic elements which writers of both English and Japanese must observe, but they also have the freedom to produce infinite variations so long as they pay due respect to those elements.

First, I should like to discuss the language of haiku. The bold use of vulgar terms is one of the essential elements of haiku. Haiku began as a revolt against the genteel tradition of waka, especially its long-established courtly diction. Waka, literally, means Japanese poetry, and in a sense it is opposed to Chinese poetry. Waka is usually written in kana, Japanese alphabetical letters, avoiding the use of Chinese characters. Waka also avoids the vocabulary of Chinese origin. Haiku, on the other hand, relies heavily on Chinese words. Let me give you a few examples:

nukiashi ni mushi no ne wakete kiku no kana

With soft stealthy steps / I cut through the field, hearing / Crickets on both sides.

What makes this haiku by Ikenishi Gonsui (1650-1722) so remarkable is the first line in which he uses a colloquial idiom, *nukiashi,* which means stealthy steps. An idiom of this kind will not be found in traditional waka. The following poem by Bashō (1664-1692) is remarkable for the bold use of a Chinese word:

Kohri nigaku enso ga nodo wo *uruoseri*
Biting the bitter ice, / A hermit mouse in a ditch / Relieved its dry throat.

The word for the hermit mouse in a ditch, *enso,* borrowed from a famous Taoist philosopher, Chuang-tzu (c369-286 BC), determines the mood of the poem, and conveys very successfully the state of the poet himself who lives in poverty and isolation.

Now, can we see a similar use of vulgar terms and colloquial idioms in English haiku? Borrowings from Chinese words would be difficult, but can we find a similar use of ink-horn terms which are generally considered to be outside the norm of the poetic language? Perusing through the February and May issues of *Blithe Spirit,* I have found many poems whose writers seem to have made conscious efforts to meet these requirements. For example:

booking in advance / for her trip to Las Vegas, / Granny touches wood.
(rasubegasu yoyaku yorokobu obaachama)

This poem impressed me mainly because of the colloquialism of the last line. In the following poem, the use of the word "hyperactive" reminds me of Chinese words in Japanese haiku.

Just watching / the hyperactive child / so wearing
(cho-kappatsu na ko wo miru dakede kutabireru)

It is true that Bashō was somewhat critical of the popularity of vulgar terms in the haiku of his day. His famous dictum, *zokugo o tadasu,* correcting vulgar terms, however, does not exclude the use of vulgar terms in haiku, it is a recommendation to use vulgar terms with a noble mind. Taking the poems in the February and May issues of *Blithe Spirit* as a whole, I feel that English haiku is somewhat conservative in the use of vulgar terms, and that there is room for greater adventure in this direction. Even Bashō himself said that waka is like the fragrance of the plum tree, while haiku is like the roughness of the pine tree.

The second essential element of haiku is the use of concrete imagery. Here again a comparison with waka is useful. Waka is usually a direct statement of one›s emotion while haiku is an expression of one›s emotion through a concrete image. There is, however, a certain amount of disagreement about the function of imagery in haiku among Japanese poets. Pre-Bashō poets emphasised the metaphorical quality of imagery. For example, Kitamura Kigin (1624-1705) says:

Spots of snow on the ground should be likened to the pattern of spots on the fabric called deer-skin, and blocks of soft snow still remaining should be likened to the rice-cakes half-eaten by mice of the sunny-season, or to the melting of the cosmetic powder on the face of the Lady of the Mountain, or to the half-torn cotton-covering of the Hag of the Mountain. If snow starts melting on the roof, you say the gargoyle has shed its disguise, and if a snow image disappears, you say the snow Buddha has passed away before the day of his Nirvana.

Here Kigin is recommending his followers to use metaphorical expression in haiku instead of simply describing natural objects. The result is similar to Elizabethan conceit. Bashō was critical of this kind of witty writing, as his disciple, Hattori Toho (1657-1730), testifies:

Go *to the pine if you want to learn about the pine, or to the bamboo if you want to learn about the bamboo, our teacher said. And in doing so, you must leave your subjective preoccupation with yourself. Otherwise you impose yourself on the object and do not learn. Your poetry issues of its own accord when you and the object become one...*

Obviously, Bashō was interested in more natural and objective expression, but we must not misunderstand his aim. He is not really denying the use of metaphor in haiku. For him the object does not have value as such, but only as long as it reveals the emotional state of the observer. What we find in the poems of Bashō and his followers is unpretentious metaphor which does not look like metaphor at all. Nevertheless it is metaphor highly charged with emotion. When we come to Masaoka Shiki (1867-1902), we feel that he is aiming for greater objectivity. He emphasized the importance of *shasei,* or *shajitu,* both of which mean sketching:

When you find something interesting in natural scenes, or in human affairs, and wish to arouse similar interests in your readers through your writing, you must describe what you see as it really is without using decorative style or exaggeration at all.

At this point, I should like to refer to the famous definition of an image by Ezra Pound as "that which presents an intellectual and emotional complex in an instant of time." It has been pointed out by Earl Miner and others that Pound was influenced by Japanese haiku. Pound's definition of the image is similar to Bashō›s with this difference: Bashō seems to emphasize naturalness, whereas Pound seems to emphasize complexity. A short poem by Pound himself can be used to prove the point:

The apparition of these faces in the crowd, / Petals on a wet black bough.

In this poem entitled «In a station of the Metro», two images are presented: the image of the bright-coloured faces among the crowd in the dark underground station, and equally bright coloured leaves hanging on a dark, wet bough, but obviously the latter is used as a metaphor for the former. In other words, Pound is more interested in expressing his thought and feeling about the condition of human beings in modern society than describing a natural scene. Hence the relationship between the petals and the faces is more complex than it seems on the surface. I know that some English haiku read very much like Pound's poem. For example:

Crocus blooms in snow,
Bright colors face the chill air;
Life›s warmth against ice.
(yuki no naka inochi no nukumori kurookasu)

This haiku by an American poet is not so complex in its thought as Pound's poem, but it has the same structure, for the poet here uses crocus as a metaphor for life, and snow and ice as a metaphor for death. When I turn to the haiku poems in the February and May issues of *Blithe Spirit,* I find many poems which read more like Shiki's sketching. For example:

rising and falling / with each gust of wind / the severed leaves
(kaze ni mau ko no ha no ugoki sorezore ni)

A water-rat / scurries along the edge / of the pond
(dobunezumi ike no hotori o kosokoso to)

In a way, I welcome this tendency. I think an overt use of metaphor is detrimental to haiku, whether in English or Japanese, as Bashō pointed out to his disciples. At the same time, however, we must not forget that metaphor is an essential element of haiku. I believe that Shiki›s idea of sketching, if carried too far, can be dangerous. If you just describe the surface of an object I think your poem becomes somewhat thin, like some paintings of the Impressionist School. Let me quote here three haiku poems by Japanese poets to show the three stages of metaphor I have been trying to explain:

hana yori mo dango ya ari te kaeru gan
More than the flowers / They seem to like the dumplings, / Wild geese going home.

This poem by Matsunaga Teitoku (1572-1653) represents the first stage, where natural objects are used as obvious metaphors for human affairs. In this poem, the poet is not at all interested in depicting the wild geese going home to the north in spring, but he is using them as a metaphor for the practical men who wish to fill their stomachs before they feast their eyes with cherry blossoms. Moreover, wild geese going home constitute a standard subject in traditional waka. The poet is, therefore, enjoying himself by playing the role of an iconoclast. In the following poem by Basho, however, the image of a goose is used for an entirely different purpose:

byogan no yosamu ni ochi te tabine kana
A sick goose falling / Into the dark, chilly night, / Slumber on the road.

In this poem, the relationship between the sick goose and the slumber on the road is not so apparent. The last line is grammatically ambiguous, for it does not make clear whose slumber it describes. It can be either the slumber of the goose going home, or that of the poet himself who fell ill during his journey. In other words, the poem is so constructed that the goose can be an independent object, or a metaphor for the poet, but a trained reader does not fail to see the subtle relationship between the two. In the following poem by Shiki, we get an immediate sense of place and time, but the poem does not go beyond the sense impression:

yuki nokoru itadaki hitotsu kunizakai
Where a lone peak stands
Still covered with snow, we have
A province border.

It is true that even here we see the landscape through the eyes of the author, who is now writing as a lonely traveller. So the subjective element is not altogether absent, but the author here is little more than an observer. In my opinion, there are too many followers of Shiki among modern Japanese poets, especially among amateur poets, so that the importance of metaphor in haiku is often forgotten. I am hoping, therefore, that English haiku poets will not follow Shiki, but they will go back at least to Basho to discover the subtle relationship between the poet and the object he is describing, and furthermore, to explore new possibilities in metaphorical expressions, using tile rich tradition of metaphor in English poetry.

The next basic element of haiku I should like to discuss is its form. Some people might say the question of the form does not exist in Japanese haiku, because traditionally, the so-called 5-7-5 form has been generally accepted as the standard. This is true in a way because at the moment most Japanese haiku are written in semi-classical Japanese which is especially adaptable to this traditional form. But if one day Japanese haiku poets should decide to write in modern Japanese, the question of the form would be a serious problem. In fact, some poets have already made this decision.

Taneda Santoka (1882-1940) is a good example. He wrote most of his haiku poems in modern colloquial Japanese. As a result, he had to discard the traditional form in many of his poems:

I pushed my way through,
I pushed my way through,
Just deep blue mountains.
wakeittemo wakeittemo aoi yama

In this poem, he has adopted a 5-5-5 scheme, but in the following poem he has adopted a 5-7-2 scheme:

mozu naite mi no sutedokoro nashi
Sharp cry of a shrike - / I can throw myself away / Nowhere.

Although Santoka uses many irregular forms, I think it is a mistake to think that he has written free verse. His poems show two rather contradictory motives. He wishes to use colloquial modern Japanese at the expense of the traditional form, but at the same time, he cannot quite ignore the traditional form. Therefore, he wishes to keep it wherever it is possible. The traditional form in Santoka's poems is like the half-erased face on the surface of a rock. In English literature, John Donne does pretty much the same thing, when he writes sonnets. In a way, he wants to destroy the sonnet form, but somehow, he wants to keep it as rigorously as other poets. I think this is what a great writer does to a literary form: he destroys it so that he can recreate it again and make it adaptable to his own purpose. In short, a literary form exists both to be observed and to be broken.

Turning to English haiku at this point, what can one say about its form? Attempts have been made to keep Japanese syllable scheme in English haiku. I have done so in this paper for an obvious reason, but many poets have found this too limiting. In my translation of Bashō, I used a four-line form, which was criticized by some people as a violation. I do not particularly wish to defend myself here, but I had hundreds of poems to translate, and I found it impossible to keep the original syllable scheme throughout. Moreover, as I have already pointed out, haiku was started as a revolt against the tradition of waka, and includes a revolt against its formalism. In translating waka, I would try to keep the syllable scheme even in English, which I have done in my translation of Ryokan (1757-1831), but in translating haiku, I thought I could take more liberty. However, I can offer no special reason for my choice of the four-line form, I only thought that the four-line form would read better, giving more weight and independence to the poem. Now perusing through the February and May issues of *Blithe Spirit,* I find most of the poets are using the three-line form, hardly paying any attention to the syllable scheme. For example:

telescope sight - / a heron / spreading its wings
(toomegane tsubasa hirogeta sagi ichiwa)

Sometimes attempts are made to get the middle line longer than the rest. For example:

almost lost / in the shimmer of water / several ducklings
(mizu haete hikari ni kasumu kogamo kana)

Sometimes, but not very often, attempts are made to keep the 5-7-5 syllable scheme. For example:

Sick horse - one hind leg
keeps kicking, kicking the long
autumn night away
(yamu uma ga ashi de keru keru aki no yoru)

One poet at least seems to prefer the four-line form:

I will show you something –
One above another,
Two evening stars setting
In a cleft of the hills.
(iza misen tani ni narande shizum hoshi)

I am not going to say which form is best for English haiku. Ultimately, the choice of the form must be left to individual poets. One poet may find keeping the syllable scheme too limiting; another many find it an exciting challenge. One poet may find the four-line form more adaptable to his purpose; another may find it too long-winded and loose. Variations within the three-line form are so great and numerous that it is not even possible to say whether there is going to be any standard three-line form in English haiku or not. However, I should like to see a little more awareness of the form among English haiku poets. It was T. S. Eliot who said no free verse is free. I think free verse works best when there is a fixed form to destroy. When we have a complete absence of form, I do not think free verse succeeds so well. In discussing the poems of Santoka I have already said that there are contradictory motives in his mind: a desire to preserve the traditional form, and a desire to destroy and recreate it. Out of the tension of these contradictory desires I think his poems emerged. I believe this applies to English haiku just as well and just as much.

Finally, I should like to discuss the question of *kireji* as an essential element of haiku. *Kireji,* literally, means the cutting word. It is a short word, grammatically a particle, which is placed either in the middle or at the end of a poem. It has the double function of heightening the emotional force of the statement, and, depending on its position, of cutting or concluding the statement. If you emphasize the first function, *kireji* is something like an interjection or an exclamation mark. In translating the famous haiku by Basho about the frog jumping into the pond, G. S. Fraser tried to make this function of kireji explicit:

The old pond, yes! / A frog jumping in, / The water's noise!

But it is the second function of *kireji* that I should like to discuss here, especially its poetic value when it cuts the statement in the middle of the poem, as in the case of Bashō's poem quoted above. When *kireji* performs this function, it is very much like a caesura, or a dash, or comma. In other words, when we have a cutting word in the middle of a poem, the poem consists of two statements, half-separated by the cutting word. There is a great deal of argument even among the Japanese haiku poets about whether a haiku poem should be a single statement, or it should consist of two half-independent statements. Bashō himself left two contradictory opinions about this issue. At one time, he is reported to have said that a haiku poem should be a combination of two things, and that a skilful poet knows how to combine two different things. At another time, however, he is reported to have said that a haiku poem should be simply like gold beaten to its utmost thinness. Among modern Japanese poets, Osuga Otsuji (1881-1920) asserted that a haiku poem should consist of two phrases making one statement, while Usuda Aro (1879-1951) maintained that a haiku poem should be one phrase making one statement. I do not wish to discuss the minute differences among the poets here. I only wish to bring your attention to the function of the cutting word placed in the middle of a poem. When this happens, the cutting word divides the poem into two phrases, each belonging to a slightly different level of meaning. Of course, the poem as a whole needs unity, so that the interaction between the two phrases becomes extremely important, but by bringing together two phrases of different levels of meaning, the cutting word gives complexity and subtlety to the poem. In other words, a clever use of the cutting word heightens the metaphorical character of haiku. Let me give you an example:

kiku no ka ya nara niha furuki hotoketachi
Scent of chrysanthemums - / In Nara, I met ancient / Statues of Buddha.

This poem by Bashō is a typical example of haiku consisting of two phrases making one statement. The cutting word at the end of the first five syllables makes the relationship between the scent of chrysanthemums and the statues of Buddha the poet saw in Nara extremely complex. On the surface level, we can say that the poem is a sketch, and that Bashō smelled the chrysanthemums placed in front of the statues of Buddha as offerings, but to me, this interpretation is unsatisfactory. Bashō visited the ancient capital of Nara on 9th September 1694. This day happens to be the Day of Chrysanthemums, and traditionally a festival was performed at the Imperial Court to celebrate this flower. Moreover, I believed Bashō remembered that chrysanthemums were brought from China as medicinal herbs about the same time as Buddhist statues in Nara. The earliest Festival of Chrysanthemums was celebrated in 685 during the reign of Emperor Tenmu (?-686). This historical association was in the mind of the poet when he combined the scent of chrysanthemums and the statues of Buddha. The result is a poem of rich imaginative quality. We go back to the age of Buddhist statues on the scent of chrysanthemums. Let me give you another example, this time, from Natume Soeseki (1867-1916):

kagerou no yume ya ikudo kui no saki
A dragonfly lands / To dream, again and again, / At a pile's top end.

This poem has the cutting word at an unusual position, namely, in the middle of the central phrase (in English, after "to dream" in the second line). This clever use of the cutting word makes the poem rather unbalanced, but in this poem, it is very effective because the unbalanced movement of the poem represents symbolically the movement of the dragonfly when it darts off from the pile's end, returning to it a few moments later to dream again before it darts off a second time. Moreover, the use of the cutting word at this position gives unusual weight to what follows immediately, namely, "again and again". Half separated from the verb by the cutting word, this adverbial phrase indicates the psychology of the observer as well as the movement of the dragonfly. So the reader senses that the observer also dreams again and again without quite achieving his dream like the dragonfly. As these examples show, the cutting word can give a great deal of subtlety and complexity to a haiku poem. In the February and May issues of *Blithe Spirit,* I find many poems using a dash to achieve the effect of the cutting word. For example:

heatwave -/ the winterwear catalogue / brings on a sweat
(fuyumono no e nimo ase juku atsusa kana)

Partly hidden / By a broken cloud - / Easter moon.
(kumo no ma ni nakaba kakurete ham no tsuki)

There is one thing, however, that worries me a bit. In many poems, the short line separated from the other two lines by a dash reads almost like a title or a summary, so that the cutting word does not really bring together words belonging to two different levels of meaning. In other words, in spite of the cutting word, the entire poem reads like one phrase making one statement. I am not saying that this is wrong. This is one way of writing haiku, but there is another way, which is, at least to me, more interesting: one statement consisting of two half-independent phrases. There are poems of this kind too, in the February and May issues of *Blithe Spirit.* For example:

daffodil morning - / looking for something / very blue to wear
(asazuisen nanika no ao o kite mitashi)

I admire this poem, as its reviewer has done in the May issue of *Blithe Spirit,* but probably for a different reason. I admire it mainly because it brings together two different levels of experience, one external and the other internal, through a successful use of the cutting word. As a result, "daffodil" and "blue" create infinite repercussions in the reader's mind. Here is another example:

on top of the moor / pissing with the wind - / distant dogbark
(no no kaze ni nyou o hanateba inu hoeru)

Apart from the question of treating a subject like pissing, which Bashō approved with some reservation, I think the poem is far better than the following poem which Bashō defended when one of his disciples criticized it:

decchi ga ou kuso kobishi keri
An apprentice boy / carrying manure, / spills it all over.

Bashō's disciple was against using the word *manure* and changed it to *water.* I do not think this saves the poem at all; in fact it makes a dull poem even duller. But in the English poem quoted above, I think the combination of *pissing* and *dogbark* creates an interesting meaning. Pissing is a natural act, so you do it with the wind, but when the dog barks, you feel somewhat guilty, but on second thought, you realise that the dog is barking as naturally as the wind is blowing. So the dogbark changes from a warning to a voice of life. I am not saying that the poet was conscious of all this when he wrote the poem, nor that the reader should interpret this poem in the same way as I do, but I am saying that this poem is a good example of a haiku poem consisting of two phrases making one statement.

Now, it is time for me to present my conclusion. The title of my essay, *Englishness of English Haiku and Japaneseness of Japanese Haiku,* may have been somewhat misleading. I must beg your pardon if I gave you the impression that I was going to make sweeping generalisations about the differences between English haiku and Japanese haiku. I hope I have demonstrated that there are more resemblances than differences between them. However, at the risk of arousing dispute and quarrelling, I should like to say a few words about the characteristic features of English haiku and Japanese haiku, as I see them. In language, English haiku uses modern colloquial English, while Japanese haiku is usually written in semi-classical Japanese, although some poets have made bold departures from this. At its best English haiku sounds more natural, but there is a danger of falling into flatness. At its best Japanese haiku uses vulgar terms within the context of classical Japanese, achieving interesting poetic effects through their contrast, but when this does not happen, Japanese haiku poems read as if they were ghosts of years gone-by. In imagery, English haiku seems to rely more heavily on sketching. At its best, English haiku impresses the reader with its vivid description, but sometimes English haiku fails to go beyond sense impressions.

The characteristic feature of Japanese haiku in imagery is its use of unpretentious metaphors, metaphors that do not look like metaphors at all, but when poets forget this Japanese haiku also fails to go beyond sense impressions. In general however, Japanese haiku seems to achieve more profundity. English poetry, of course, has a long tradition of metaphor, beginning with Anglo-Saxon kenning, and going through Elizabethan and Metaphysical conceits, and Romantic and Symbolistic metaphors, and coming to Surrealism of this century. But in general, English metaphors are radical metaphors, and whether radical metaphors are suitable for haiku or not are a matter for dispute, but I think English haiku will gain more by exploring a new territory of metaphor. In form, English haiku seems to enjoy more freedom, while Japanese haiku is strongly governed by the traditional syllable scheme. What we must not forget is that haiku was started as a revolt against the formalistic tradition of waka. For a haiku poet, therefore, the form is there partly to observe, but also partly to destroy. I think English haiku poets will gain more by having more awareness of the form, while Japanese haiku poets will gain more by making bolder departures from the traditional form. In the use of the cutting word, Japanese haiku poets seem to be more resourceful than English poets, partly because they are more accustomed to the use of the cutting word, but mainly because the English language has no words that play the same role as the cutting word. However, I believe that the poetic effect of the cutting word can be achieved in the English language by the use of a dash, or three dots, or a comma. If English poets remember that the role of the cutting word appearing in the middle of a haiku poem is to put two half-independent phrases together to form one unified statement, I think they can achieve greater complexity and subtlety in their poems.

My final statement is this: I am not quite sure if English haiku has really achieved its Englishness, for I believe English haiku is still in its making. But anything in its formative years is more interesting than anything in its decaying years. I think there is a great danger that Japanese haiku will cease to be attractive unless Japanese haiku poets make serious efforts to renovate the old tradition. Already in 1946, a famous Japanese critic, Kuwabara Takeo said that haiku was dead in his provocative essay called "A Secondary Art". I do not share this opinion myself, but I can see the danger of Japanese haiku falling into a secondary art. I believe that one way of getting out of this condition is for Japanese haiku poets to study overseas haiku. Perhaps English haiku poets can make contributions in this direction in future.

Carol Rumens

Kettle Talk

This conversation takes place between a young man, 'The Blithe Spirit', a keen, but not yet prominent BHS member and aspiring haijin, and a young woman, 'The Red-Blooded Poet', who has just published her first book of poems with *Bloodaxe* and of course writes opinionated reviews for the literary magazines.

They are in Blithe's kitchen. Red has called to return the haiku books he lent her in exchange for two newly published volumes of 'ordinary' poetry. These volumes are *Rembrandt Would Have Loved You,* Ruth Padel (Chatto) and *Broken Dishes* by Michael Longley (Abbey Press).

The books Red is returning are *The Iron Book of British Haiku,* Ed. David Cobb and Martin Lucas, *Jumping From Kiyomizu* by David Cobb (Iron Press) and *darkness and light* by Martin Lucas (Hub Editions)

Blithe: Mind if it's teabags?
Red: Yes, I was hoping for a tea ceremony. No, a teabag' s fine
Blithe: So. What did you think?
Red: I'm in culture shock. Didn't someone say that reading haiku was like being pecked to death by a flock of doves? It was like being strangled by a bonsai tree ... overdosing on cherry-blossom ... drowning in a dewdrop ... suffocating in a ...
Blithe: OK, OK, point taken. No need to use *quite* so many similes, I think.
Red: Sorry, just having a wallow. Pigging out after the starvation diet.
Blithe: Starvation diet? Maybe that's good. You only taste things properly when you're really hungry.
Red: Some of those haiku slipped down so fast I didn't notice the flavour unlike your tea.
Blithe: Too strong?
Red: No, I like it strong.
Blithe: There's an art to reading haiku, of course. We talk so much about the art of writing them, but ignore the art of reading them.

Red: I was exaggerating. Some of them did make an impression. I liked Martin Lucas's dog sniffing among the poetry stalls and David Cobb's one about being slapped in the face by the sight of a nun's black stockings on the line. I liked most of Cobb's poems actually. But then I discovered a lot of my favourite haiku were really senryu! In all these books I preferred the renga and the sequences, especially when they built up a bit of narrative. It's not stuff the purists like, though, is it?

Blithe: I'm an impurist myself.

Red: I like to meet another person when I read poetry. Sometimes when I read haiku I get very little sense of an individual ego being present.

Blithe: But you're not supposed to. I must say I enjoyed reading your books and I've made up my mind to read more non-haiku poetry. But I did get fed up with the I, I, I! Sometimes it almost embarrassed me; I couldn't concentrate on the poetry even when it was very good. For instance, I kept on wondering about Ruth Padel's lover and thinking what a bastard he was. Haiku expresses the world, not the self, that's why it's so refreshing.

Red: But it's such a limited world! Admit it, there's something awfully middle-class about English haiku. I always imagine these retired people in dressing-gowns, padding around their perfectly trimmed lawns and making notes on the birdsong. Nothing intrudes on their Eden, except when they kill an insect - by mistake, of course, because they're nature-lovers.

Blithe: Absolute rubbish!

Red: I made a list of all the flowers mentioned in the latest Blithe Spirit. Lilies, bluebells, michaelmas daisies, magnolia, chrysanthemums, wisteria, daffodils, asters, charlock, cherry blossom, jacaranda.

Blithe: And what about the trains and coffins and newspapers and loudspeakers, not to speak of the smell of chips? You're being unfairly selective. Not that I'm making any apology for flowers. Even if you're a *Bloodaxe* young revolutionary living in a Neasden tenement, you've probably seen the odd dandelion or bought a bunch of daffs. Your man Longley' s got a 'Daffodil' poem, by the way. He's very keen on flowers. I like his work a lot: it's often very close to the haiku spirit.

Red: He never simply describes his flowers, though. The Daffodils poem is an elegy; a lot of his flower poems are really people poems. Have you noticed how he likes to weave in the person's name? So you get a wonderful sense of human individuality being valued. You couldn't have a haiku elegy, could you?

Blithe: Haiku poets are deeply aware of death and passing time.

Red: Death in the midst of life, yes I know. The wasp at the picnic, the bin-liner in the cornfield - all the old clichés.

Blithe: I'd rather call them paradoxes. They're what poetry's all about, surely?

Red: I think what poetry is really about is language.

Blithe: You're sounding suspiciously post-modernist. You'll use the word 'ludic' any moment now.

Red: Why not? Art is play.

Blithe: Not just play.

Red: And haiku is all climax and no foreplay.

Blithe: It plays with rhythm. Think of all the variations you can have on a mere 17 syllables - or fewer. No haiku is rhythmically identical to another.

Red: You could have fooled me. They're rhythmical clones, a lot of them. I'll admit it's hard to do anything original with stress. If you make it fall on a trivial word it can ruin the poem. I remember this one, listen. (She flicks through a back issue of Blithe Spirit)

What kind of tree
is flowering? I do not know –
but the fragrance

Blithe: The great Basho. I love that last line trailing away into the unsayable...

Red: OK, but what about the second line? - is *is* the kind of word you tuck away inside a line, not expose at the start. I don't like lines that begin or end with *of* either. Some haiku poets do far too much of this.

Blithe: Of course ordinary poets don't?

Red: They do, yes, but they're more likely to get away with it. Haiku exposes this kind of ineptitude - it encourages it! And about that last line. *Fragrance* is far too refined. A lot of haiku vocabulary is.

Blithe: Blame the translator. But you must have liked some of the 'Iron' poets: Jackie Hardy comparing a rose to the bouquet of her lover's sweat, for instance?

Red: Yes, I liked that. And I enjoyed the richness of vocabulary in the Scots dialect poems.

Blithe: Did you understand them?

Red: Not entirely, but that's partly why I liked them. I like my poems a bit opaque.

Blithe: So you'd allow a few flowers as long as they're in Latin?

Red: Just one or two. But no bonsai trees.

Blithe: You'll be drummed out of *Bloodaxe* young revolutionaries if you're not careful.

Red: You know what I really think? The whole concept of haiku in English is a kind of translation. It belongs to a different aesthetic, a different set of ethics, as well as a different language. That's OK, but poets should work harder at naturalising it, using all their linguistic resources - even rhyme!

Blithe: Have you ever tried to write one?

Red: Yes, but I had to scrap it because it had a metaphor. Honestly, it was like trying to boil a kettle over a night-light. I gave up.

Blithe: Well, I'll tell you what I think about a lot of your sort of poetry. It's like boiling a kettle - just a little domestic kettle - in an industrial furnace. More tea?

Gabriel Rosenstock

The Stairway of Surprise

Reflections on Poetry and Haiku

Somebody said 'nobody writes poetry about parsnips.' Haikuists may - and can and must if they are alive to the moment-to-moment reality of the world. The freedom of haiku is precisely this aesthetic governance in which the subject can never be in bad taste, given it is informed and inspired by the arresting quality of a haiku moment; in the words of Nadezhda Mandelstam, 'a vehicle of world harmony.'

Early Irish lyric poetry had a compressed form and a blessed, clear-eyed view of nature which makes writing haiku in that language a logical continuum of almost 2,000 years of poetry:

> The small bird / let a chirp / from its beak: /
> I heard / woodnotes, whin- / gold, sudden /
> The Lagan / blackbird
> *(The Blackbird of Belfast Lough, trans. Seamus Heaney)*

The Russian linguist, Viktor Kalygin, traces the Irish word *file* (poet) to the Indo-European *wel*, to see. I believe that the art of the haiku teaches us to see. Without, it I would not have 'seen' the following, or written this haiku / senryu:

> Sop ina ghob / dá nead - / féasóg ar an éan!
> *A beakful of straw / for its nest -- / the bird with whiskers!*

Whether the haiku poet relates to all religions, one in particular – the warmth of I Tantra or the coolness of Zen - or none, by 'seeing into the life of things' he makes his art sacred. Gabriel Mistral affirms this in *The Artist's Decalogue (IV): Beauty will not be your excuse for luxury or vanity; it is a divine exercise ...* Rumi and Háfez affirm this truth in every line. As do Kabir, Tagore, Angelus Silesius... But let us see how poets and haikuists tend to differ in their approach. The great Portugese poet Fernando Pessoa wrote:

The startling reality of things / Is my discovery every single day, / Everything is what it is.

The Irish poet, Seán O' Riordáin, wrote 'Bhi gach rud nite ina nadur féin...'

Everything was washed in its own nature.

But the haiku poet does not *tell* us this. He shows us. Pessoa goes on to say: "I was once called a materialist poet and was surprised, because 1 didn't imagine I could be called anything at all. I'm not even a poet. I see... "

The haikuist doesn't have to tell us this. He/she *sees* and *shows.* Haikuists are 'Technicians of the Sacred' - the phrase comes from an anthology from the University of California Press, edited by Jerome Rothenberg, *Poetry from Africa, America, Asia, Europe and Oceania.* The Shamanistic literature of native peoples is a recommended diet for haikuists and humbles us. We know so little of nature!

We may or may not agree with Ralph Waldo Emerson, but we cannot lightly dismiss his lecture of 1833, *The Uses of Natural History,* in which he stated that 'The whole of nature is a metaphor or image of the human mind.' And he says in his *Essays* (1841), 'There is one mind common to all mankind.' Emerson claimed that the insights of poets were truths and that poets use words that 'mount to Paradise / by the stairway of surprise... ' Haikuists perform this function more consistently than conventional poets, which is why I'm looking forward to Robert Bebek's next book *Sanctum* more than I am looking forward to any new book by a living mainstream poet.

Ruben Dario wrote: 'This is my curse: To dream. For poetry is an iron vest with a thousand cruel spikes that I wear around my soul. The bloody paints let fall the endless drops of my melancholy...' If Dario's curse was to dream, the haikuist's blessing is not needing to. Paul Celan wrote:

"I need a form that my style cannot discover, a bud of thought that wants to be a rose... "

Might that form have been a haiku - for him and for hundreds of other poets? We'll never know.

It may be a generalisation, but I'll risk stating it anyway: poetry is very often in the business of skirting the issue, discursively and descriptively, while haiku gets to the point. Neruda is not quite getting to the point, in the way a haikuist does, when he writes:

"I copy out mountains, rivers clouds. I take my pen from my pocket. I note down a bird in its rising or a spider in its little silkworks. Nothing else crosses my mind. I am air... "

The haikuists will notice that the word 'I' is used not once but four times in this passage. Such commentary on one's own art seems to be an incessant behaviour pattern among mainstream poets, as in the Catalan poet's declaration: 'He donat la meva vida ales paraules ... ' *I have given my whole life to words ..* (Salvador Esprin). Acceptable enough as the opening line of an autobiography, but of a twelve line lyric? A bit wearisome, I say. The haikuist shies away from such statements, eschewing self-indulgence, self-consciousness, self-everything... Rilke goes on a bit, does he not?

"To write poetry is to be alive. For a God that's easy. When, however, are we really alive? And when does he turn the earth and the stars so they face us?"

No wonder Rodin told Rilke to go off to the zoo, to look and to see!

Marina Tsvetaeva says: 'A poet's speech begins   a great way off...'

The haikuist would disagree and bring the focus much nearer home. Poets who sing the sad obfuscations of interiority often project an image of the dying Chatterton. But unless we know them, we don't have any image of J.W. Hackett, George Swede, Bruce Leeming, Marcel Smets, Alain Kervern, David Burleigh, David Cobb etc.? Why do we not find more haiku in mainstream anthologies? Is there a critical prejudice at work which believes haiku is water-colour, poetry is oil? If Buson can be compared to a water-colour Impressionist in the following remarkable haiku, then let's hear it from the water-colourists:

the evening breeze / blows water to the blue heron / whose legs are rippled

To those reared on conventional poetry Buson's haiku will have all the shock of *nouvelle cuisine* to a system used to generous portions of roast beef. Yorkshire pudding, roast potatoes, veg and gravy, served in a familiar pub and washed down with real ale.

But we shouldn't overstress the differences between haiku and conventional literature. If we wish to see what they have in common we will find that all types of literature are peppered with hidden haiku:

leafy island ... / flapping herons wake / the drowsy water-rats

This is an 'extracted' haiku from *The Stolen Child* by W.B.Yeats. With the minimum of editing - dropping a definite article or an adjective or two, and arranging the title text in a three-line format - you will be surprised how many hidden haiku exist, not only in conventional poetry, but in novels, plays, short stories, nature and travel sketches, letters, diaries and so on ...

frost broken up / gaslights reflected / on the wet pavement

No, you'll never guess where that hidden haiku came from - *Sketches by Boz,* Charles Dickens. And:

Silence; the last bird passes / in the copse / hazels cross the moon

from *The Widow in the Bye Street,* John Masefield. What a fantastic project it would be if haikuists in America, the Caribbean, Britain, Ireland and Australia began to explore the English-language literatures of their respective countries and produced an anthology of hidden haiku for the new millennium. Any takers?

I'll conclude these reflections with a conversation I had on this topic with the poet, Noel Griffin:

GR If there is *a Western prejudice against haiku, might this be due to the dominance of the epic tradition, Homer, Virgil, Milton, Dante, The Táin, Beowulf - to the displacement of the Celts in Europe and, latterly, the bourgeois fantasies and urban realism which colour contemporary prose and verse?*

NG Undoubtedly - but even more than that, the nature of the Western poetic tradition itself, which leans toward the discursive and narrative, the play of ideas, essentially. But ... not ideas but things, the plum in the fridge, the red wheelbarrow, as William Carlos Williams would have stated, he being a one-man revolution against the tendencies of Modernism as propounded by T.S.Eliot.

GR Pound and the Imagists (1912-1917) *also counteracted trends, being open to the ancient poetries of China, Greece and Japan, and published haiku and haiku-like verse.*

NG They had sympathies with what one might call oriental poetics, but then they had sympathies with almost every vital literary tradition - Italy, Provence etc. W.C. Williams was the only one who stuck to his guns and really did practise what he preached. He still remains a beacon in this respect.

GR Let me read you something written as far back as 1920, by the American poet, Max Bodenheim. It's almost as if he anticipated the emergence of haiku in English: 'The old emotional eloquence, dramatic ecstasies of phraseology and suave oratory with which most poets have always addressed birds, trees, flowers and the lives of men, is disappearing, and in its place there has been a struggle on the part of the poet to wrestle with the concrete forms about him, and in the heat of this fight, suddenly awakes to find that he has been gripping different parts of himself .. · 'Good, eh? John Clare, G.M.Hopkins, and in our time Heaney and the late Hughes, celebrate the Anglo-Saxon thingness of things and a spiritual closeness to nature. Is it the Romantic influence and the temptation of Latinate grace that clothes the thingness of things?

NG I fear we're opening a can of worms and many other things besides. Yes, there would definitely seem to be a great deal of truth in this. Western poetry since the Renaissance looked over its shoulder at the classical tradition as a kind of validation of its own worth. The consciousness was one of the State or the Empire or, put more simply, Society. In many respects this was inevitable and brings us to the question of complexity: complexity of society, complexity of consciousness, perception, inspiration...

GR *Simplify! Simplify) as Thoreau said...*

NG Which brings us back to haiku.

GR *Many mainstream poets have lost the gift of perception. The Candamaharoshana-tantra states:*

> When you see form, look!
> Similarly, listen to sounds,
> Inhale scents,
> Taste delicious flavours,
> And feel textures.

This wisdom is being lived by haikuists. Our craft is spiritual. You can argue about syllables, rhythm, season words, the influence of Zen and so on, but the fact remains that haiku are being written today in dozens of languages, which elate one, which chill one, which bring one back to the awful mystery of being and our relationship to natural phenomenon.

Ken Jones

Zen and the Art of Haiku (dedicated to Jim Norton)

such a sky
the ache of loss is answered
and returned entire

" We know in our bones that there is something odd, something queer, about everything, and when this contradictoriness has a deep, religious, poetical quality, when the whole thing stands revealed and we see right through it to this side, we weep with uncontrollable joy, or laugh with irrepressible grief"
- R H Blyth 1

What is it about haiku that imparts that mysterious little whiff of insight, so difficult to describe and yet so strangely satisfying? I would like to offer some pointers from my experience as a long term Zen Buddhist for whom the Way of Haiku has become a valued part of my practice.

Characteristically we endeavour to secure and console our fragile self-identity by processing, shaping and colouring the raw experience of existence, Even - or especially - in the face of discouraging external circumstances, our mind strives to maximise the "feel good" factor both emotionally and intellectually, helped and amplified by a social culture which includes plenty of imaginative literature, The worst of this offers temporary escape from who we really are; the best offers a sometimes magnificent creative and cathartic treatment of our existential evasion, However, as *imaginative* literature it remains ultimately subjective in the sense used by Blyth as "the state of mind in which a man looks at the outside world, or at himself, as he would like it to be".2 The example he quotes from Byron would be hard to beat:

> And Ardennes waves above them her green leaves,
> Dewy with nature's tear-drops as they pass,
> Grieving, if aught inanimate e'er grieves,
> Over the unreturning brave.

For Buddhism our root unease originates in the countless and subtle ways in which we try to evade, by action, thought and emotion, the totally open experience of just how it is and how we are. Trying to make it otherwise has been described as a lifelong lawsuit against reality, which we can never win. Spirituality itself, even Zen Buddhism, may be expropriated by the needy ego as the ultimate evasion. Here is a beautiful warning from the eighteenth century Zen Master Hakuin:

> At the north window, icy draughts whistle through the cracks,
> At the south pond, wild geese huddle in snowy reeds.
> Above, the mountain moon is pinched thin with cold,
> Freezing clouds threaten to plunge from the sky.
> Buddhas might descend to this world by the thousands,
> They couldn't add or subtract one thing. [3]

Ultimately the only effective remedy is, in Blake's words, to learn to "cleanse the doors of perception" and let reality flood in. As all the spiritual traditions affirm, this brings a sense of joy and release and an ability to live more fully and freely in the world - and in the moment.

Zen is a school of Buddhism concerned with the cultivation of a profound down-to-earth awareness of this "suchness", unmediated by doctrine or other concepts. Haiku are the most thoroughgoing expression of literary Zen. They are also one of the several meditative "Ways" (like calligraphy and the minimal ink paintings, *zenga* and *haiga)* whose form both gives expression to insight and helps to deepen it. The "haiku moment" is thus no less than a tiny flash of an ultimate reality which in fact is just what is under our noses. Haiku which most clearly embody "suchness" as the ground of our being I shall, in the Blyth tradition, call "Zen haiku" and it is with these that I am particularly concerned. Exceptionally they may be quite didactic, like this from George Swede (which sums up the argument so far):

> After the search for meaning
> bills in the mail

Empty of self-need

It follows that haiku must spring from a mind open and unobstructed by any urge to make something of the reality that has come to the poet's attention. Those who go searching after haiku will find them shy and few and far between. Look for them and you will not find them. Don't look for them, and they are not to be found. Of subjective meddling the 13th century Zen Master Dogen observed, "When the self withdraws, the ten thousand things advance; when the self advances, the ten thousand things withdraw." And Basho advised that "When composing a verse let there not be a hair's breadth separating your mind from what you write; composition of a poem must be done in an instant, like a woodcutter felling a huge tree or a swordsman leaping at a dangerous enemy." 4

Just washed / how chill / the white leeks!

Contrariwise, Bruce Ross identifies a "tendency in the fourth generation of American haiku writers of the late seventies, eighties and early nineties unfortunately to frequently offer catchy moments of sensibility that often rely on obvious metaphoric figures. These American poets desire to create 'haiku moments'. But a subjective ego, call it sentiment or call it imagination, intrudes upon their perception of the object."5 Typical is the poem by Steve Sanfield quoted later in this paper in another context.

"How it is" doesn't come with meanings and explanations attached to give us the illusion of a more secure grip on it. Allusive brevity is one invariable characteristic of the haiku form. We have an itch to add in order - as we fondly suppose - to clarify. Too much verbiage muffles the spark; the shorter the poem, the more space for the reader. And the reader, too, may have an itch to explain. Thirty long lines to kill three short ones! A haiku derails rationality; why try to put it back on the rails? Bashō (through Lucien Stryk) makes the point:

Bird of time / in Kyoto, pining / for Kyoto

If haiku were no more than a reflection of how it is ("so what?") they would not engage our attention as they do. But they express how it is *as experienced by a human being, within our shared humanity.* These two elements are precisely set out in this verse from the *Zenrinkushu* 6: "Rain of no sorrow falls on banana leaves ... A man, hearing it's pattering, feels his bowels cut". Haiku, in Martin Lucas's words, are "open metaphors" for our human condition and resonate with that condition. They offer a glancing opportunity, without the poetic prompting of another, to accept for ourselves how it is. Such pure acceptance has qualities of compassion, release, quiet joy, subtle humour. It is well known to the mystics, like Julian of Norwich: "All shall be well, and all manner of things shall be well". Haiku moments offer a little bit of existential therapy shared between writer and reader, a little bit of mutual compassion. In David Cobb's words (borrowed from Gustav Holst and Paul Nash) they combine "tender austerity and the mystery of clarity." Of all literary forms haiku are, in the current tell-tale slang, the least "in your face"; they have the least "attitude". Indeed, they may leave us momentarily suspended in an emptiness which nevertheless feels authentic and moving, as with Shiki:

> The long night / a light passes along / the *shoji* [screen]

At the other extreme the reader may just occasionally he prodded with a question, as in this example from Bashō:

> In the dense mist / what is being shouted / between hill and boat?

The sense of metaphor may be particularly strong when the poet has his own feelings in mind. In this example, old age is deeply felt by Shiseki. He acknowledges the self-pity that comes with it, but he does not massage this feeling with the any expressions of consolation:

> My old thighs / how thin / by firelight

However, these "open metaphors" retain their power only so long as readers leave them open and do not hasten to fill them with their own meanings. R H Blyth warns: "Where Bashō is at his greatest is where he seems most insignificant, the neck of a firefly, hailstones in the sun, the chirp of an insect... these are full of meaning, interest, value, that is, poetry, but *not as symbols of the Infinite, not as types of Eternity, but in themselves.* Their meaning is just as direct, as clear, as unmistakable, as complete and perfect, as devoid of reference to other things, as dipping the hand suddenly into boiling water." 7 Explicit symbolism narrows the metaphor, takes space from the reader and leadens the lightness. Some Japanese regard it as a peculiarly Western haiku vice, and it is very seductive, as in this from Scott Montgomery:

her silence at dinner
sediment
hanging in the wine

Traditionally haiku poets have taken nature as their subject matter, as being more contemplatively accessible. But when nature turns dramatic only the best haiku poets can both express the drama and retain the haiku spirit without tipping over into subjective melodrama. In such highly tuned haiku the translator also will be put to the test. Here are two examples from Basho, translated by Lucien Stryk, with all the dramatic down-to-earth energy of Zen:

Mogami river, yanking
the burning sky
into the sea

Shrieking plovers
calling darkness
around Hoshizaki Cape

Perhaps human affairs were assumed to be more likely to excite the poet's impulse to comment. But this is not necessarily so, as the growing number of "social haiku" bear witness. The top one is by an American, Donald McLeod, and the other, by Peter Finch, is from an industrially depressed Welsh valley:

Unemployment office / a metal chair/ scrapes across linoleum

Through dense firs / light of a wrecked car / burning

Varieties of awareness

Undistorted by self-need, reality displays characteristics of transience and insubstantiality which, deeply experienced (as at times or lifetime crisis) may feel very threatening. Meditation enables a gradually prepared opening to them and joyful release from the lifetime effort of denying them at a deep existential level. When "how it is" ("suchness", *sono-mama*) is "empty" of the weight of self-need we feel a sense of release, of lightness or spirit. This is the *karumi* experienced in miniature in haiku, many of which give intimations of this "emptiness". In some instances it may move us very deeply: *yugen* - profound awareness to which we cannot put words. In Japanese culture certain mood responses, of elusive and overlapping meaning, have been identified. Unless appreciated in the spiritual context of Zen these easily become no more than haiku conventions or "values", or Japanese mannerisms. "Willow pattern haiku", haiku *a la Japonaise,* may result. Thus Bruce Ross refers to "the stylistically self-conscious underscoring of Zen-like experiences" to be found in many contemporary American haiku poets.[8]

Sabi is an acceptance of the "emptiness", insubstantiality and vulnerability of phenomena (including oneself). But it is an acceptance coloured with a gentle, compassionate sadness, a delicate frisson, and not of stoic indifference. In Brian Tasker's words, *"Sabi* is a kind of pure and sublime melancholy and detached emotion which is not received in a self-centred way but simply honoured for what it is - a symptom of the human condition. *Sabi* is the existential aloneness that can only be resolved by acknowledging its inevitability coupled with the joy and gratitude that can arise from its acceptance."[9] Consider the following haunting example from Bashō (loneliness, deserted, aged, wild):

> The loneliness
> of this deserted mountain
> the aged farmer
> digging wild potatoes

On a more superficial view *sabi* can refer to anything that is old, worn, tranquil, mellow and dignified. Like the other haiku "moods", in the absence of real insight it can all too easily lend itself to tired and well worn "oriental" haiku.

Wabi essentially denotes respect for the ordinary, the commonplace as opposed to the sensational. Simplicity, restraint, austerity are related meanings, with "rustic solitude" as a rather more mannered expression. Here is a nice contemporary example from Gary Hotham:

coffee / in a paper cup - / a long way from home

When the self withdraws its confirming sharpness and specificity of perception it leaves space for a more subtle, subdued, low key beauty to manifest. This is *shibui,* as in the following from Martin Lucas (silent, white, empty):

first darkness of dusk / silently a white owl flies / in the empty lane

Aware is the mood of transience, defined by Makoto Ueda as "sadness or melancholy arising from a deep, empathetic appreciation of the ephemeral beauty manifested in nature, human life, or a work of art."[10] It commonly translates as a nostalgic sadness connected with autumn, as with Marlene Mountain:

faded flowers on the bed sheet / autumn night

Finally, another very Zenny haiku mood is that of understated humour, sometimes black or tinged with irony - especially irony. It typically arises when one of our cherished delusions impacts with reality, and life momentarily lives us with a wry grin. Here Alexis Rotella and I respectively face a new day:

Undressed –
today's role dangles
from a metal hanger

Worn old feet
in worn old slippers –
really mine?

And the gentle ironies of matrimony seem to make for better haiku, in the Zen sense, than breathless passion. These two, from Karen Klein (left) and George Swede, were close together in the September 1997 *Frogpond:*

too hot to make love
too hot
not to

A sigh from her
a sigh from me –
two pages turn

The Zen of the cutting line

The majority of haiku achieve their main effect through a device called "the cutting line" or "eye opener". Some Zen preliminaries may help us to understand more profoundly how this device works. In order to free their students from the conventional self-assuring perceptual patterns, Zen teachers commonly resort to mutually contradictory words and phrases: iron women give birth; the sun rises at midnight, or, in this verse by the C15th. Master Ikkyu:

> Hearing a crow with no mouth
> cry in the darkness of the night
> I feel a longing for
> my father before he was born. 11

So characteristic of all spirituality, paradox is only baffling, only paradoxical, to a mind unable to step out of a logically structured world of *this* defining *that.* In all spiritual traditions, what *is* is the same as what is not; one thing is all things and all things are one thing. There is all the solidity of the world of form in "a wooden hen sits on a coffin warming an egg" (Hakuin again). But it is empty of "sense" - "pure nonsense" - in that the self cannot confirm the self by *making* any sense of it. In Buddhist terminology, form is in fact "empty" - of the order, solidity and permanence we need to attribute to it. In this by Bashō, both time (spring) and place (a hill) exist in *suchness,* empty of conceptual referencing. The hill is "nameless" and it is the "thin mist" shrouding it which makes spring time.

> Spring has come / a nameless hill / is shrouded in thin mist 12

In Buddhist terminology, the power of Zen haiku lies in their embodiment of form-and-emptiness. The best of them come to us out of the moment in an insight so right, yet so beyond our ordinary habitual perception, as to dumbfound us. We find ourselves saying more than we mean and more than we know.

Two lines set the scene and a third, cutting line throws them out of gear by switching attention to a different perception, sparking across the gap between the phrases and momentarily illuminating the whole poem in a fresh light.

Our customary - and solidified - perceptual associations are fractured. Self momentarily loses its foothold. Selfless space ("emptiness") opens for an instant of naked clarity. We have been caught off balance. Trying to figure it out is like figuring out a joke: we miss the point. Occasionally the cutting line is wholly contradictory. Thus Soda (1641-1715), expressing *sabishisa* (spiritual poverty):

In my hut this spring
there is nothing -
there is everything 13

Faced with such paradoxes Blyth advises "some vivacity of energy .... lest the intellect arrive and split hairs. "They must be "swallowed in one gulp", like Yamei's pheasant:

In one shrill cry / the pheasant has swallowed / the broad field 13

It would be possible to attempt a classification of different uses of the cutting line. There is, for example, the double cutting line, where the second line magicks the third into being as a throwback illumination of the first. RH Blyth (in a different connection) quotes Kikaku:

The beggar wears / Heaven and Earth / as his summer clothes 13

The cutting line provides a ready, specific device in haiku-making and lends itself to the cleverness of what I call "artful haiku" which lie at the opposite end of a continuum from "insightful haiku". This doesn't make them "better" or "worse", even as a genre, let alone individually. Most haijin probably write and enjoy both. Good "artful haiku" can be quite clever at tweaking our fancy - and a bit more - as in this one by Steve Sanfield:

sleep on the couch she says / cutting his fantasies / in two

Altogether different is the distinction I would like to make between "broad" and "narrow" ends of the spectrum of insightful haiku. The broader profoundly illuminate our whole human condition, and are what I have specifically in mind as "Zen haiku"; the narrower do so in a more limited and specific way.

However the use of the words broad and narrow is not intended to refer to the quality of the haiku. Here are two examples, broad (about the shortness ... and yet ... of life) and narrow (about the tedium of matrimony), from Buson and Issa respectively:

In a short life
an hour of leisure
this autumn evening

Those two tired dolls
in the corner there – ah yes,
they are man and wife

Note that although Issa's is the narrow one it is more than merely "artful". The man and wife are dolls: the metaphor is open.

Finally, there is a Zen perspective on the optimum conditions for the making of haiku. Two conditions seem to be needful. First, there is the priming and internalising of the form - getting into haiku mood and haiku mode. Hearing or reading haiku, and particularly sharing in a group, are valuable in this respect. For presumed contemplatives, haijin have usually been a sociable lot! Secondly, and more important, is the opening to a contemplative state of mind. My own experience of solitary meditation retreats of a week or more may be of interest here. The meditation I use is that of "bare awareness" *(shikan taza),* in which the mind is a mirror, not a lens. Whatever comes up is simply observed, without mental comment, and dissolves like a bubble. After some practice the mind becomes still for quite long periods. This transparency carries over from the meditation periods. Primed with "dry" haiku (through reading) it translates into haiku "readiness". I am far from being either a gifted meditator or haiku poet and it is usually not until the second or third day that haiku begin to flow freely.

For company
an empty chair

Bruce Ross has argued that the writing of "the fourth generation of American and Canadian haiku poets... attests to the presiding importance of Japanese haiku values to the haiku form as a whole."[14] Some awareness of the Zen Buddhist tradition underlying those values can be helpful, and this now flourishes vigorously in the West. This is not a matter of taking on board some oriental philosophy or modelling classic Zen haiku; quite the contrary - in Zen parlance that would be "adding legs to a snake." As Blyth robustly demonstrated, Zen is not the preserve of any one national culture or institutionalised religion. He found (even if highly selectively) an abundant Zen spirit in European culture and in Christianity. It is a deepening of contemplative poetic sensibility that is at the heart of the matter.

References

1. RH Blyth, *Haiku vol.* 1: *Eastern Culture* Hokuseido Press, Tokyo, 1981. pp 199-200.
2. RH Blyth, *Zen in English Literature* & *the Oriental Classics;* Hokuseido, Tokyo, 1942.p72.
3. *Zen Words for the Heart: Hakuin's Commentary on the Heart Sutra,* translated by Norman Waddell; Shambhala, Boston, 1996.
4. Quoted by John Stevens, in a footnote on p25 of his introduction to *Mountain Tasting: Zen Haiku by Santoka Taneda;* Weatherhill, New York, 1980.
5. Bruce Ross, ed. *Haiku Moment;* Tuttle, Boston, 1993. p.xxi.
6. Soiko Shigematsu, *A Zen Forest: Sayings of the Masters,* Weatherhill, New York, 1987.
7. As for (2) above, p.49.
8. As for (5) above, p.xxii.
9. Brian Tasker, *Haiku and Zen;* Barebones Press, 16 Wren Close, Frome BA11 2UZ pp.38 & 39.
10. Quoted by Bruce Ross as for (5) above, p.xxiv.
11. *Crow with No Mouth: Ikkyu 15th* c. *Zen Master;* versions by Stephen Berg; Copper Canyon P., Port Townsend, WA, USA, 1989. p.17
12. As for (1) above, p115.
13. As for (2) above, pp186,186 & 159 respectively
14. As for (5) above, p.xxvii

Lee Gurga

Haiku in America

Haiku occupies a unique position in American culture. A few childhood favorites aside, the average American would rather have a tooth pulled than read a contemporary poem. And I realize how serious a situation this is, since I am a dentist! But while Americans in general have little interest in contemporary poetry, most Americans have at least heard of haiku and often have a surprising affection for it. When they think of haiku, most Americans think of a three-line poem in 17 syllables. This is the way it is taught in elementary school, and apparently, this is also the way it is taught in college writing programs. Even professional poets go on for years publishing three-line 17 syllable statements as if they were haiku poems. I am not going to talk about this understanding of haiku today, as I will assume that everyone here has a deeper understanding of what haiku is or at least what haiku can be. I will take as a basis for this discussion the understanding that haiku is a short poem, that this poem, to quote part of the HSA's definition, "records the essence of a moment keenly perceived in which nature is linked to human nature," that this short poem in English is of unspecified form, that it has some reference to non-human nature and that it is generally composed of images. A concise definition of haiku that I once heard from Bob Spiess is that it is a poem that "presents images that reflect intuitions." It is important to note that haiku thus defined do not present thoughts, ideas or tell stories.

Originally, many of the people in the States that were interested in haiku were so because they were interested in Japanese culture or in the philosophy of Zen Buddhism as it was popularized there in the 1950s and '60s. I will characterize this group by saying that their primary interest in haiku was in its use as a vehicle for spiritual development. Because of this group's belief that the kind of haiku developed by the Japanese masters, and Bashō in particular, is a useful tool for this purpose, this group has had a great interest in studying the characteristics of classical Japanese haiku, its history, its philosophy, and its technique. What was available for this study in the 1950s were the books of your great expatriate, R.H.Blyth, Harold Henderson›s books *An Introduction to Haiku* and *Haiku in English,* and Kenneth Yasuda's *The Japanese Haiku.* Later on, these books were supplemented by others, particularly Bill Higginson's *The Haiku Handbook.* Using these resources as a basis, and a commitment to truth as a guiding principle, North America produced several haiku poets of a high level of accomplishment.

More recently, as haiku magazines have proliferated and as anthologies of English language haiku have become widely available, more people have come to haiku because of an interest in general poetry or because of an interest in using poetry as a form of self-expression. It seems that many of these people are more interested in experimenting with haiku as a vehicle for expressing their own thoughts than they are in experimenting with themselves in order to find out what haiku has to offer them. In other words, these people's interest in haiku as a vehicle for self-expression takes precedence over their interest in haiku per se. As a result, we have people writing minimalist poems, concrete poems, visual poems and word puzzles of various sorts and calling their efforts haiku.

In the early days of American haiku, when people looked to haiku to provide a new way of experiencing the world around them, most haiku were based on actual experience. Today, however, many of the poems being written and published are no longer based on the poet's personal experiences. We find that in some cases, poets will imaginatively alter experiences to produce a poem of greater impact; poets will base poems on scenes in photographs, on movies, on television programs, or on items in the news, on pure fancy, or even fantasy. In other cases poets will create haiku – or senryu-like poems by manipulating stereotypes. Of course, a certain amount of experimentation is essential to the continued vitality of haiku. However, several questions arise: Is it in haiku that we share our insights, those "images reflecting intuitions?" Is haiku a form in which we can display our wit? Does the creation of the poem as an object take precedence over the truthfulness of the content? Is it some combination of these? These are fundamental questions we need to consider carefully as we go about the business of creating English-language haiku.

Haiku in America has what might be called an "amateur status." In great part because they have not really understood its properties and potentials, professional poets in America have looked down on haiku as an inferior form. Many of them have assumed that so short a poem must necessarily be easy to write. Of course, you and I understand that the brevity of the form creates one of its greatest challenges: there is nowhere to hide, nowhere to explain what you *really* meant to say. One of the results of haiku's lowly status is that it has been in America, as it has historically been in Japan, to quote Bill Higginson, "a literature written for a popular audience and involving people from all walks of life as authors." While this is undoubtedly one of the reasons for haiku's wide appeal, it has created some serious problems for haiku in America. One of these problems results from the fact that anyone who has the time and the resources can successfully produce a haiku journal. Because some people will support a journal that publishes their own work regardless of its poetic merits, sometimes journals of vastly inferior quality continue successfully for years. While this "success" might be beneficial for the emotional health, or as we say, the "self esteem" of the editors and contributors, the continued existence of these journals contributes to the perception that it is not possible to write worthwhile haiku in English. Another aspect of this problem is the general unavailability of appropriately critical reviews of haiku books in our journals. To some extent, neophyte poets depend on these reviews to learn what is good and what is bad. If reviewers are unwilling to take poets to task as well as to praise them, it will be difficult for the art-form to advance beyond the stage of the dilettantism of which it is sometimes accused.

Speaking of reviews brings another matter to mind, that of assessing what is going on in haiku in countries other than one's own. The fact is, it is as difficult for you to keep up with what is going on in North America as it is difficult for us to know what is happening here. This is one of the primary reasons I made the journey to be here with you today - I wanted to get to know you and your poems better. If any of you happen to be interested in keeping up with what is being written and published in North America today, I would suggest that you consider subscribing to our journal *Modern Haiku.* One of the policies of the journal is to review all haiku related books sent to it, and even, as in the case of the Waning Moon Press books, some that haven't, but that the editors consider to be of interest to the haiku public. Another resource that is now available to those interested in assessing the progress of English-language haiku is Jim Kacian's *Red Moon Anthology.* This annual attempts to bring together in one book the best haiku in English that have been published in the previous year. I'm sure many of you are already familiar with this book as your haiku have already appeared in it.

So there are a few observations on North American haiku. With your indulgence, I would now like to share some thoughts about the development of the haiku poet.

According to Robert Lowell, "A poem is an event, not the record of an event." Of course this is an ideal, rarely achieved in any poetic form. How are we to make an individual haiku into an event? A haiku is composed of two ingredients: the event or experience and the poet's mind. It is the combination of these two things that can potentially make the haiku itself into an event. To write haiku, then, also requires two things: that we cultivate our powers of attention and perception so that we don't miss the event, and that we cultivate our "poetic mind" or "haiku mind" so that we are able to transform our experience into a poem.

According to Makoto Ueda, the Japanese poet and theorist, Shiki said that there are three stages in the development of a haiku poet: *shasei* or sketches from life, selective realism, and *makoto* or truthfulness. In the first stage, the poet simply records what he or she experiences. The purpose of this stage is to develop the poet's perceptual abilities, to teach the poet to avoid intruding his or her thoughts and feelings into the poem, and to develop the craft of translating perception into language. This is perhaps the most difficult stage for Americans to endure, since it requires that poets *not* express themselves, that they *not* strive for effect, but that they simply develop their powers of perception and learn to record their perceptions in language. Since this effort frequently results in flat, uninteresting poems lacking in significance (the so-called "so what?" haiku), few people are willing or able to stay in this stage long enough to open themselves to the world as it actually is. For this is a key element of haiku: haiku record the world as it is rather than as we would like it to be. After the poet has developed a sufficient maturity of perception and craft, he or she is able to begin to understand what makes up the essence of each scene or experience.

Shiki suggests that when poets have achieved this understanding, they may move on to the next stage, one that Ueda calls "selective realism," but one for which apparently Shiki had no specific name. In this stage, the poet attempts to select out the essential elements from each scene or experience, and to express this essence in language. The art of selective realism can be said to have been achieved when the poet is able to perceive, select and express the true nature of things. In other words, only after having sufficiently experienced the world as it is, is the poet able to select from or rearrange actual scenes in order to create a poem that both reflects truth (in its ontological sense) and is a poem (that is, an art-form in words). I would say that this is the highest stage to which any of us can reasonably aspire. If one has reached this level of achievement, one could truly say that one is a poet, that is, one is making an original contribution to human understanding through the imaginative use of words.

Is there anything beyond this? For the poet who has attained this level, Shiki suggests that the final step is to begin to examine and express the poet's own interior reality. Shiki called this *makoto* or "truthfulness." Contemporary haiku master Yatsuka Ishihara refers to this as the "landscape of the heart." In this most advanced stage, the poet connects exterior and interior in a seamless expression of reality. The early 20th century (US) haiku poet, Aro, quoted by R.H. Blyth, calls this *makoto,* "the truth we create in living with energy, seeking something." *The truth we create in living with energy, seeking something.* Indeed!

I think Shiki's theories are a useful framework for understanding the potentials of poetic development. As you may already know, however, one of the biggest problems for the poet is to be able to accurately assess where he or she is. For myself, having composed haiku on and off for some 30 years now, I would like to think that I am solidly in the second stage, that of selective realism. I would like to think I am, but find that many of my attempts at "selective realism" are merely attempts by my ego to intrude into the poem, attempts to produce poems that will be judged by others to be good or clever or profound, rather than ones that achieve the true goal of selective realism, which is to make the poem even more "real" than the actual experience. While poems I have composed in this manner are sometimes appreciated by others, I have found that they are rarely satisfying to me; they generally don't pass my own "smell test." As a result, it is necessary for me to return again and again to the discipline of detached observation. As I am sure many of you realize, this issue of ego versus true receptivity to reality is one of the most persistent and distressing issues of haiku.

Can we ever hope to enter the third stage? Shiki's own poems of the third stage were written in the final years of his life when he was fighting a losing battle with tuberculosis. Perhaps one needs the unrelenting focus produced by the experience of facing death to fully develop one's perception and expression.

There is some wisdom in all this as well as a warning. Sometimes young poets try to start off by experimenting with the limits of haiku before they have fully absorbed the essential elements of the world around them and developed a complete understanding of what makes haiku haiku. As I mentioned earlier, it is difficult to stay in the first, or "boring," stage, long enough to sufficiently develop one's powers of perception and expression. For people raised in contemporary Western "instant culture," the tendency is to try to "jump start" their haiku by beginning in the 2nd or 3rd stage. For some very talented people this might result in successful haiku, but for the vast majority of us, it simply produces a short Western poem, either lyric or confessional, that strains for effect, but without what has been referred to as *haiku essence,* the essence of reality. Fine haiku do produce what Wordsworth called "the shock of mild surprise." What could be more American than to amplify this shock until it blows us away?

Robert Lowell remarked of free verse, "I never dared write it until I was about forty. If it doesn't work, if the rhythm isn't right and the experience isn't right, you have nothing... " It might be fruitful to consider this remark in relation to haiku. Most Japanese haiku masters are in their 60s and 70s and 80s. As I find myself approaching my 50th year, I am beginning to understand why.

Matt Morden

Haiku on the Internet: The Next Great Wave.

The world of the Internet can be compared to your local pub. It can be pleasant to drop by for a drink once in a while, but you wouldn't want to spend your life there. That said, haiku is fast becoming the poetry of the Internet and there is much to interest the occasional visitor to cyberspace. Since a quick glance down the BHS address list reveals a scarcity of e-mail addresses, this article seeks to highlight the opportunities offered by access to a computer for those interested in haiku. [now nearly everyone has web access – ed.]

Firstly, it is necessary to debunk a few popular myths about computing in general and the Internet in particular. Access to the Internet need not be expensive - many local libraries and all colleges and universities are hooked up to the World Wide Web. Enrolling on a one hour a week course in any subject at your local college will give you free use of this resource. Additionally, these institutions will often allow you a free e-mail address for correspondence. Many people now have Internet access at work and if all else fails you could buy a computer.

You don't need to know how a car works to drive one - and the same applies to computers. If you can click a button with your finger you are away.

The Internet is not just for young people. I estimate the average age of people submitting to haiku sites at between 50 and 60, but it might be older still. Those later in life often have more time to make valuable contributions to the Internet haiku communities. They usually know more about haiku too.

Haiku is the most popular form of poetry on the World Wide Web for a number of reasons. At present, the majority of web pages and mailing lists are based in America, where the profile of this type of poetry is higher than the UK. The brevity of the form means that posting haiku onto a mailing list can be done in a few minutes. Typically, haiku poets use simple language which can make haiku more accessible than 'mainstream' poetry, and there are a number of web-based haiku competitions. All of these factors help to raise the profile of the form.

For haiku enthusiasts, access to a computer can open up a whole new world. A poet in a geographically remote location has access to hundreds of fellow poets at the click of a button. There are a number of forums where haiku can be submitted just to be read or for discussion. There are dozens of editors requesting e-mail submissions for their on-line haiku pages. The possibilities for *renga* and *renku* with poets around the globe are great.

Typing 'haiku' into an Internet search engine reveals thousands of sites related to this form of poetry. These range from the excellent (a few) to the appalling (many). This is because on the Internet 'haiku' has become a generic term for all short free-form prose on subjects from Spring, through Spam to the Spice Girls. Writing computer error messages as 'haiku' has become very popular and prompted a recent article in *The Times* on the form.

There are two main areas on the Internet that are likely to be of interest to haiku poets. The World Wide Web is a massive collection of web pages which often combine articles on haiku with poetry, graphics and music. Anyone with even a basic understanding of computers is able to produce one of these pages. This makes the process very democratic, but does not always mean that the information presented (or haiku) are of a high standard.

Perhaps the easiest way to access the more informed haiku web pages is through a gateway site, such as the pages put together by Mark Alan Osterhaus which have the following URL (site address)
<http://ww.execpc.com!ohauslhaiku,html>

As information on the World Wide Web can be easily linked together, the 'links' page on a site such as Osterhaus's means you can move easily from one site to another (the so-called 'surfing' of the web). All of the following pages are linked to the Osterhaus site.

Acorn editor A C Missias has written perhaps the best description of contemporary haiku on the web.

It can be found at <http://www.webdelsol.comlPerihelionlacmarticle.htm> .'

Ryu Suzuki's *Logos and Haiku* pages feature many of the 'speculations' on haiku written by Robert Speiss, editor of *Modern Haiku,* the longest running English-language haiku magazine. The URL is <http://www.bekkoame.or.jp/.v ryosuzu/WHATHAIKU.html>.

The first port of call for many haiku poets is the *Shiki Internet Haiku Salon,* based at Matsuyama University in Japan. The Shiki team run an informative website - <http://mihan.cc.matsuyama-u.ac.jp/~ shiki> as well as three very popular mailing lists.

Other recommended sites include Jane Reichold's *Aha Poetry* <http://www.ahapoetry.com> and Dhugal Lindsay's homepages <htlp.//www2.ori.u-tokyo.ac.jp/Ndhughallhaikuhome.html>.

Gerald England, editor of New Hope International and Aabye's baby runs a UK based haiku mailing list, *Haiku Talk,* <http.//www.nhi.claranet.hktalk.htm>. Other UK-based haiku websites include John Barlow's *Snapshots* magazine site which features another good definition of contemporary haiku, <http.//www.mccoy.co.uk/snapshots/start.html> a and ai li chia's *still* magazine pages <http:www.into.demon.co.uklindexl.htm>

The Irish magazine Haiku Spirit's site <http:www.dublinwriters.org/haiku/index.html> features the haikualive mailing list and some interesting articles by David Cobb and Gilles Fabre.

These sites are a small number of my favourites. By the time you read this the information will probably be out of date and there will be another dozen haiku sites on the web. If you go looking, you will probably find them before I do, and that's one of the beauties of the Internet.

Tōru Sudo

Progress in Haiku in the Past Hundred Years
from *Haiku As Theatre* Shin'yasoshosha Tokyo Japan *12/1/98*
Trans. by Hiroaki Satō

Shiki Masaoka (1867-1902) who played an important role in starting modern haiku, said there were two types of progress in haiku: the beginner becoming an adept and the adept 'advancing into areas' not explored by the 'ancients'. He went on to say, 'I don't have to point out that true value lies in the latter,' and noted that Hekigotō KAWAHIGASH1 (1873-1937) was representative of that kind of progress. Elsewhere he wrote: 'As the population increases and education spreads, people's tastes will inevitable become variegated in thousands upon thousands of ways; so, in response, will literary and artistic expressions. The short poetic form of haiku exists for the same reason and, for the same reason, haiku changes as the age changes.'

Thus Shiki was flexible and accommodating as to the actuality of haiku. Yet if you ask whether the strategy for change he proposed has had any effect in the past one hundred years, my answer has to be: 'No real effect.'

When you look at haiku as they have been written in the last hundred years, you at once notice three main developments:

1. The predominance of flower-bird-wind-moon haiku with the emphasis on the idea of *shasei,* 'sketch', that Shiki advocated.
2. The adherence to the traditional approach that accepts the 5-7-5 syllable form, seasonal words *(kigo),* and *kana, ya,* and other cutting words *(kireji)* as essential.
3. The ambiguous treatment of the questions of dimensionality and layering of language.

All this has worked to flatten haiku, distance it from, shall we say, 'poetic inspiration', and dilute Shiki's goal of turning haiku into a literary genre that represents a comprehensive art form. In fact, you might say that all haiku has done in the past hundred years is to construct a genre of brief, 'impressionistic poems'.

In order to spawn strong and insightful haiku in the coming century, we must re-examine what has happened in the past century and propose some guidelines for new haiku. We must carefully examine the haiku writer's imagination, identity and style, and deep psychology, along with this century's dominant ideal of *shasei.* We must liberate haiku from its restrictions and consider incorporating cosmic, universal, humanistic and religious sensibilities. For haiku to be rich and fertile, we must abandon superficial, ocellar perspectives.

Seisensui OGIWARA (1884-1976) said haiku had two elements: 'fluidity' and 'condensation', suggesting that he could write haiku only by allowing these two opposing forces to contend with each other. Of the two, 'fluidity' is hard to define, but I take it to mean the willingness to illuminate perceptions hitherto not captured. If my understanding is correct, it should encompass views that are cosmic, universal etc., which I've just mentioned. It should also mean the embodiment of the author's imagination, identity and style and so forth.

Seisensui's 'condensation' is what comes with the fixed haiku form 5-7-5 syllables - that is, the haiku's basic strength of drawing things together into a set confinement. At the same time, Seisensui advocated the creation of *shintanshi,* 'new short poems', in addition to the so-called *jiyuritsu,* haiku that do not stay within the confines of set syllabic patterns or syllabic count. In his view if something can't be confined in a set form, it shouldn't be.

Some of the haiku written in the past hundred years that I consider significant in the creation of future haiku embody Seisensui's notions of fluidity and condensation.

> *Lying in the grass I hear the sound of clouds flowing in the sky*
>
> Hōsha SERITA (1885-1954)

This haiku, composed of 6-8-5 syllables, illuminates correspondence between self and sky that combines visual, auditory, and tactile senses. Almost Whitmanesque, it shows the readiness to accept an object or objects into a poet's inner world. Hōsha was a lifelong insurance man who was inspired to write haiku by Seisensui's arguments.

The flesh grows thin these are large bones

Hōsai OZAKI (1885-1926)

Composed in 8-8 syllables, this describes human physicality in the ultimate state with intrepid insight. Hosai, a graduate of the Imperial University of Tokyo, drank himself into poverty and died a mendicant monk. His pieces were published in Seisensui›s magazine and Seisensui posthumously collected his pieces in a book he named *Taiku (The Big Sky).* (A substantial selection of Hosai's haiku in Hiroaki Sato's translation can be read in *Under the Big Sky I Don't Wear a Hat,* published by Stone Bridge Press in 1993).

Litvinov isn't the name of a wine, my friends

Eibō NICHI (1910-1993)

Litvinov here is the Soviet politician, Maxim Maximovich Litvinov (1876-1951) who served as foreign minister from 1930-1939 and as ambassador to the United States from 1941-1943. He was particularly known for his efforts for peace and international co-operation. Eibō, who worked for the government as a monitor of Soviet radio broadcasts, was arrested for his anti-war haiku in 1941. This piece of his sounds like a pronouncement in ordinary conversation, though the total syllabic count comes to seventeen.

Sleeping lotus: cleanse the flesh with something that isn't death

Kusatao NAKAMURA (1901-1983)

Kusatao, a self-proclaimed prophet, did his best to bring religious dimensions into his haiku. He was the leader of the Humanity Explorers school of haiku. This piece was written in 5-8-6 syllables.

Under a rainbow we humans I am alone

Sōsōshi OGAWA (born 1921)

This piece, written in 5-7-6 syllables, seems to consider the future of earth as well as an unchanging aspect of humanity. A note appended to it says, 'At Assisi', and the collection that includes it says, 'The world kept swaying, moving in various ways, and my haiku appeared to exist slightly out of key with the tremors.'

The other land breeze stirs moves eternal cedars dust

Ban'ya Natsuishi (born 1955)

This piece incorporates phrases from the *Amida Sutra* and evokes the Pure Land, a Paradise for all sentient beings. It is said that when a wind rises and stirs the bo-tree (Bodhendrum), under which the Shakyamuni attained enlightenment, ineffable music begins and reaches the farthest corner of the universe. The fact that the haiku is written entirely in Chinese characters and the reading given in katakana syllabary adds to the sense of religious recitation. These haiku remind us that *hai* of the word *haiku* originally implied the dynamic ability to extract the essence from reality, recognise it for what it is, and if necessary criticize or differentiate it. For haiku for the coming century, we must work to recover that ability.

Geoffrey Daniel

Against the Tide:
Antecedents of the Haiku in English Literature

If you happened to strike up a conversation with a stranger on the Clapham omnibus, you might well get round to the subject of English poetry. And if you were to ask for a sample of what constituted typical English poetry, you'd likely get something of the following from Shelley: [1]

> Hail to thee, blithe spirit !
> Bird thou never wert,
> That from heaven, or near it,
> pourest thy full heart
> in profuse strains of unpremeditated art.

(and another 20 such verses].

It is unlikely, however, that you would be offered Soshi Chihara's [2]

> I catch
> my kid come running
> skylark field

I am, of course, demonstrating the obvious - these poetries are poles apart in many significant features: their length, their construction, their diction and their tone at the very least. Moreover, their spirit is importantly different: Shelley, using the bird as a symbol of inspiration, transforms the creature itself into human terms, ascribing to it "rapture ... love ... joyance ... gladness"; it is "an unbodied joy" .... "like a poet hidden/ in the light of thought"; and a device by which to measure Man's lot. Chihara, on the other hand, simply offers the facts to speak for themselves, and appeal to associations in the reader's mind. He furthermore celebrates a relationship and a moment of humanity, set in a context of birds and field that we can detail for ourselves - man and nature intermingled, but autonomous, of a value each within itself.

What is the point then, you might ask, of the present investigation suggested by the title: the relationship of modern haiku to what has gone before in English poetry? I suggest that if tradition matters, and if a nation has a demonstrable predilection for certain kinds of art, then we may be able to predict the chances for the future of any particular kind of imported form. However, if traditionally English poetry is found to be completely at odds with the spirit and form of haiku, we may see no point in trying further to evangelise. [And there may be no further point in a British Haiku Society, for example...]

I take the spirit of haiku to be simplicity, a focused and tangential vision couched in deliberately commonplace language, accessible to all readers and listeners, appealing to their experience of man and nature. It deals with the stuff of the senses. It is precise and capable of dealing with all subjects. It is meditative and non-judgemental.

Certainly, the first 1000 years of English poetry show little congruence with these points. In general, early English art was something done by expert practitioners to a passive audience; initially oral and communal, later a solitary book-readership. Poets were separate beings; poetry was not something that ordinary people could do. They were guides, working in a heightened diction and with superior insights, developing their ideas in full, with cunning and musical crafts, working to established patterns and traditions. [Even as succeeding centuries brought in foreign influences, these were assimilated and became part of the tradition: the Italian sonnet became the Shakespearean, for example.] Their work stretched understanding and language to the limits, but it was only accessible to a cultured minority, those who didn't have to labour for their bread and for whom ballads, bread and circuses were the limit.

Traditionally, the subjects of art were also limited to what was appropriate: the great themes of love, death, religion and the heroism of myth and legend. The religion of that first millennium after literacy is an instructive example to consider. As it was for poetry, spirituality was for specialists, the priest behind the altar ministering to the masses in rituals unchanged over centuries. [Innovation was not to be encouraged: that was the path to heresy.] At best, Nature was decorative, an embroidered or symbolic backdrop to the more important concerns of Man; at worst it was to be feared and controlled, red in tooth and claw and part of that unholy trinity "the world, the flesh and the devil". The senses, by definition, were evil, as were all material things that did not lead away from themselves to a contemplation of higher heavenly things. Compare haiku?

It is always possible to find oddities, however, moments and poets who have more in common with the haiku approach [although whether this is by chance or design is a moot point]. Andrew Marvell had the closest and earliest to what might be a haiku moment in his "Thoughts in a Garden" and his mind "Annihilating all that's made / To a green thought in a green shade". However, this startling image is of course merely one part of an argument, carefully connected, not the central image. In common with the other Metaphysicals, what seems to be a genuine interest in things for their own sake [Bashō " learn of the bamboo from the bamboo" etc] is more likely an intensive use of extended metaphor and symbolism. Donne's "The Flea" tor example I would take to be no more than a clever idea; certainly, real fleas did bite people in those days, and blood could be intermingled. But this is squarely in the tradition of a "conceit", merely a witty extension of metaphor that provides the basis for some argument. He actually gives us nothing of the thing itself, no real description: the idea and argument are what really matter.

Continuing my [admittedly sweeping] over-simplification - into the eighteenth century, Pope and Dryden took English poetry to its most mannered and polished versification. Satire and the rhyming couplet carried the tone of the Age: a smart, sneering artifice in which Nature was merely pastoral and Man was his manners [skim Pope's "The Rape of the Lock" for the ultimate in this vein]. It is not until the Romantics in the late Eighteenth century that we find a serious break with the tendencies and traditions I have been describing. The leaders of the revolution [not unrelated to the political events of the time] were Coleridge and Wordsworth, with Shelley, Byron and later Keats, in revolt against what had been unfolding in this age of Classicism.

Wordsworth has been too well examined elsewhere to need much analysis here. Suffice it to say, he made great claims for the primacy of everyday speech over poetic diction; and for the centrality of both humble subjects and natural things. Moreover, "The Prelude" gives us some of what I take to be the first fully realised references to what could be haiku moments, what Wordsworth referred to as "spots of time", formative moments of realisation that shape the spiritual nature of a person [3], although in his usage they were as much moralistic as anything. Other Romantics could handle moments of intensity, too: Keats' stout Cortez, "motionless on a peak in Darien" [4]; Shelley gave us in Ozymandias a snapshot of man's puny arrogance against the scale of nature's indifference [5]. But in the end, Romanticism went down the traditional way, moralising, intellectualising, drawing it out, wallowing in self-referential emotion. The old battle cry of accessibility through "a selection of language really used by men" [6] became lost.

Through the nineteenth century, poetry ran as traditional as ever: Tennyson ruled the waves, despite what Blake had given us in simplicity. John Clare is much vaunted as one of the first pure and haiku-like Victorians, with his rustic descriptions. I'm afraid I find him generally inconsequential and the producer of what is frequently unilluminating doggerel. Those who were moving closer in spirit to what haiku find in the world were the prose writer Richard Jefferies, who with his "It is eternity now" [7] managed to define perfectly the haiku moment; and Browning who approached it in "Two in the Campagna" - finding that moment of suspension between two people in love.

Whilst the lonely voice of Gerard Manley Hopkins was opening up new possibilities at the end of the century, Ezra Pound characterised "the common verse in Britain from 1890 [as] a horrible agglomerate compost... a doughy mess of third hand Keats, Wordsworth, heaven knows what, fourth hand Elizabethan sonority blunted, half-melted, lumpy" [8]. In other words - the English tradition at its fullest and worst. However, into this new century also came new influences, particularly the French *symbolistes* who had themselves begun to discover short Japanese poems. Thus it was the haiku first made its appearance in the Edwardian years before the First World War. T S Eliot was beginning to write in a way which would change English poetry for ever. His free verse and symbolism take us closer to the possibilities of haiku literature: away from the constraints of consistent rhyme and meter; from the extensive and traditional patterning; from the poetic diction of *doths* and *haths* to the language of the city, the *demimondes* and the pub. The image, the symbol became central, rather than merely metaphorical colour; this was the *"objective correlative"* he took into the wasteland.

A group of writers formed in the years just before the First War who took this idea of the image to the heart of their writing. Known as "Imagists", they based their ideas upon the theories of T E Hulme and Pound among others. Hulme was writing from the desire "to produce the peculiar quality of feeling which is induced by the flat spaces and wide horizons of the virgin prairie of western Canada" - a response many haiku writers would recognise; his inspiration had come through philosophers such as Bergson and Schopenhauer, who had recommended" [the man who] gives the whole power of his mind to perception ... the quiet contemplation of the natural object actually present, whether a landscape, a tree, a mountain, a building, or whatever it may be, inasmuch as he loses himself in this object."

In 1908 Pound defined the image as the "intellectual and emotional complex in an instant of time" and declared his aim "to paint the thing as I see it". He looked for "absolutely accurate presentation and no verbiage" and "a fine language, departing in no way from speech save by a heightened intensity [i.e. simplicity]". Later he wrote "Use no superfluous word.... go in fear of abstractions" and "language is made out of concrete things. General expressions in non-concrete terms are a laziness." Others like Ford Madox Ford agreed that "poetic ideas are best expressed by the rendering of concrete objects"; F S Flint counselled "direct treatment of the thing" and "to use absolutely no word that did not contribute".

At its best, the movement produced poems like Pound's "In a Station of the Metro"

> The apparition of these faces in the crowd;
> Petals on a wet, black bough

Or HD's poem on Hermes that begins "The hard sand breaks / and the grains of it / are clear as wine" However, theory was one thing; the practice was in many cases very different from both what Pound was doing and what they all claimed to be at. John Gould Fletcher could begin a poem on "Dawn" with "Above the east horizon / The great red flower of the dawn / Opens slowly, petal by petal."

And Aldington produces "Like a gondola of green-scented fruits / Drifting along the dark canals of Venice, / You, O exquisite one, / have entered my desolate city." In the end it is perhaps not surprising that the movement folded: too many different points of view; too many inferior poets, also.

And perhaps, too, what I have been arguing throughout: the English tradition reasserted itself. Fletcher himself wrote about his contemporaries, "their attempt has not been altogether successful... intense and concise grasp of substance is not enough; the ear instinctively demands that this bare skeleton be clothed fittingly with all the beautiful and subtle orchestral qualities of assonance, alliteration, rhyme and return". Later he noted "It was the fault of Imagism never to let its devotees draw clear conclusions about life ... [it led] its disciples too often into a barren aestheticism which was and is empty of content... poetry merely descriptive of nature as such, however vivid, no longer seems to me enough; there has to be added to it the human judgement, the human evaluation." Added to this moralising function, the need for complexity and narrative remained. In particular, the horrors of the First World War demanded space for their complete depiction, and for the voicing of the emotion and judgements that naturally arose from their experience [9]. The inter-war years saw a growth in polemic, too: Auden arrived, political awareness was heightened and the arts became the vehicle of analysis and protest. Writers needed other tools for the job than minimalism, to explain, to persuade, to make sense of a brave new world. The earlier fascination with image had been subsumed into the flow; its greatest legacy was concision and ellipsis.

Which brings me back to my opening hypothesis: Imagism was English poetry's chance to assimilate the haiku and make it work. Ultimately, it didn't. The conclusion may be then that the English are just not suited to this kind of writing, and therefore it has little future. However, since the Second World War a great deal has happened to weight the scales back in favour of poetry like haiku, and I think it actually stands a better chance of acceptability than ever before. The reasons for this are complex, and by no means all to be applauded.

Firstly, tradition of all kinds is now under attack; after a century of free verse, free love and the inalienable freedom of the individual, there is scant respect for anything simply on grounds of its tradition. If it doesn't appeal, it's out, whether it's politics or literature. Furthermore, moralising is out too, as the hold of the once Established Church on national consciousness diminishes, and morality becomes regarded as a merely private affair. In its place is a meditative and often undirected "New Age" spirituality that has naturally made use of haiku-like material for its inspiration. If there is a new religion and morality to replace the old, it is perhaps "eco"-centred: saving the world has a very different connotation now from what Tennyson would have understood. With it comes a new veneration for Nature, especially given the huge eco-industry that revolves around it, not to mention the Green politics. Furthermore, the *here and now* has the ascendancy: what is tangible counts for as much as anything these days. This is related to an increasing stress on the physical and sensual: people are encouraged to focus on their senses, in a self-centred way. Poetry therefore that is based squarely on the things of the living world and on sensual experience has great attractions.

Aiding the spiritual revolution has been the influx of exotic influence, one result of the greater global communications revolution, supported more recently by the Internet. [Notable, too, the rise of web-based haiku sites: the relative simplicity of composing haiku on-line is encouraged by the interactive nature of these sites, almost like chat sites - almost indeed like the first renga events.] The increasing and rapid exposure to other cultures through travel, education and immigration has relegated what was the mainstream English tradition to merely one among a number of possibilities. Related to this is one result of the growing pluralism of British society: the centuries of English literary tradition are considerably harder for non-native speakers to cope with, whereas a poetry that requires simplicity, directness and shortness will find a grateful audience.

There are more seriously regrettable reasons for the popularity of minimalist writing these days. I mean in particular the growing unwillingness [or inability?] of the educational establishment to require serious study of pre-20th literature, or indeed of any really challenging material for those other than specialist students. This dumbing down of British culture, the ascendancy of the sound bite, has ensured that little early poetry will be offered as a model. The haiku, however, offers an instant fix. It is like the recorder, that instrument of a thousand Primary school music lessons: anyone can get a tune out of it in seconds; whereas a flute takes for ever. So too, if a child has words and wit enough to make three lines, there will be some teacher to tell her how good a haiku it is. Read any school anthology. Remember your childhood music lessons...

Yes, for better or worse - whatever antecedents haiku might have had, however unpropitious the signs have been - conditions are more right for them now than ever. It has not been easy: the haiku came into this century as an alien form, too short, too unmusical, too amoral; generations of readers and writers before us would have snorted in derision at the claims of the haikuist to be taken seriously; many still do. However, it has been adopted with passion by enough of us to get it a passing mention in the National Curriculum, even while the prescribed lists of Great Writers are being deregulated. We're not there yet, however: Cobb didn't make it to Poet laureate this time; Gourlay will not be in the Poetry Chair at Oxford, either. And we may well have to accost quite a few more strangers on the Clapham omnibus before we hear any of the BHS membership quoted as a "typical English poet".

NOTES

1 "Ode to a Skylark" P B Shelley
2 "Haiku World" Kodansha 1996 ed. Higginson p.71
3 "The Two Part Prelude Wordsworth" CUP 1985 [Part One 1.288 - 374] "
4 "First Looking into Chapman's Homer" J Keats
5 "Ozymandias" P B Shelley
6 Preface to "Lyrical Ballads" 1798 W Wordsworth
7 "The Story of My Heart" Richard Jefferies, Longman 1883
8 for this and all subsequent references to Imagism see "Imagist Poetry" ed. Peter Jones, Penguin 1972
9 I am indebted to Colin Blundell for sowing the seeds of this idea.

W A Grant

Taneda Santoka 1882-1940

He was a drunken, solitary, poverty-stricken, ordained Zen priest who had failed in everything he had tried except, perhaps, writing a free-style form of haiku which has now made him one of Japan's most popular poets.

Somewhat surprisingly perhaps, there are more accounts of his life and his haiku writings available than perhaps on any other Japanese poet, ancient or modern. His haiku were vital and admired for their unadorned style and were representative of what can be called the 'New Haiku Movement'

matsu was kata muite aranami no kudakeru mama

the pines careen the way the rough waves crash

To Santoka, haiku was written Zen; spontaneous, sharp, clear, simple and direct, with no artifice and no striving for effect. He never used any literary or historical allusions nor refined expressions and kept very much to everyday language. His haiku were easy to understand and possessed a beautiful rhythm, assonance and onomatopoeia. This unfortunately cannot easily be translated into English, but the following gives you an idea:

Azami	thistle
azayaka na	brilliant
asa no	morning
ame	rain
agari	finished

His non-traditional haiku were direct observations of nature, the landscape he wandered through and of his daily life and experiences. He didn't obey many of the rules of style, form or content of traditional haiku, a fact which John Steven's freeform translations of Santoka's haiku, *Mountain Tasting - Zen Haiku by Sanika Taneda* (a book I can't recommend too highly) clearly demonstrates.

Born Shoichi Taneda on the 3rd. December, 1882, his early life was somewhat tragic. He endured the suicide of his mother when she was thirty-three and he was eleven and later the failure of his own marriage, the suicide in 1918 of his younger brother, Juro, the death in infancy of his other brother and an early and lifelong addiction to saké. He had a younger, married sister, but she never welcomed him and on one occasion when he visited her, she asked him to leave before the neighbour's saw him. In 1902 he enrolled in the Literature Dept. of Waseda University, Tokyo. There he took the pen name Santoka, which means 'Burning Mountain Peak'. He began drinking heavily and suffered his first nervous breakdown, leaving the university before he could complete the first year's requirements.

His father was a landowner, a business man and a womaniser. In 1907 he sold off some of the family land and bought a sake brewery which he opened with Santoka; in 1909 he arranged a marriage for Santoka that proved less than satisfactory. By 1916 they had lost everything and were bankrupt; in 1919 Santoka left his wife and went to Tokyo to seek work and by 1920 he and his wife were legally divorced. In December 1924 he attempted suicide by standing in the path of an oncoming train, but was rescued and taken to a Zen Temple. Perhaps it was his proximity to the religious life, coupled with despair caused by so much suffering that resulted in his profound desire for a change of direction and through the study of Zen he found what he felt to be his true vocation; in 1925 at the age of forty-four he was ordained a Zen priest, assuming the name Koho.

Thus he began his pilgrimages and wanderings which were to continue until his death on 11th. October, 1940 at the age of fifty-eight. Leaving the cities he followed very much in the tradition of the great Zen eccentrics of the past - Ryokan, Ikkyu, Bashō, Rotsu, Issa, Li Po, Tu Fu and Ozaki Hosai of wandering and begging and it is calculated that he walked more than twenty-eight thousand miles during his travels.

Hotto tsuki ga aru Tōkyō ni kite iru.
At last! the moon and I
arrive in Tokyo.

Occasionally he would settle in a small hermitage and experience the extreme poverty, loneliness and hunger which his lifestyle brought. Giving himself completely to mujo (impermanence), sabi (solitude) and wabi (simplicity) he was thus the true Zen beggar monk who always travelled alone and flowed with the clouds and the water. Whenever he did try to settle anywhere, he found that after a few months contact with other people brought hatred, conflict and attachments and so he felt forced to resume his wandering and to seek again his own particular freedom. His life of continual travel and abandonment of everything that was stable or permanent, a life lived in the present moment and reduced to essentials, enabled him to achieve the Zen nature and outlook with which he sought to imbue his haiku writing. His only possessions were his black priest's robe, his begging bowl and the large, woven straw hat to protect him from sun and rain. Other items that he might have carried along with all the wandering monks of the period, could have included a staff, a journal, pens, brushes, inks, several pairs of straw sandals and a shoulder pack.

Each day he would rise at 4.30am, bath, chant the morning prayers and after a tiny breakfast start out on his journey. He would generally beg for about three hours, stopping in front of houses and chanting Buddhist mantras, visiting no doubt some fifteen to twenty homes before he had enough for his daily needs; sometimes he would be chased away, beaten or abused. Every evening he would record in his journal the name of the inn where he had stayed, his daily expenses, the sights he had seen and his thoughts concerning them. His journals - haibun - became a self-portrait, including such intimate recordings of his innermost thoughts and feelings that often he felt he was growing too attached to them and would burn them or throw them away.

Drinking cold water at the end of a day's travelling and finishing the evening with warm saké were Santoka's greatest joys. Once he described his most intense happiness as 'one room, one person, one light, one desk, one bath and one cup of saké'. His diet mainly consisted of water, rice, saké, umeboshi (pickled plums), takuan (pickled radish), yudofu (boiled soyabean cake), rice cakes, hot peppers, raw fish, tempura and scallions - traditional peasant fare found everywhere in Japan .. Though very inexpensive, when properly savoured it was in fact quite delicious and it is probably because he kept to such a simple diet he never really fell ill; when he did, he apparently recovered fairly quickly, typically perhaps through the further self-administration of more saké.

One typical Zen practice that Santoka was scrupulously careful to observe was to be satisfied with any amount and not to waste anything. His three precepts which were virtually his religion were: *Do not waste anything; do not get angry; do not complain.*

His three vows were: *Do not attempt the impossible; do not feel regret for the past; do not berate oneself*

And his three joys: *Study; contemplation; haiku.* (perhaps one might add a fourth - *sake).*

Sake wa nai tsuki shimtjimi.

No saké;
I gaze at the moon.

Santoka's Zen was not Zazen (sitting Zen) or Dogen or the Koan Zen of the Rinzai sect. His method was more akin to that of the ancient Chinese monks who sought realisation and awakening through the practice of walking and contact with nature on long pilgrimages from one mountain temple to another. Such pilgrim monks were solitary figures attached to no master or temple; walking was their meditation and begging their accepted discipline; Santoka's real monastery was the back roads, mountain paths and sea coastlines of Japan.

Just before his death he wrote:

I find myself in great difficulty. I don't know if I'll eat today or not. Death is *approaching. The only thing I am able to do* is *to make poetry. Even if I don't eat or drink I cannot stop writing haiku.... for me, to live is to make haiku. Haiku* is *my life.*

Barefooted and naked of breast I mingle with the people of the world.
My clothes are ragged and dust-laden and I am ever blissful. I use no magic to extend my life; Now, before me, the trees become alive.

Caroline Gourlay

Some Thoughts on the Writing of Haiku and Longer Poems

In considering my response to the question do I write haiku in the same way that I write longer poems, I thought it a good moment to ask myself whether or not I believe haiku to be a form of poetry. As regards most aspects of haiku, there are varying opinions on this. In *Traces of dreams,* Haruo Shirane persuades us that Bashō saw himself in the context on the Japanese literary tradition and therefore must have thought of haiku as poetry and himself as a poet. R H Blyth on the other hand, maintained that a haiku was not a poem. ‹Haiku ... has little or nothing to do with poetry, so-called, or Zen, or anything else›. *(Haiku:* Vol I Eastern culture) He goes on to say what he *does* think haiku is: ' ... a way of living, a certain tenderness and smallness of mind that avoids the magnificent...' none of which to my mind rules out haiku as poetry. In fact, I believe that it *is* poetry, for if a haiku isn't a poem, what is it? It certainly isn't an epigram, a statement, or an aphorism; neither is its brevity a barrier to its claim to be poetry-several poems that find their way into collections and anthologies are no more than two or three lines long.

That said, it seems that there are comparatively few people who approach the writing of haiku and the writing of longer poems with the same degree of interest or seriousness. Many haiku poets, to give themselves a change, will occasionally write a longer poem but probably don't bother trying to get it published, and we know that some mainstream poets make it their practice to limber up with the writing of haiku in order to get themselves going on what they regard as 'proper' poetry; for them haiku is a means to an end rather than an end in itself.

So, what is the difference between the method employed in the writing of a haiku and that in writing a longer poem? Having talked to several people who do practise both, it would appear that most have no difficulty in working on both simultaneously. I would like to be able to do this, but I find I can't; for some reason when I am focussing on haiku I don't seem able to write longer poems and vice versa. Although I believe that haiku is a poetic form, it is somehow unlike other poetry and consequently my approach for writing it is different; I almost feel that I inhabit different frames of mind, almost different selves, depending on whether I am writing haiku or a longer poem.

As every haiku writer knows, for a haiku to be effective it has to pack its punch in very few syllables - there is no time for an experience, idea or narrative to build up or unfold. The haiku has to be right here, *now* - indeed it cannot be set in the context of time, for it is instantaneous, fleeting, eternally present. A good haiku must demonstrate the only reality which is the present and will come out of an awareness of the true nature of existence, making connections below the level of rational thought. Three haiku that are good examples of this come to mind-ones that I feel were not consciously thought up, but have come to the writer unbidden:

Medical reprieve
wandering the streets
empty handed *Ken Jones*

breakfast in silence-
both halves of the grapefruit
unsweetened *David Cobb*

custody battle
a bodyguard lifts the child
to see the snow *Dee Evetts*

There is nothing contrived or derivative in any of these; they are first hand, authentic. In their different ways all three reveal profound truths about human nature and have a quality that lifts them above the ordinary. Why would a medical *reprieve* leave one 'empty handed'? With the rational mind the opposite would be true; but one knows immediately that it is absolutely right.

Every good haiku points to the here and now, whether it deals with a moment relating to nature, or human nature, or successfully links the two moments of intense awareness that can only be arrived at during those comparatively rare occasions when we are truly living in the present. The writing of haiku is, if not a way of life, a way of seeing. However, we do not always achieve this ideal of fully engaging with the moment; for most of us any ordinary day brings its pressures and preoccupations when all we can do is sit down, knowing that what we attempt will probably be second rate. But that isn't a reason not to write on a daily basis; there are techniques that can be employed, exercises that we can do that will help us to make language work for us. This aspect of working at it applies to the writing both of haiku and longer poems. I have never subscribed to the view that the 'poet' should wait until the spirit moves before sitting down to write. Waiting for 'inspiration' means that it will come less and less often. Writing is a craft and should be practised as such; only if the tools of the trade are kept in good shape is the writer prepared when the Muse does decide to visit.

The brevity of haiku demands a high degree of intensity and every syllable has to be not only the right one, but the *only* one. Maybe the reason that I cannot write longer poems at the same time as I am concentrating on haiku is because when I focus on the latter I build up a kind of 'haiku mind' (or 'haiku no-mind'); I begin to form the habit of living more intensely in the present, of seeing the 'ordinary' as extraordinary. Writing a longer poem demands as much attention and energy as writing haiku, but maybe not in the same way. It requires different skills and, in certain respects, more stamina. In many longer poems the dictates of the form - villanelle, sonnet or whatever - discipline the poet, whereas in haiku the spirit is considered more important than the syllable count. Also, with the writing of longer poems, a familiarity with the subject one is writing about is necessary. Norman McCaig could not have written with such authority on countryside matters if he had not had a deep knowledge and appreciation of the natural world; likewise, Derek Walcott could not have written *Omeros* had he not immersed himself in the Greek myths. No haiku writer needs any such specialised knowledge, just (just?) an ability to *see,* to appreciate the moment and record it with accuracy.

One can be more relaxed about writing a longer poem; it gives one greater leeway than a haiku, for the writing of it will probably be spread over a period of time - anything from days, to years. You can meet it in the past, your own and/or the poem's, accompany it through the present and follow it into the future. There is a sense in which a poem is never finished; it can stretch and yawn, venture up alleyways, only to return and change direction if a particular foray proves unsatisfactory. A writer can start a poem, nudged by a phrase or image that takes root in the mind, an idea that might open interesting doors, not knowing how the poem will end or which aspect of the writer's experience or vision it will finally represent. One can leave it and come back to it; so long as it continues to hold one's enthusiasm and remains alive in imagination, it will eventually flower. These kinds of liberties can never be taken with a haiku. If you don't grab the haiku the instant it makes its appearance, the moment is gone, like a lizard leaving only its tail in your hand. With a poem there is more slack, greater room for manoeuvre; you can return to it, alter it, hone it and if you lose the original theme yet keep the impetus, a fresh approach, even after years, will often carry you through to a different but still valid result.

Many feel that the main difference between haiku and mainstream poetry is in the use, or non-use, of metaphor, simile, aphorism and anthropomorphism. There is insufficient space here to deal more than superficially with this topic, but suffice it to say I feel that in these areas there is more of an overlap than is often supposed. The writing of all poetry, haiku or otherwise, depends on using what is appropriate in the given situation rather than in the keeping or breaking of rules. Where anthropomorphism is concerned, I believe that unless used with the greatest subtlety it weakens all poetry and should be avoided. Aphorism in haiku is always inappropriate, telling rather than pointing, working through the intellect rather than the senses. Simile, which can be effective in longer forms, also rarely seems to work in haiku, lessening tension and taking up too many valuable syllables, but metaphor is more complex and used correctly has an important place in all poetry - it is a powerful tool in the hands of any poet and one of the most effective ways of creating meanings on different levels. It is not always appropriate in haiku: the kind of wild, idiosyncratic metaphors that make Sylvia Plath's and Anne Sexton's poetry so vivid and memorable, for instance, would be quite out of place in so short a form since the writer would lose touch with the reader.

Another area in which haiku and the writing of longer poems share common ground is in the extraordinarily difficult business of saying what we really mean, or rather *knowing* what we want to say. So often we think we are clear about what we want to communicate until we pick up the pen, then somehow the words elude us and we find that what we thought was a strong idea or image in our minds is only an intimation. Hunting down what lies behind this vague, yet pressing, reality takes a surprising amount of concentrated energy. It is so much easier to let the mind slide over what it was that first caught our attention and search out something more accessible. But though it might be more accessible and familiar, it will be less interesting, for herein lies the danger of derivative writing and clichés - the easy option. The difference between a strikingly original poem or haiku and a second rate one depends on the integrity of the writer. John Burnside, a poet I greatly admire, has just such all ability to honour the original purpose of the poem; his poems are well worth reading for their integrity and individuality and for their intelligent use of language.

Harold Henderson has said that 'haiku is more akin to silence than to words'. This statement sums up for me the main difference between it and other forms of poetry. Because haiku is more akin to silence than to words does not mean that it is not a valid form of poem, but it does mean that in some essential way it is different from other forms. In conclusion, I would say that because I perceive this to be an important difference, I can only approach the writing of haiku in a different way from the writing of a longer poem. Perhaps this difference is felt by many poets, even if they are not consciously aware of it, and accounts for the fact that at the moment anyway most tend to write either haiku or longer poems but not both. It remains to be seen which direction haiku will take in the future. If the view that haiku is ' ... evolving ... into a new genre of short poetry that enables each individual to express something important in a few words' (Ban'ya Natsuishi) supersedes the view of haiku based on the spiritual origins of the classical Japanese haiku - those encompassed in the 13 states of mind considered necessary for the writing of it, then it is almost certain that haiku will become indistinguishable from other forms of poetry. Its brevity, however, will never be in question. More important than having something 'important' to say is having the desire and the ability to say it effectively. With so few syllables in which to do so, this will always challenge the haiku poet in a unique way.

Martin Lucas

Spooks, Spectres and the Haiku Spirit

Are there any rules governing the composition of haiku? The rules appear to have a sort of spectral existence, combining insubstantiality with a frightening power to intimidate. I've never actually seen any rules, all I've seen are guidelines and a set of conventions characterised as an evolving consensus. To misinterpret such guidelines as rules is detrimental to the haiku spirit. If the 'governors' of haiku, the editors, were to insist on rigid constraints the result would be ossification. I've seen no evidence that this approach is being advocated, at least in theoretical essays, but I suppose it is possible to discern a drift towards homogeneity in some publications. The third edition of *The Haiku Anthology,* for example, maintains the level of quality of the second edition, but is noticeably less adventurous. But can we be sure that this is the result of an imposition of a constricting template? Is it not perhaps a consequence of the sheep-like timidity of the poets themselves, or, more healthily, the result of some mutual imitation and the establishment of a common poetic language? Stanley Pelter seeks to speak up for the 'governed' by warning that haiku is 'becoming a programmatic discipline in which taboos break through the veneer of tolerance'. [1] This fear-factor, real or imagined, introduces an unhelpful mistrust into the relationship between poets and editors. Against this, I feel a need to renew my editorial vows, as it were, and underline my own commitment to openness. At the same time, I wish to make three key points which, I suggest, have the potential to provide a constructive underpinning for any further discussion of 'rules'. If we work with these points in mind, we can maintain a sense of proportion and read and write with the courage of our convictions. Each point is illustrated with what I trust are pertinent examples.

[1] **Haiku needs both a centre of gravity and an open boundary.** Haiku needs to cohere, or it ceases to be a genre. The various attempts to define the genre have been necessary to provide that coherence. More useful, perhaps, is the practical cohesion established by the mutual intelligibility of the work in a high-quality journal or anthology. But these centripetal forces must be balanced by a commitment to questioning and continued evolution. The borders between

haiku and senryu, haiku and tanka, haiku and poetry, haiku and non-haiku, are indistinct and mutable. Creativity necessarily challenges prevailing perceptions and encourages continual refinement of the sense of what is possible. We are looking at a two-stage process. The initial creation requires a free spirit, but the subsequent submission to the editorial filter is a necessary discipline. Editors can establish a culture of shared values, by being selective rather than wildly eclectic. This isn't the iron hand of tyranny; it is simply the application of principles. The individual poem, however, exists at a single point along the axis between safe centre and daring boundary; it can't simultaneously occupy both extreme positions. For the poet, then, it is only necessary to prioritise each moment of inspiration, forge without fear, and leave to others the judgement of whether, or where, the work 'fits in'.

One very good reason for slackening the reins a little is the recognition that the historical Japanese understanding of haiku is less narrowly confined than our own. Timid reflex reactions can't possibly equip us to appreciate Japanese haiku, which evinced a broad range of possibilities long before the rise of the avant-garde. We have heard, for example, that objectivity is prized and subjectivity isn't. If this is our catechism we are unprepared for poems such as these:

Pomegranate seeds -
how many must I eat
to end my loneliness?

Takako Hashimoto 2

Taking the sort of breath
one takes before confession
... I swim

Yasuko Tsushima 3

Although personal in expression, there is nothing impossibly private here: the poems are open, and we can enter into their spirit. If this kind of 'subjective' stance is beyond us, we are impoverished. We need to extend to embrace it.

[2] In order to ensure an open boundary, **we must encourage sensitive reading practice.** We must respond to each new poem on its merits, rather than by measuring it against a checklist of attributes. The perfect encapsulation of such a position is Colin Blundell's

not a real haiku? / chuck it out of the window / and see if it flies [4]

In other words, what matters is whether the poem works; however it works. Genre definitions are a secondary consideration. It will assist this process if we shift the emphasis of commentary to the act of reading rather than writing. As Maurice Tasnier pointed out in Blithe Spirit 11/1, speculation on the state of mind of the poet at the time of composition can lead us into a morass of confusion. [5] A haiku is a work of art, not a statement in a witness-box. Whether or not there is such a thing as 'haiku mind', it is highly problematic to attempt to use it to gauge a poem's worth. Collating a variety of readings, on the other hand, conducts the debate in accessible terrain. One reward of the workshop process of sharing readings is that we become aware of a broad measure of agreement and specific areas of disagreement. Not all of us prefer strawberries to raspberries; presumably all of us prefer strawberries to straw. This is the application of taste, discernment and appreciation, rather than the cumbersome invocation of 'rules'.

General principles, then, must always give way to the individual case. For example, the injunctions against simile and metaphor, although based on sound poetic judgements, cease to serve us once they harden into absolutes. It is very difficult to use these techniques in a way that doesn't undermine immediacy, but occasionally it is possible to find successes where the evocative power of the poem is enhanced:

Walking through leaves,
the beech mast underneath
popping like seaweed.

Billy Watt [6]

school gate
mothers unravelling
a tangle of children

Maurice Tasnier [7]

At first sight, Billy Watt's simile fails because it proclaims an exactness of comparison that can't be justified: only seaweed pops exactly like seaweed. But the merit of the poem is a by-product of the simile: it captures a drift of attention, unifies the 'actual' beechwood with the remembered seashore, and commends both actuality and association to the imagination of the reader. Maurice Tasnier's 'tangle', meanwhile, is a fine example of poetic economy.

It enables, rather than hinders, appreciation of the familiar scene and in no sense is the metaphor clumsy or obtrusive.

[3] **When commenting on haiku, think in terms of resources** rather than rules, virtues rather than defects. The rules that seem so intimidating are generally expressed in negative terms: no simile, metaphor or personification; avoid isolation in subjectivity, ornate diction, adjectival clutter, artificial concision, padding, redundancy, etc.

All such 'rules' are merely the shadow-side of a much more vital list of desirable qualities. The moods of *sabi, wabi, aware and yugen* all characterise attractive features of haiku, but they have yet to acquire sufficient currency in English. But we *can* identify: space, groundedness, honesty and transparency as strengths. Space is achieved by restraint, and has been identified as 'wordlessness'. It has many applications, including allowing the poem to be completed in the imagination of the reader, not intruding and pre-digesting the experience with interpretative comment. Groundedness means writing close to actual experience, locating the poem in the concrete and specific rather than the abstract and general. Honesty is being true to the nature of things rather than the mundane matter-of-fact. It relates to suchness, the power of things to speak for themselves, as it were, the inner life perceived by the eye of the artist. Transparency means that the language of the poem honours the moment of which it speaks. It does not draw attention to its own status as poetry. These qualities combined result in simplicity and immediacy, or presence: the barriers between writer and reader collapse in a moment of sharing. Personally, I also seek, and respond to, authenticity, the vivid sense of a thinking, feeling mind at work, which can't be achieved by compliance with external criteria.

Where the rule-bound mind detects problems, the creative spirit sees opportunities. One application is a commitment to imaginative truth, a higher value than scientific literalism. Many concrete nouns have power as 'keywords' in the sense that they open up the poem, making connection possible. There seems to me to be no reason why such keywords cannot include imaginative elements, so long as they possess a collective currency and do not erect barriers of privacy. One such keyword which I am keen to welcome is 'ghost'.

Here are four examples of possible uses:

alone on this hill
ghosts of discarded kites
drift into the sky

Annie Bachini 8

These chestnut floorboards,
Worn to a dark mirror
By the feet of ghosts.

Alan Maley 9

moonless night
ghosts singing
in the long grasses

Giovanni Malito 10

midnight
on the river
the ghost of a swan

Frank Dullaghan 11

The keyword does not necessarily open up the poem in the sense of facilitating a paraphrase - although only in the Malito poem is paraphrase at all difficult - but what it does achieve is the stimulation of a rich array of imaginative associations. It enhances both a sense of silence and an awareness of absence. This possibility hasn't been outlawed and nor should it be: we need such resources.

Without ground rules, dialogue is not possible; it would degenerate into formless chaos. As writers and readers, we need to feel that we are engaged in a process of dialogue, and the 'rules' are in place to facilitate, rather than frustrate, that process. But creativity always implies the potential to transcend limitations, and there is no value for editors in legislating against creativity. I believe we *are* open to challenge, to the unexpected, and reports of the stagnation of haiku are exaggerated. But the important point is that it is precisely confidence in the strength of our centre of gravity, a sense that the fundamental criteria of haiku have become soundly established, that propels the form to greater openness. With that security, haiku can unfold without disintegration. It's not, and never has been, poetry-by-numbers; it's an intuitive thing. Let's trust our intuitions.

1 Stanley Pelter, 'Haiku Pensees 2' in *Blithe Spirit* 11/2, p52
2 James Kirkup, *A Certain State Of Mind* (University of Salzburg, 1995), pl3
3 Ban'ya Natsuishi (ed.), *Haiku Troubadours 2000* (Ginyu Press, 2000), p167
4 Colin Blundell, *My Dog Reads Haiku* (Hub Editions, 1992)
5 cf Maurice Tasnier, 'Of Sheep and Goats and In-betweens' in *Blithe Spirit* 11/1, pp12-14
6 *Presence* #14, p16
7 *Time Haiku* 13, p6
8 *Blithe Spirit* 5/3, p13
9 David Cobb & Martin Lucas (eds.), *The Iron Book of British Haiku* (Iron Press, 1998) p69
10 *Presence* #13, p25
11 *Presence* #8, p30

Wim Lofvers

From the Radish Field

In the afternoon of August 9 1956, a fine sunny day, the doorbell rang at my quarters in Rotterdam, where I lived as an intern of the surgical ward of the Harbour Hospital. A pretty young lady entered my room to bring me a birthday present. She was a nurse in one of the wards. Her present, which turned out to be a small German edition of Japanese haiku, was the beginning of something that would become of increasing importance in my life. *Vollmond und Zikadenklange [Full Moon and the Sound of Cicadas]* was among the early translations of classical haiku poetry into a European language. On the page that gave:

Wieder schwand ein Jahr unci ich trage immer noch Pilgerhut und -schuh,	another year and I am still wearing pilgrim's hat and shoes

Bashō

there was a note: *'Das Menschenleben ist eine Pilgerschaft'* [Human life is a pilgrimage ...]. How true, I thought, and I took the idea with me for the rest of my life.

Stimulated by my acquaintance with the young lady, I soon knew the greater part of its contents by heart. It became a sort of cultural backpack which I took along with me when, as a naval surgeon, I was sent to 'Dutch New Guinea', as it was called then - now Irian Jaya. We were at the time 'at war' with Indonesia, which country claimed the large island as its political inheritance, while the Dutch kept up a stubborn resistance to the world's opinion. So I spent a few years in our last lonely outpost in the Far East on a destroyer, which was patrolling in an almost deserted archipelago. In those days I was a great admirer of Somerset Maugham, and much of what I experienced I viewed in the rather melancholy light of his writings.

But of far greater and more lasting influence was the little haiku volume. It gave me a feeling that it might be possible for me to express my own relationship with my surroundings in the austere, measured structure of a haiku. Having grown up in an anthroposophical atmosphere I had come to the conclusion that a spiritual background must be recognisable in the lines of a haiku. And on reflection I made a decision to shape thoughts in the '5·7·5 way' when observing something that impressed me as essential. I still remember this inward decision as one of the important moments in my life.

In those days the earth was still of enormous dimension, and nature seemed endless and unspoiled. A feeling of general responsibility for its continued existence had not yet sprung up. There was still left in us, human beings, a trace of an attitude of amazement with which we looked at our surroundings - at least, there was in me. Looking back I realised how much had been lost in the fifty years that passed since. The world revolved without the help of electronic gadgets, and the three windows (the car windscreen, the monitor of our computers and the TV screen) had not yet spoiled our interest in nature.

When flying back to the Low Countries I took my chance to make a stop in Tokyo and as a result of this visit I cherish the memory of Fuja-san and the Road to Edo. Soon after my return I wrote:

at dawn already
I saw the high window
traversed by gulls

which seemed a premonition of future ambitions. The interesting thing is, though, I remember the moment and situation when it was written.

In Holland I found my wife, and with her I decided on a further adventure, this time going to the North of Norway. As a district doctor I served the local population of the Vesterålen, well North of the Polar Circle, mostly by boat. From early boyhood I was a sea scout - I had had the secret wish to be a sailor, and this existence was the fulfilment of my heart's desire. In the dark days of winter I found my way across the fjord with my skipper in our wooden boat, guided by the Northern Light. For two months the sun hid behind the Lofoten Ridge and on the day it returned a son was born to us. Spring, coming late, was an explosion of flowers and green across the desolate grey landscape. The contrast between the Tropics and the Polar region has remained a basis of my relationship with nature.

A sedentary life followed as a country doctor in the small town of Sneek in Friesland for thirty years, in which I gradually learned to listen to the worries of other people. The existence was made acceptable to us by the many trips we made with our gaff rigged boat. There is intense satisfaction and, consequently, gratitude, at listening to the sound of halyards tapping against the mast and waves lapping against the wooden hull, when lying safely at anchor in a snug creek, the oil lamp lighting the tiny cabin, and one's best friend snoring on the other bunk.

In the end, however, this way of life became a repetition of events, the landscape gradually lost its former charm and it occurred to me that it was no longer necessary to experience freedom in *this* way. The boat was sold - at too low a price – and with little pain and regret. My friend died, too, prematurely. I wrote:

from the haze
  an old moon rises, teaching
    me how to be alone

I now acquired a cylinder press on which I spent many an hour, trying to print the poetry I meant to impress the world with, My private press was appropriately called *It's Time*. Looking back now this 'Longing to Appear in Print' presented itself as a moment of supposed adulthood as a poet. I believed that at last the day for publication had come after some years of wrestling with ways of expressing myself.

Now I see that this, too, was a station I had to pass, a moment of consciousness of the increasing part poetry had come to play in my life. Printing and binding my work seemed a satisfactory way of offering my modest poetical potential to the world. It takes many years and many failures, errors and mistakes to become a real printer, though, and this I was to learn bit by bit. It is but right that one should use one's own literary output to experiment with. So the break between luncheon and consulting hours was filled up with typesetting, and many a patient may have wondered what strange medicine had left those black marks on my fingers.

But after many a happy hour at my Asbern press a lead intoxication became evident, an affliction that probably worsened the beginnings of deafness which I had inherited from my grandfather.

to grow deaf, OK,
but if I don't hear you any more,
September rain ...

This led to my decision to retire to the countryside, The press was sold and a printer bought, and so I entered Modern Times, determined not to become the 'mouse-arm slave' of my PC by carefully dividing my time spent between the PC and more healthy hours amongst the vegetables in our garden, My press was renamed *The High Word* because now we lived on Friesland's highest hill, *It Heech,* a full *11 meters* above sea level.

I became a sort of amateur-editor now. One of my more interesting projects is the production of *Radish,* a series of A8 size booklets, made from one A4 sheet, offering 32 small pages to haijin who wish to present themselves to their literary friends. The title, Radish was taken from Issa's

The turnip puller
points the way to me
with a turnip

I replaced the turnip with a radish, in the conviction that I am, and always will be, an apprentice; this seems to me the right Zen attitude, necessary in my relationship with both haijin and haiku itself. Another discovery was the close connection between garden work and writing ku.

fresh snow-
beyond the garden fence
the pure land

Either subject requires devotion, much care and attention, love for whatever my surrounding may offer, and in the end, now and then, my efforts will yield something to present to others. Also both have greatly increased my respect for other workers in the field.

his father's hoe:
a pilgrim's staff to
the old gardener

This reminds me of the *Bhagavad Gitâ* (13-1) where Krishna says: 'The body is a field, Arjuna: he who knows it is called the Knower of the field.' All outward things belong to the field, from which the Knower may learn. This is what the garden is to the turnip puller, this is what his surroundings mean to the haijin, Issa's poem became the motto to the Radish series, in which recently the 25th volume was published, *l 'Année Haiku* de Daniel Py from which I quote:

Sur les pommes du matin le soleil vient boire	On morning apples the sun comes to drink

I'm proud too to have done a volume for David Cobb, which was called *Just an Alphabet of Haiku.*

When serving the Dutch Haiku Circle (HKN) as its president for some years (they could find nobody else) I got acquainted with many poets and so it was not difficult to find authors whose poetry I could edit. I discovered how much more interesting it is to study and publish *other* people's work than to go on navel-staring at my own ku, This new view of life also led to the foundation of an independent international haiku magazine by myself and Milivoj Objedović, a Croatian refugee who wanted to meet somebody in Holland who was as much interested in haiku as he was: this is a recent ku of his.

Sijena na suncu- koračamo da bih izmjerili vrijeme.	Walking in the sunlight, I measure my shadow.

Our acquaintance led to founding *Woodpecker,* a biennial publication offering space to an international public of authors. It has been alive and kicking for seven years now and - after one or two years of being subsidised - it is now financially independent, surely something rather uncommon in our literary world; but it must be said that all the jobs are done by the Staff on a voluntary basis; we have some very qualified people, among whom I wish to mention Gerda Naarding-Tukkors, our excellent translator. It is a pleasure to get in touch with poets all over the world and to be able to offer them space to share the best of their work with their colleagues elsewhere. This has meant writing in English and in other foreign languages, which has given me much pleasure. Doing this one makes interesting observations: using somebody else's language is like wearing their clothes, a thing that, even if you have asked permission, may cause a feeling of unease, however much you love the language. It is like being an actor in a play. In the end you feel you have to put on your own well-worn old jacket again.

Another thing I have noticed is that language is more specific than belonging to one whole nation; everybody uses their mother tongue in a different way and so is a co-creator of its new developments. This is reflected in haiku. Language is very close to the soul; it is an intimate phenomenon.

More intimate than language is music. While my speech makes contact with other people possible, this contact is limited to my countrymen only; when I make music I have access to everyone in the world. Music seems to be the highest of all arts, because its instrument is least physical - and so most spiritual. This may make haijin a bit more modest. Our ku reflect our best moments, those moments we like to call our 'haiku moments', though this phenomenon seems to be unknown among Japanese poets. I don't mind; haiku, anyhow, has become rather independent of its mother country. We may respect, even revere that country but need not necessarily follow *all* its ways and rules regarding haiku any more.

Biographical data are nothing but the thin shell of what I have come to look upon as an inner biography, which one may read in my ku. Though I have discarded 99% of these myself and others maybe cast away three quarters of the rest, still there may remain some from which the personal 'Narrow Road' I went down could be traced. Another name for a haiku could be 'biogram', since it is the smallest possible description of an essential moment in the poet's life; and threading a series of them on a string would give the reader a reasonably exact description of the author's way in life.

> the choir left
> but the singing remains
> in the May evening

For a few years now I have been a pupil correspondent to a Japanese haiku teacher of the old Bashō school; I believe she is of my age but she is very severe in her lessons. It is not at all easy to accept someone else changing your ideas and ku, and I must say her approach has made me rather rebellious now and then. In defence, I gathered all the basic philosophy and mysticism I could muster to spread out before her, but it has not as yet led to a common point of view.

It is clear, though, that she makes a point of my ku having to 'rise from nothing', i.e. from an inner attitude that is free of bias, judgement, personal emotion etc. whatsoever. That I have not succeeded in reaching such an emptiness will surprise nobody. We have reached a point where both of us seem to be rather out of breath; and this may be a good basis to continue. *Atman* and the German *Atem* (Dutch *Adem),* Breath, are linguistically connected. But she requires me to even let go of *Atman,* while I say that *Atman* is my true spiritual self without which all being ends. Well...

> old pail
> teach me how to pray
> without complaining

Lying awake in the middle of the night, listening to the winter wind (difficult because of my hearing problem), I have come to believe I am writing ku as a way of showing my gratitude for being alive and to account for my life. Thomas Merton writes *(Thoughts in Solitude):* 'Reading ought to be an act of homage to the God of all Truth. We open our hearts to words that reflect the reality He has created or the greater reality which He is.' If this is true for reading, it is all the more so for writing, because the writer is, in a way, a minor instrument of God.

I think writing should be done without emphasis; but it is precisely this which is I find so difficult. Avoiding emphasis is one thing that I think characterises haiku.

Much poetry has to be discarded at a later stage. I wonder when I will stop throwing away my own creations. Maybe this is necessary as a proof of selfcriticism. Learn from the pine tree, Bashō said; I looked at the poplar and found it throwing its cotton-wool seeds all around in a careless way.

I discovered that, because of the 'hidden laws' of haiku, it was impossible to express any philosophy in a direct way and it became quite clear to me that the haiku way was open only to observations, free of subjectivity and judgement. This is affirmed by Bashō›s

> yield to the willow
> all the loathing, all the desire
> of your heart

which seems to give a clear indication of how to follow the Road on which he is our guide. But only a very few people seem to agree with me on this point. So I feel alone; but this is of no importance. That too, is a feeling easily yielded to the willow or the poplar.

Akiko Sakaguchi

An Introduction to Haiga (part 1)

The existence of haiga arises from the incompleteness of haiku.

The highest quality combinations of words and pictures were achieved by Bashō and Buson, but at their time there was no word *haiga.* Buson called his works *haikai no sōga,* that is, a simple, rough drawing for haikai. In the calligraphy of Kanji, there are three types, *kat* (strict style), *gyō* (a slightly rougher style), and *sō* (very rough style), and *sōga* came from this *sō* style. The word *haiga* was first used by Watanabe Kazan in 1849, and he declared in his book that the first *haiga* artist was Shōkadō Shō jō (1584·1635) and *haiga* had been developed by Ryūhō (1595- 1669), Bashō (1644-1694) and Buson (1716·1783). Buson in particular brought *haiga* closest to perfection.

He drew some works of illustrated 'Okuno Hosomichi' (by Bashō) and quite recently one of them has been rediscovered. Buson included these important words in his letter accompanying his illustration for 'Okuno Hosomichi': 'To illustrate a work, it is not fitting to employ *kai* style as in a strict sketch. The *sō* style is best suited to such work as it is full of *hai,* so I drew it a little bit light and comical.' Here is a recent version of the Buson haiga of *Okunohosomichi:*

I found a good explanation of *haiga* in *The Genius of Haiku* (p120): *'Haiga* are compositions in which poetry, calligraphy, and painting, or drawing, complement each other, blending together in the spontaneousness of their execution and the compression of their style. [Like] haiku and the art of Tea, and Flower arrangement, *[haiga]* are not much in little, but enough in little. It is in *haiga* that we see most clearly, directly and instantaneously the nature of haiku, its willing limitations; its 'sensation-ism'; its unsentimental love of nature; its lack of *iki,* elegance; its appreciation of imperfection; its skilful unskilfulness; its 'blessed are the poor'; its combination of the poetic vague and the poetic definite; its human warmth; its avoidance of violence and terror; its dislike of holiness; its turning a blind eye to grandeur and majesty; its unobtrusive good taste; its still, small voice.' Though I can't understand or agree with all this completely, I feel that it is generally in line with what Buson wanted to say.

These examples are taken from a textbook sent to me by my haiga friend, Kiyoko Fukutomi, written by her haiga teacher Kurusu Kota who is a haiga master. These examples perhaps point up the difference between *shasei* and *haiga.* Kota says, 'I don't want you to draw according to patterns. To draw without patterns, it is important to look at the object carefully and to sketch accurately, and then to simplify and draw your haiga. It is important to base the haiga on the sketch. Don't try to draw skilfully or to get any praise. Draw and enjoy innocently and spontaneously.'

Haiga means two ways, one is a drawing with haiku and another is a drawing which has *hai* (= lightness of spirit). To begin, let us draw lines ...

A A Marcoff

Some Thoughts on Haiku, Poetry and Healing

Three cheers for Leslie Giddens *(Blithe Spirit 11/4),* Cherry Taylor *(Blithe Spirit* 12/2) and Diana Webb (in the foreword to her haiku booklet *Dancing Stones)* for highlighting an aspect of haiku I should have written about myself long ago. I remember that while living in Japan the haiku I was shown in translation seemed for the most part childish and banal to my mind and I once dismissed haiku altogether as 'a cultural nod of the head'. However, after a year of intense pressure teaching English to 450 different High School students six days a week, learning first Kendo and then Karate (intensive training often seven days a week) and studying Zen and Japanese language and culture, I suffered a serious breakdown and coming back (somehow) to England went through six years, on and off, of clinical depression, during which I was hospitalised three times.

During those difficult years I tried to hold on to what I knew about Zen (though sadly my teacher in Japan had died) while I worked as a library assistant, gardener and kitchen porter at a Home for the Blind, lavatory attendant, car-park cleaner and maintenance man, and service areas operator (glorified dustman at a new shopping centre). The job as library assistant lasted for six months during which I sometimes cleaned books in the children's department for eight hours a day. The only way I survived was to keep a notepad to hand and - wondering if I had misjudged haiku - to jot down poems that seemed peaceful and beautiful to me in this 'prison' in which I had to work - beautiful in the sense *of yügen,* a word taught to me by Professor Richard Storry when he said that the Japanese think that W B Yeats lived in a world of yüjen. Once I wrote 64 of these short poems in one day and, although many of them were rubbish, some few did seem worthwhile.

hands folded
reach in to the mind
& find -   you

the backlash of the salmon
leaping up the stream:
            this is your past

spilled circle blossom
in the pink veil of the stars:
face to face

An acquaintance had told me that Bashō was the Japanese Shakespeare. I recalled being flown to the island of Okinawa, the home of the Karate Sect I belonged to, for special training. On a day off, I was taken round the clifftop fortifications built by the Japanese to defend the island: I was shown a chamber where a Japanese officer, realising the battle was lost, wrote a haiku on the wall before taking the pin out of his grenade; this deeply impressed me.

Whether the poems I was producing were haiku or not did not concern me at the time. I was using memory (of Africa, Iran, France and Japan - thank you Eric Speight and Stanley Pelter) to write in a therapeutic way of things it seemed healthy to think about in the circumstances. For example I remembered seeing flamingos in the distance on the lake of the Ngorongoro Crater in Tanzania when, at the age of 17, I crossed Africa in one year, and I wrote:

silence of the crater:
distant pink
emancipation

As I cleaned those books in a room without a window, this poem seemed to capture 'a lifetime burning' in a moment (to paraphrase T S Eliot); I reached out to the space and light of Africa and Eternity and realised for the very first time that haiku could be wholesome, beautiful, deep and healing.

I continued to write haiku for years, finding moments of clarity, focus, perspective and peace as I went, until I was employed at last on the other side of the fence as a member of staff at a huge psychiatric hospital in Epsom, where I was an Occupational Therapy Helper and where I was to find that reading and writing poetry (and haiku in particular) were highly successful as therapies for people with depression and many other disorders. A number of my patients told me they liked to memorise my poems, claiming that these gave them great peace of mind.

It was then that I realised that my haiku had become an expression of the Zen I had studied in Japan, that Zen was essentially about *compassion* and that 'a haiku a day keeps the doctor away' (James Kirkup), What I had been through in the previous six years was what St John of the Cross had called 'a dark night of the soul' in which I sought, fought and lost touch with God again and again, until eventually I had the clarity to write:

> the snow of thinking
> covers the earth
> with a white thought

I should add that my experience had been described long ago by the Sufi poet Rumi in Persia (the land of my birth):

In the driest, whitest stretch/Of pain's infinite desert, /I lost my sanity, /And found this rose.

Poetry and haiku writing had played a huge part in my coming through depression to the joy and peace of mind I now have, and I am sure that today the reading and writing of haiku have become deeply connected to my everyday sense of well-being.'

Alison Williams

The Alchemy of Haiku

Alchemy is much misunderstood and, it must be admitted, much of the reason for this lies with alchemists themselves. There is a long tradition amongst them of obscurity and indirectness, of anything but plain speaking. Some might say of deliberate obfuscation. They claim that their work is derived from basic truths and that it is a practical art rather than a theoretical philosophy, and yet they seem unable to state plainly what the truths are, or what the practice consists of in such a way that others can emulate their skill.

This is the first point of similarity between alchemists and writers of haiku. I would like to suggest that there are two further aspects of these subjects that bear comparison. A particular kind of symbolism and, perhaps, the goal of the practitioner.

Alchemical symbolism is dependent on a world view which was taken for granted in medieval times, but which has been widely discredited by the modern materialist and scientific orthodoxy. There are three interrelated aspects of this world view. One is that the world of matter is transient, and that there is an eternal reality beyond the natural world.

The second is that symbolism is not of a merely metaphorical nature but is concerned with discerning real correspondences or equivalence, in the light of which seemingly very different things can be recognised as sharing essential qualities. The third is that these essential qualities are graduated from the lowest to the highest and are capable of transmutation.

The Emerald Tablet of Hermes Trismegistos 1, the nearest thing to a straightforward statement of alchemical principles that exists, begins, 'In truth, certainly and without doubt, whatever is below is like that which is above, and whatever is above is like that which is below.'

Dawn -
the rising mist
turns to gold

To the medieval world view it is obvious that the sun and gold share qualities and that these qualities also have their counterpart in the human body and soul. Today these correspondences, if they are noted at all, are seen as either archaic poetic fancy or as coincidental. Thus a BBC science web site [2] recently noted: 'Mars, the Roman god of war, has always had a special fascination for us. Indeed, there is even a slight connection as both blood and Mars owe their red colour to iron and oxygen.'

R.H. Blyth [3] denied that haiku was symbolic: ' ... it is necessary to state with some vehemence that haiku is not symbolic, that is, not a portrayal of natural phenomena with some meaning behind them ... There is no separation between the thing and its meaning ... One thing is not used to imply another thing. 'I would suggest that what he is denying here is that haiku is symbolic in the limited, metaphorical sense. If there is a symbolism in haiku, and surely there is, it is of the kind that seeks to discern the shared essential qualities in natural phenomena and in the human being's inward experience.

a chained bike
up to its hubs
in yellow leaves

Perhaps the most common misapprehension about alchemists is that they are concerned with the transmutation of lead into gold as a means to wealth. It is true that, throughout the history of alchemy, there have been those 'charcoal burners' who wanted only to discover a formula to get rich quick. This was not the concern of the alchemist who was inclined to devote a lifetime to his work and to have more in common with a hermit or monk than with seekers after worldly riches.

The true goal of the alchemist depends upon an understanding of the concept of correspondence discussed above. In this context the physical transformation of lead into gold can only be achieved in parallel with a corresponding transformation *of the alchemist himself.*

Is our goal to discover the formula for writing the golden haiku? Or is there some other goal which, if diligently sought, will transmute our leaden efforts into something of a higher grade?

I. Titus Burckhardt. Alchemy: Science of the Cosmos, Science of the Soul. Fons Vitae, 1997. Translated from the German by William Stoddart, (First published by Walter-Verlag Olten und Freiburg im Breisgau, 1960) p196

2. http://news. bbc.co. *ukl* 1/hi/sci/tech/3093693

3. RH Blyth. A History of Haiku. Volume I. The Hokuscido Press, 1963. pp13-14

Jesse Peel

Intertextuality in Haiku

Literary allusion as 'a method of expanding meaning is used frequently in Japanese haiku, but often eludes Western readers, or even modern Japanese, who may not have the literary background necessary to appreciate many allusions'. *Haiku Handbook* gives classical and modern examples: On pp.12-14, Buson's *willow leaves fallen / clear waters dried up stones / one place and another* seems, at first glance, a little thin on meaningful substance; but its multi-layered allusion to a particular willow tree spans back some five and a half centuries from a waka by Saigyō (1118-1190), through a nō play by Nobumitsu (1435-1516) and Bashō's Narrow Roads of the Interior (1689), to the 18th century, where Buson (1716-1784) adds a final touch of metaphor to comment on the 'modern' decline of Bashō's haiku method. On pp123-124, an example of allusive variation' is given: *an empty elevator/ opens / closes (J* Cain, 1969 becomes *the elevator / opens ... / vacant masks/ ... closes* (F. K. Robinson, 1976). 'Elevators presumably may be empty in more ways than one'. My own variant is *the lift doors open / full ... / and close - / too damn quick* (a busy department store at Christmas).

In general, allusion within literary texts is used to illustrate or enhance the subject, or to undercut it ironically; but other writing need not be the only source of referential material - well known persons, places, or events might serve as well. The modern term 'intertextuality' (which includes allusion) refers to the multiple ways in which any writing uses, echoes, or is linked to other texts; and the word 'text' might have wide definition. I find some 6% of my haikai writings to be intertextual; (I prefer the term 'haikai' for my own writings). *Dangerous pavements / caterpillar - mind you don't / step on any cracks* echoes Seamus Heaney's *Dangerous pavements / But I face the ice this year / With my father's stick.* The colloquialism *'mind you don't'* can be read two ways: caterpillars are not superstitious. *Effortless, the sun / cuts shadows out of morning frost ... / the beginning of art?* echoes Bashō's *The beginning of art - / the depths of the country / and a rice planting song.* R Aitken *(A Zen Wave)* translates Bashō's first line as *The beginning of culture - /.* My own variant means 'art'. But *Neighbours secateurs? / No - feasting sparrows swing high / stems of Pampas Grass* (compare *Clods of earth / seeming to move? / No - quail* Naitō Meisetsu); *One last search of my room ... / all I wanted from life - / where did I leave it?* (compare *There is nothing / in my desk drawer / I open it and look in* Ozaki Hosai); and *I nose the fine glass / of elderflower spritzer ... / summer's almost gone* (compare *Wrapping my hands round / this teacup's old yellow glaze - / September going* by Kōko Katō) ... these last three haikai are all examples of totally independent writing that lack any intentionality of reference at all. That they compare to other writings (discovered much later) only points to the commonality of certain human experience: they allude to the text of life itself.

Might *Haiku Handbook* have commented a little more on the use - or non-use - made of allusive methods by Western writers? Judging from *The Haiku Anthology* (Cor van den Heuvel), up till 1986, at least, North American haiku writing seemed fairly committed to developing styles dependent on the plain juxtaposition of simple images for their effects; and newcomers to the scene at that time might well have thought that the use in haiku of allusion (of the literary variety at least) was valid only for the Japanese. *Haiku Handbook's* directive - that haiku language 'must be utterly clear, stripped of all impediments to sharing', might have been read by some as prohibitive to the use of all allusion (consequently seen as being just as bad as metaphor in closing off the writing to a reader's interpretative freedom, even though *Haiku Anthology* and *Haiku Handbook* do comment on the not infrequent use made of allusive variation by poets of both East and West). What evidence is there that the creative climate has changed since? Not a lot, it seems to me. But then my opinion is based on little more than what I read in UK haiku publications: few Japanese haiku (whose translations may mislead, and whose allusions, if any, may be culturally obscure anyway); and little up to date transatlantic writing. But flicking back recently through 10 years of *Blithe Spirit,* I found little evidence of allusion that deepens the text. Maybe I missed much. Where, for instance, was *How pleasant - just once / not to see Canary Wharf / through morning mist* by Martin Lucas, that I came across some 6 years ago? (an ironic allusive variation to one of Basho's haiku - for *'Canary Wharf,* substitute *'Fuji').* As if in pre-emptive rebuke, while I was writing this, *Blithe Spirit* 12/4 came through the door with Ken Jones' *Long grasses / through cracks in tarmac /*

planners' dreams (the irony here gaining much from its soft voiced allusion and pivotal ambiguity); and Stanley *Pelter's fallen leaf / how could I mistake it / for a butterfly* (after Arakida Moritake) - which I nearly missed!

It isn't necessarily easy to pick up other writers' allusions. Allusions don't have to wave frantic flags at the reader; and they might be anything from semi-private to full up-frontal, from simple sensory to complex mental. Also, as with extended metaphors in Western poetry, some allusions in haiku may well work best when one is least aware of them. Take for instance my *always one leap ahead, / wet sand spurts / precede my feet,* conditioned by Ruth Robinson's *a splashed frog / leaps ahead / of my watering can.* Any beach-stroller will surely have noticed this phenomenon; a few may even have sensed that it reminded them of something (without being able to pin down what); but who hasn't chased a frog with a watering can? Observation and word entering my mind together, *'leap'* was retained for its spontaneity. More privately, consider

slowly
turning
turkey
carcass
suspended
over silent snow
the sun sets

Only a few classical piano enthusiasts are going to get the slightest twinge of allusional recognition here (a vision of *Le Gibei,* from Ravel's *Gaspard de la Nuit,* which pictures a criminal left to hang outside the city gates. In the reddening sun, his body slowly rotates). But the writing stands well enough on its own; and notes only serve to expand any sensual appeal it may already have. More complexly, consider *Spring weddings ... / the wind scatters confetti / over old graves. 'Spring',* the immediate word, deflects attention from the allusion to Philip Larkin's *The Whitsun Weddings:*

> *... the wedding days*
> *Were coming to an end. All down the line*
> *Fresh couples climbed aboard: the rest stood round;*

The last confetti and advice were thrown,
And, as we moved, each face seemed to define
Just what it saw departing: children frowned
At something dull; fathers had never known
Success so huge and wholly farcical;
The women shared
The secret like a happy funeral; ... (extract)

... but the distinction between Spring and Whitsun hardly matters; the dance of Life is, at all times, only the flip side of the dance of Death. Larkin might well have thought of the ephemerality of Mayflies while writing his poem.

Back in 1991, *(An ABC of English Haiku,* progenitor to our present *Composite View),* David Cobb wrote, 'Japanese haiku are riddled with allusions to famous Literary works and historical events. The margins of allowable allusion in English still have to be charted. The furthest I've dared go is: *on the stroke of noon / the snow-gown of the cypress / is turning to rags* '. Well, I rather like this haiku, despite it seeming a cocktail of reference, metaphor and marginal anthropomorphism. But 'allowable' and 'dared' are hardly positive words, and between '94-'96 *(Towards a Consensus; Haiku for All; Haiku - Then and now),* allusion gets scarce further mention. Then, in *The Nature of English Haiku,* we find 'other matters ... subject to fashion as well as personal taste ... include ... allusion' and 'Allusions were much favoured by Bashō, but are riskier these days, when even well-read people do not all read the same works'. In sardonic mood, one might ask, 'are we then to dumb down haiku to the level of our worst-read readers?' More moderately, we might ask 'Was it only Bashō?' or 'Were allusions understood by everybody in classical times, then?' Anyway, all such writerly caution needs is the observance of a few technical guidelines. Finally in *English Haiku: A Composite View,* we find 'The desire for "presence" does not rule out allusion. One of haiku's achievements is to relate present and past (as represented by literature, legend, history), hinting at the transience of the former and the enduring quality of the latter, so that our living experience fuses in a common paradox'. Well, that seems a bit weighty; surely allusion might have lighter purpose too? Most importantly, is anyone listening to such advice? Having occasionally spoken to English 'doers of haiku'* who seem of the opinion that literary allusion, at least, has little or no place in English haiku; and having also had the quaint experience of having some of my own haiku liked well enough until their allusive depths were revealed, ("Oh, but that's too difficult - haiku should be more immediately readable ... "), I'm inclined to be somewhat dispirited. I find it depressing that 'we' are willing to give so much time to discussing terms such as *immediacy, particularity, incompleteness, unguardedness, directness, deep playfulness* etc. (terms having all the subjective indefinability of wine bibbers' jargon), yet choose to ignore the objective and glaringly obvious: that the use of allusion always was, and, according to *Haiku Handbook* (1985), seemingly still is, a part of haiku tradition in Japan. Allusion works! By turning simple images into potentially more complex ones, it produces yet one more (or is it two?) of those allegedly sought after haiku qualities: *depth* and *layers of meaning.*

So what guidelines might be suggested for the use of allusion or any other form of intertextuality in haiku? Well, I suggest that referential material might be 'anything that works'- for light or serious purpose; but unless one is writing imaginary haiku perhaps, it should not be contrived or sought. Nor should one go around with likely references in one's mental pocket, just itching for the opportunities to use them. Referential material should be evoked naturally by circumstance, drawn to the surface of awareness from one's subconscious by the lure of the right moment. That way one maintains makoto, sincerity or whatever, by making the freshness and spontaneity of the language and the freshness and spontaneity of the moment one and the same thing. For instance, it shouldn't really stretch belief to accept that, on having my path crossed by a green squidgy thing with multiple legs, I just might - quite innocently and almost without thinking, have come out with *Dangerous pavements / caterpillar.* 'Deep playfulness'? Search me; but certainly, in such circumstances only the deliberate act of erasure or editing out could be considered as contrivance. James Hackett *(The Zen Haiku)* advises 'Never use obscure allusions ... real haiku are intuitive, not ... intellectual'; and I'd mostly go along with that. Certainly, one shouldn't use allusions simply to display the brilliant mind. Besides which, allusions are far more likely to be immediately effective if they work first on the senses rather than the intellect. But it might be reasonably argued that if a haiku is already independent of any allusion that it contains, then it cannot matter much if that allusion carries unobtrusive erudite baggage? Who'd notice, except the few readers who might enjoy a discovered bonus? *Most importantly,* all haiku should stand independent of any allusions etc. that they contain. Explanatory notes might be supplied as appropriate; in the absence of such aids, allusive haiku should never deny a reading to those who do not share the writer's 'erudition'.

* Apparently, in Japan, one asks, *Haiku o nasei masu ka?* (literally, *Do you do haiku;* and 'To write haiku', means to put in calligraphic form, (Yagi Kametaro; Messages from Matsuyama). Our editor further informs me that the word *poet* has its roots in Greek, where poet = *poietés* (a maker or doer of things).

A Comparison of two haiku:

the silk-tearing / biwa's current / autumn's voice (Buson in *Haiku Handbook)*

Written from on the spot experience, this haiku concludes a haibun *('Uji Visit).* Haibun title and haiku's opening line reference a poem by the T'ang Dynasty poet Po Chü-I.

> *a silver jug suddenly dashed crystal fluid spatters*
> *armored cavalry rushes out swords and spears resound*
> *song gathering to the end stroke with care struck*
> *four strings one sound* like tearing silk (extract)

Biwa and Ujl are both rivers; Buson and Po Chü-I both lovers of the social pleasures of life in the capital where there is access to art and music, etc. But Po Chü-I's poem relates to a time when he has been sent to live in some provincial outpost, and describes the ambience - particularly the sounds - of an evening on the river; *'like tearing silk'* forms a small part of a complex sensual image that captures the sounds of both river and distant lute music; and the whole poem evokes feelings of intense nostalgia for the life missed elsewhere.

Buson, too, experiences the rural life away from the capital; and faced by the mountain torrent of the Uji, he remembers Po's lines. By use of his allusion, he manages to fuse all of the intensity of Po's feelings with his own - plus whatever extra is carried by the seasonal *'autumn's voice'.*

Buson would have had a select contemporary readership familiar with the Chinese poets - one that would probably have needed no help to understanding; although the haibun does cite the alluded to poem and relevant extract. But can an unannotated translation of this haiku be understood by modern westerners? Does it take too much imagination to grasp that *'the silk-tearing'* is metaphor for the sound of a river? Even missing out on all that the alluded to poem has to offer, unknowledgeable about haiku and season words, might one not still intuit *something* out of *'autumn's voice'.* Overall, might one not get *some* sense of nostalgia for things lost? Whatever, what's underlined here, is *how* Buson's allusion was inspired; also, that in classical times at least, it was not frowned on to write 'erudite' haiku.

Over the gravel sea, / a river in the trees - the sound / of children's voices

No haibun, no footnotes: access to meaning is through the poem itself. This apart, the 'haiku' has not a little in common with Buson's. I wrote this spontaneously from the immediate experience of visiting a formal Japanese garden. The poem images the wind in a stand of pines mingled with the distant sound of children playing, and it references two lines by Seamus Heaney: *The riverbed, dried up, half full of leaves. / Us listening to a river in the trees.* Now, poetry scraps can be released from the subconscious by events similar to those that caused them to be written in the first place; and at such times, one really shares with the poet. But when these scraps reach the surface of awareness, they may well have dragged with them more cognitive, yet no less spontaneous associations that overwrite with symbolic meaning - for the writer at least.

How accessible is this haiku? Does one need to have read Heaney, or an analysis of his lines to reach a reasonable interpretation? *'a river in the trees'* intends to evoke a sense of rushing water or the sea; and to reinforce this interpretation, the second line ends with - *'the sound'.* But when second line runs into third, *'of children's voices'* an ambiguity is created as to what has been heard, (Buson wrote in his haibun, 'The sound reverberating in mountain and valley confuses human speech'). Only *'over the gravel sea'* risks causing problems for readers. Some may not know that a common feature of formal Japanese gardens is a carefully raked area of gravel that symbolises the sea, while tumbling rock-falls symbolise mountain torrents etc. But then, maybe we can learn from other peoples' haiku? Would Buson have expected everybody to understand his allusions? In fact, this haiku has not deviated far from current standard practice - two juxtaposed images to evoke a shared sense. Doesn't the sound of wind in trees, sea surge, or children's voices evoke, in older persons at least, a sense of nostalgia for something lost or undefined? Admittedly, we need Heaney's first line for any autumnal sense; and it requires knowledge of both Heaney's lines to release the hidden 'erudite' baggage (such as it is). Heaney may well have been metaphor-ing a need to find a new poetic voice from an old source. When I wrote the above, I happened to be thinking about the English haiku. But if nobody knows that, does it matter much?

To conclude: should we actively strive to use allusions in haiku? Definitely not! Nor need we become literary scholars in order to write haiku. I have tried here to provide a spectrum of intertextuality in haiku/haikai writing, and to suggest that all of us, irrespective of background, must have assimilated plenty of referential material that might enrich our writing - if we let it. I'm suggesting that, as creative writers, we should try to keep our minds more open, ridding them of what might well be misconceptions; and that we be not so quick to edit out the dreaded 'literary excess' when it appears in response to instant perception. Perhaps also, as intelligent readers, we should accept that haiku might be written to a range of literary strengths, just as we accept that Western poetry has its Wendy Copes and its T.S. Eliots. Might not Buson have known similar times? Surely, we owe it to Haiku to protect *all* the important elements that have contributed to its tradition. How sad, if West (and East in imitation of the West) lost one of the foundation stones of Haiku's literary status, either through misconception, or because raising the creative stakes became too much like hard work. Who knows what Western poetic interest might not be stirred by an infusion of Buson-style writing?

Canada geese at grass - / no time to stop and stare, / just peck and go.

A flock of geese moving like a shoal of fish - no time for anything except feeding. Two allusions suggest Man's position in an increasingly techno-corporate world: *What is this life if, full of care / we have no time to stand and stare?* (W. H. Davies) *Just wash and go* (Shampoo commercial jingle). Despite all its post-analysis, this writing wrote itself, spontaneously, in exactly the above form.

Quite fortuitously, it might even, from a distance, nod towards Bashō: Learn from the geese what it is to be a goose. Spontaneity works - if you let it.

*

Presentation of this article at the BHS Ludlow Conference at the end of April 2003 drew two comments; only their gist is given here; neither question is *verbatim,* and I apologise for any errors:

HR: Surely, one needs to be steeped in literature to be able to generate worthwhile allusions?
JP: I used the term 'intertextuality' to forestall this question. The suggestion is that the mindscape of the syllabically challenged haiku might be expanded by the use of spontaneous (not contrived) referential material without bending 'the rules'. Such material might be a single word, a colloquial phrase, a line of poetry, a historical reference - *any material that works,* as long as the end result is compatible with some aesthetic standard. For instance, the scent of *'May-flower'* through car windows might suggest a sense of adventure; *'blowing in the wind'* might mentally transform a shower of leaves into thoughts; *'one night cheap hotel'* (T.S.Eliot) might set just the right world-weary tone for a particular haiku; looking for four-leaved clovers on *'Culloden moor'* might prolong a reader's thought. Of course, the more marinaded the haiku poet is in 'real literature', the more likely it is that 'real literary allusion' will appear in his or her creations. At least, that's the theory; the thing is, it rarely seems to. I'd hate to think that our 'really well read' members were stifling all spontaneous allusions at birth so as to pursue some ideal based on simple imagery. Both methods seem to have had equal validity in haiku history.
ML: So far, I've not been really impressed by any western attempt at allusive haiku writing.
JP: Sure, but then *'so what* sickness' afflicts simple imagery haiku too. What I'm suggesting is that we won't know what may be achieved by acceptance of allusive methods, especially in the hands of those best equipped to use them, until we make the effort - both as writers and readers. And I'm certainly not expecting the sudden emergence of small miracles of haiku literature. Technical and cultural factors (differences between classical Chinese and modern western poetry for example) will probably stop us ever writing

haiku like, or as effective as, Buson's *willow leaves fallen* or *the silk-tearing.* But from my position of limited reading, I feel that western haiku is due some 'new' technology (technology which in this case seems scarcely to have been tried out) in order to produce something of more varied interest - that more people will accept. The way via *Intertextual City* seems a better literary bet than the road to *Surreality.*

I found Ken Jones' allusive comparison of developers with warriors stimulated thought as well as humour. Despite the different translations of Bashō's *Fuji* haiku (Aitken v Blyth), many might now think of this as, *one can have too much, even of a good thing; what then the bad?* Your variant thus has enjoyable valid humour, even if 'not great haiku'. And for myself, I was pleased simply to be able to spontaneously respond to both previous *elevator* variants and *Haiku Handbook's* comment on them. Regarding Buson's use of allusion, *Haiku Handbook* says, Buson's allusions 'never appear without the clarity and power of a strong sensory image'. But his two haiku quoted in this article still seem to fall into two categories. *willow leaves fallen* encourages us to think (through metaphor) as well as see; *the silk-tearing* seems the stronger haiku because it links strong sensory haibun imagery to equally strong sensory imagery of allusion, requiring us only to see and hear (could the haiku have been written without the haibun?). Whatever, my own *over the gravel sea* seems category one - one for 'thought'; so does *turkey carcass* (except that the allusion is not obvious, and needs notes).

In a recent haibun - *Thoughts, Words, Writing* - I wrote 'Tai Haku, the Great White Cherry, much valued in Japan, is said to have vanished from Japanese culture somewhere between the 18th and 20th centuries, only to be restored from a 'new' clone found in an English garden'. That was a fortuitous metaphor; although, of course, haiku has never vanished from Japan. However, what I was suggesting was that this new clone must, while retaining its parental ('genetic') constraints, develop within the space afforded by its new cultural surrounds. It should reflect *our* approach to life, *our* seriousness, *our* sense of humour (not just *deep playfulness)* etc. And Western humour there should be, as well as Western colloquialisms etc. For myself, I am very unsure as to the nature of what I am writing, but I have felt for some time now that true haiku can only exist in the country where the tradition lies: that all else can only be 'haiku equivalent', different, though of no less literary value. To ask 'what constitutes haiku' in relation to Eastern and Western forms seems hardly worthwhile. I refer to my efforts as haikai, because I feel that too close an allegiance to the principles of so called 'true' haiku precludes experimentation into finding a true English form; while the use of haiku to describe some of the experiments tried out by others seems misleading. On the other hand, the experimental use of intertextual methods seems a step in the right direction, in as much as it seeks to restore a seemingly ignored, yet important, traditional technique.

*

Ah, Jayzus! And isn't Man's whole life one huge bloody constraint in which he struggles to perfect his tiny song. And isn't it the givin' up on it that's the sickness?

Stanley Pelter

Haibun - Here There & Everywhere

Over the past few years there has been a flurry of haibun activity. Now there is a plethora of criteria with plenty of discussion about its possible characteristics. Discussions and arguments trip from one person's magazine to Society Journals. Ariseth the Need, Cometh the accidental Committee!

The desired outcome seems similar to that believed achieved in the haiku debate: a socially acceptable consensus, broad enough to digest a modicum of divergence sufficient 'to constitute an agreeable and satisfying continuity of discourse'. This ensures that the range of incompatibility is limited. Only acceptable are variants within a single problematic. What would happen if discourse shot beyond containable agreement, beyond the psychologically and emotionally secure?

There are perhaps insufficient historical antecedents; source material is relatively limited and often second-hand. A vacuum exists. Many suggestions derive from a haiku mould. Some are rigid, others broader but tentative. If this goes on it will result in a tradition producing a similar mind-set to that of contemporary haiku. Competition Judges and Editors will base decisions upon parameters now being decided. Even what seems open and flexible soon fixes, limits, confines, makes for pastiche, a 'follow-my-leader' mentality. Much present bravado consists only in disobeying structural limitations. Beyond this, we remain tied to ancient maestros, commentaries and interpretations. It would be useful to ask: What might be the shape and dimension of, reinvented haibun?

Where is the 'debate' now? What aspects are considered too important to exclude? Where are the edges of acceptable disagreement? What is so beyond doubt it is beyond dissent? Here is a dollop of what is felt should form part of this hybrid form: incorporate existing characteristics or haiku; add 'literary' and 'arty' qualities to 'embellish' the prose component; haiku and prose should integrate; haiku can detach from the prose; haibun is more effective without two or more haiku set next to each other; the work ends with a haiku; haibun 'shows' not 'tells', but should contain a variety of layers and be expressed with musicality; an epiphany is the high aim but, failing that, it is important to integrate haiku and prose to create and build a unity in which both major elements are enhanced; authorial reflective impositions are desirable: subject matter is broad, but there should be only small doses of exposition; it is not an accumulation of 'sound bites'; it should be elliptical in the haiku tradition; there should be unity in diversity; abstract and conceptual words are shunned, depending more on vibrant and glowing imagery; no emotional outbursts; it should be an in-depth, creative piece of work, not just the recording of stimuli; the writer's 'detachment' is essential; there is a 'right' proportion of haiku to prose; senryu in haibun is, in the West, acceptable; 'story' climax is not relevant; haibun contains the essential 'lightness' associated with haiku, and makes use of unexpected and contradictory images, irony, wit, paradox, ambiguity, enigma; haibun, for Bashō, is writing in the style of haiku, (though his haibun style was one of continuous development); sacrosanct - it *is always a combination of haiku and prose, and the dialogue between them is the gut.* Where is the space for *invention?*

What would adventurous Basho have made all of this? Perhaps he would have absorbed Eisenstein's practical and written work *(Film Form, Essays in Film Theory);* he might have used and developed the devices employed by great Japanese Film Directors like Akira Kurosawa (in *Rashomon, The Seven Samurai)* who made moving montages with interposed and vibrant images, created awesomely sensitive 'light' yet dense layers of atmosphere, effects and mood. Would he carry a cadcam on his travels, and be accompanied by a cameraman with editing equipment at his base studio? Would he go on physical walkabouts? What would he mingle and mangle with haiku, let alone haibun, if he were to reinvent it now? The world moves on...

I have re-read many haibun, plus and minus haiku. I do not find unless, unless very short, easy to finish. At best they leave but a faint memory, a hope that they were fiction, and a concern that the 'literary' effects were so hard won. there are a few exceptions: some of Helen Robinson's and, occasionally but brilliantly, David Cobb's haibun have integrative and unifying power. But mostly the haiku are preventative, not enhancing, and the prose lacks those qualities considered core to the haiku genre. Many leave that dulling 'so what' taste' in the mouth.

Why not invent without constraints, question the unquestionable and remove the safety net of Japanese commentary! This might free us to brainstorm, to open hitherto 'impossible' doors. Can haibun, for instance, be conceived within a form of self-contained prose imbued with the *'spirit' of any Age in which people find themselves alive?* If not, why not'! Can *the* haiku be subsumed, or integrated into the body of the prose? If not, why not! Devices should be reviewed; emphases altered; others introduced; there there might emerge different balances between them. There may be value in, say, a controlled cliché-based approach, different uses of musicality, sentence contrasts, uneven rhythms, unusual 'literary' syntax - the equivalent of discords in music or complimentary colours in painting. Is it possible that haiku could act as an image that works by juxtaposition rather than merely being related or integrated by connection? Presently we are repairing rather than playing the instrument. At the moment there is a disconnect between intention and invention. Might we not excite ourselves by adopting 'the-world-is-our-oyster' stance rather than staying roped to that same old creaking wooden bridge, watching Hokusai's 'Wave' approaching ever closer?

Evidence for the above has come, with thanks, from at least the following:

Haibun: What are We Up To... ?	*Presence* 15	Ken Jones
A Few Timely Heresies about English Haibun	*Blithe Spirit 10/3*	David Cobb
Creating Haibun	*Blithe Spirit 10/3*	Ken Jones
Concerning Free Range Haibun	*Presence 15*	Allan Jarrett
Letter from Ludlow	*Blithe Spirit 12/3*	Jesse Peel
Thoughts, Words, Writings	Hub Editions	Jesse Peel
Haibun in Progress	*Blithe Spirit 10/3*	Jo Pacsoo
Review- Mice in the Living Room	Frogpond*XXV:3*	M. McClintock
The Cosmological Eye	Dobson	Henry Miller

Matthew Paul

A Winger's Shadow: Haiku and Sport

In telling people of my intention to write this paper, the reaction was inevitably one of surprise or indifference: "Haiku and sport - they're incompatible, surely?" Indeed, at first sight, the competitiveness and all-action speed of sport would seem to be the antithesis of haiku spirit; but I aim to show, however, that sport, even in its most commercial varieties, is a subject matter that can lend itself to the writing of poignant senryu and profound and moving haiku:

in the bedroom mirror
the old slow bowler
bowls at himself 1 *David Cobb*

shielding his eyes
with his baseball glove ...
first geese 2 *David Elliott*

As these examples demonstrate, it is perhaps not surprising that the (to non-adherents at least) arcane complexities of cricket and baseball account for most of the sporting haiku written in English to date. It is worth remembering that baseball is followed passionately not just in North America but in Japan also (although cricket seems to have been somewhat lost in translation to the Far-East so far). The *Haiku Anthology* includes some fine baseball-themed haiku that celebrate the slow, patient build-up of excitement within a game:

at shortstop
between innings
Sparrows dust-bathing 3
Alan Pizzarelli

summer afternoon
the long fly ball to center field
takes its time 4
Cor van den Heuvel

Like haiku itself, baseball and cricket are often dependent upon the elements:

October rain
the tarpaulin ripples
across the infield 5 *Alan Pizzarelli*

a faint hiss of rain-
the sound of cricket repeats
on television 6 *John Barlow*

If anything it is surprising that cricket, with its obvious summery associations, and its potential for 'moments', hasn't made more frequent appearances in haiku. Both Cyril Childs, in New Zealand, and myself have written cricketing haiku sequences, but there is scope for so much more:

cricket locker
an odour of mushrooms wafts
from the practice gear 7 *Cyril Childs*

the breath between
appeal and decision -
pigeons fly 8 *Matthew Paul*

Cricket with all its attendant, sometimes bizarre, terminology - 'rain stopped play', 'short leg', 'howzat', 'silly mid-off', and so on - could probably fill a quarter of an English *saijiki* on its own, and I have no doubt that it will continue to inspire haiku poets for as long as the game survives. Like it or not, tennis plays an equally essential role in the English summer, but appears to have had a disproportionately minimal impact on haiku to date:

switching channels
from tennis to tennis...
the sun comes out 9 *Martin Lucas*

tense match-
at the drinks break the umpire
keeps his distance 10 *Cyril Childs*

The conclusion to be drawn, maybe, is that lone-combat sports do not inspire haiku poets in the same way that team-sports do, but the contrary ought to be the case; after all, the loneliness not just of the long-distance runner but of the individual sporting participant *per se* would be rich with existential moments of *sabi* and *aware.* So far, though, apart from the odd few poems on chess –

afternoon cafe / the captured chessmen / in an empty cup 11
Michael Ketchek

that has not been the case. I am not certain if the buttock-wrenching grapple of sumo wrestling has gripped the imagination of Japanese *haijin,* but one could be forgiven for thinking that golf, horse-racing, judo or even snooker or darts might by now have inspired their western counterparts.

The national sports of the USA and of this country have also failed, by and large, to engage the haiku imagination, despite their apparent centrality to our respective cultural identities. Websites such as *Football Poets* (www.

footballpoets.org) proliferate with nearly-haiku and nowhere-near-haiku; the real thing surfaces only occasionally; Alec Finlay's Baltic Mill football haiku project produced slogans rather than genuine haiku; but the rare examples published in haiku journals thankfully contain the classic haiku ingredient of the fleetingness of the moment:

Late summer practice-
footballs in the end zone
gathering shadow 12
Barry George

beneath the floodlights
a winger's shadow
darts in four directions 13
Matthew Paul

The pomposity of superstar footballers and stereotypical cigar chomping coaches, managers and chairmen has, happily, been targeted too –

stadium tour / a pigeon struts / in the manager's box 14
Matt Morden

But we can't all be superstars of course and, far removed from the glamour and over-paid hype of professional sport, the simple innocence of childish enthusiasm has inspired other writers:

penalty:
I place the ball on the spot
I painted myself 15
David Cobb

The last kid picked
running his fastest
to right field 16
Mike Dillon

The sharp-eyed will have noticed that all the examples here are by male hands, not out of choice but of necessity: I was unable to find a single sport-related haiku or senryu by a female writer, which was a surprise, given that sport, in the main, is thankfully no longer the preserve of men and boys.

Sport, like life in general, is of course multi-faceted and universal, from the kick-about in the park or street, to the crazed bravery of the charge down a ski slope, to the great crested grebe courtship rituals of synchronized swimming. In all its forms, it produces strong emotions - adrenalin-pumped *machismo,* tears of defeat, or complete and utter apathy for non-followers - and telling moments both of high and inconsequential drama. I see no reason why haiku and senryu cannot portray the emotions and subtleties of sport and inspire great writing that we can all enjoy, regardless of whether we are sporting participants, devout or armchair fans or - in some cases-bored rigid by all of its many varieties.

calm evening
the ballgame play-by-play
across the water 17
Jim Kacian

September dew-
the last-man-in
with a yellowed bat 18
David Cobb

1 *A Bowl of Sloes,* Liverpool: Snapshot Press, 2000, p.17
2 Ed. Cor Van den Heuvel: *The Haiku Anthology* (3rd Edition) New York, WW Norton 1999 page 37
3 ibid pg. 154
4 Ibid pg. 229
5 Ibid pg. 154
6 Snapshots 3, July 1998 pg. 6
7 Presence 20, May 2003 page 29
8 Blithe Spirit 9.2, June 1999 pg. 13
9 Snapshots 9, 2001 pg. 40
10 Ibid pg. 19
11 Ed. Jim *Kacian/Dee Evetts, A New Resonance,* Winchester, Va, Red Moon Press 1999 p. 106
12 Snapshots 8, 2000, pg. 37
13 Snapshots 7, 2000, pg. 21
14 Snapshots 6, October 1999, pg. 16
15 Ed. Colin Blundell, *Home* (BHS Anthology), Sutton Bridge, Hub Editions 1996
16 *The Haiku Anthology,* op cit., page 33
17 Ibid, page 95
18 Snapshots 5. January 1999. page 10

Kōta Karusu (tr. Susumu Yamane & Kiyoko Fukutomi)

First Steps in Haiga

What Is Haiga?

Haiga is an art form associated with haiku: haiga is derived from haiku. Kenkich Yamamoto (1907-1988) a literary critic, said: 'I cannot appreciate haiga, It is often over-simplified and lacks the depth of real art.' I agree with this opinion in the sense that generally speaking, modern haiga is very poor in artistic qualities. To be artistically sound, haiga has its starting point in haiku calligraphy: rightly conceived, haiga is the expression of poetic sentiment in harmony with haiku, drawing and calligraphy artfully combined.

The relationship between Haiku and Haiga

In order to create haiga, first of all you must study and understand the depth of haiku: essence of haiku is that it does not contain the poet's complete feeling or thought but leaves a space for each reader to develop images different from those of the poet; this creates a second and a third conceptual world. This is the charm and the heart of haiku,

Then you learn some elementary points of haiga art and calligraphy.
Haiga is a kind of intellectual play which can result in a rich creativity; the essence of haiga is not necessarily in the finished product but in the process of its creation; the haiga artist plays in the realm of poetry. Here is an example of such play:

Iwakura no Kyōjo koi seyo Hototogisu	*The crazy woman in Iwakura village weeps bitterly being reminded of her old lover when she hears the song of the little cuckoo...*

Iwakura is a small village in the suburbs of Kyoto, the old capital of Japan with a waterfall famous for healing 'the crazy'. According to Japanese literary tradition, the hototogisu (cookoo) reminds one of love.

The haiku is by Yosa Buson (1716-1783), one of the greatest haiku poets to succeed Bashō (1644-1694). He was an excellent artist, the originator of haiga. In his haiga, the hototogisu is flying over two hydrangea flowers which don't appear in the poem itself. One might ask why Buson included these flowers?

In short, Buson has gone beyond the obvious content of the poem to play with the thoughts that might be inspired by the symbolism. In the ancient period 'hydrangea' would have reminded the reader of night and love, especially that which is changeable and passionate; the haiga may convey the idea that this love is tragic because a hototogisu was said to spit blood when it cries. Such symbolic expression which plays with the spirit of haiku is called *Nioi-tsuke;* there is a match between poem and drawing that goes beyond but is intimately linked to the poem where the haiga started.

Beta-tsuke or *Jika-tsuke,* on the other hand, is the plain and direct inclusion in haiga merely of whatever appears in the haiku; this would lack depth.

The only way to learn this process is to do it yourself; a theoretical approach is not helpful. As the English proverb suggests, 'practice makes perfect'.

The Unlimited Freedom of Haiga

The expression of haiku spirit in haiga should be free from any ready-made pattern. I have seen haiga textbooks that demonstrate the process of drawing step by step but I do not recommend this approach; it is important to use good textbooks just as a starting point and then set out to develop your own style.

The Importance of Sketching

When you begin haiga without slavishly following the textbooks, sketching is most important. Observe and sketch anything in detail without imagining that scientific detail is necessary. Your original sketch has to be refined and simplified In order to make good haiga.

You need to have a way of seeing that enables you to select what is worthy of being drawn and to decide how to simplify in order to get to the core of the beauty of the natural world.

Blank Space in Haiga

Unique in Eastern art is the great value placed on blank space. Haiku is, in a sense, the poetry of silence; likewise, haiga is the art of emptiness. An important factor in haiga is the beauty of blank space. The poet's soul and feeling flows into the blank space; it is not just an empty vacuum. Even the calligraphy, however skilfully done, should never intrude on the emptiness of the drawing.

Use of Colour

There are two ways of using colour in haiga: one is to fill the drawn lines with colour: the other is to use colour initially. The colour does not have to be true to life, but must create an artistic atmosphere and add to the depiction of the subject: incomplete or overflowing colouring has exquisite charm.

When colour is used from the first directly on to the paper, you can try, for example, to dip your brush in yellow and then only the point of the brush in red; you will immediately get red, yellow and orange. The accidental results of this process can be very thrilling but you need to be aware that some colours will not harmonise either with each other or with a true expression of the spirit of the haiku you are starting with. There should not be too many colours in one haiga; colours should be appropriate to the atmosphere of its haiku.

The natural world is full of powerful and exciting colours. Though we might wish to copy them, they remain mysterious and so full of variety that any attempt to recreate them is highly unlikely to succeed; choose few colours and use them symbolically to make a dignified haiga.

Haiga and the Drawings of Children

Children immerse themselves in the process of drawing; as a result what they produce is full of joy and happiness. Children don't think about the techniques of art nor are they concerned with being praised for what they do, at any rate to start with. Their thoughts about drawing come from the purity of childhood. This is how haiga should be.

Expected Qualities of Haiga

It is possible to get too concerned about what a haiga should be like. Don't worry yourself about that; what you have to think about is permeating the drawing with your feeling and soul. Take from the natural world whatever appeals to your aesthetic sensibility and draw it freely in your own way.

We do come across many haiga artists who have studied haiga for a little while and yet act as if they had mastered it. Haiga cannot be mastered in a short time; your personality has to become one with haiga.

Observation of Excellent Models

A person who has worked with paper currencies for a long time has a quick eye for false banknotes! When you attend art exhibitions you are able to appreciate good pieces of work; observation of good haiga will influence your work. The starting point for creating haiga is to depend on your own perception to sketch freely from inside yourself so that what you draw becomes an expression of your character. Begin with familiar objects-vegetables, wild flowers, animals. Simplify in order to capture their essentials. You could try copying outstanding haiga from the past in order to get a grasp of the artist's techniques and points of view.

Calligraphy

After a drawing is completed, with the blank space well balanced, the next step is to think about how the haiku may be harmoniously added calligraphically. The beauty of blank space must be considered carefully in order to allow the calligraphy to find its proper place.

Stretching myself at ease,
I look up at
the peaks of clouds *Issa*

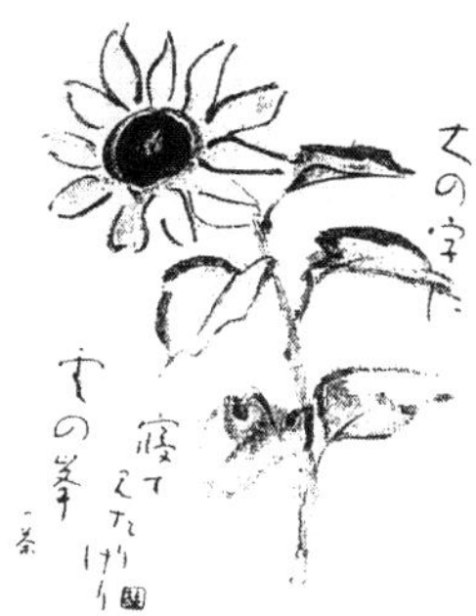

There is an English proverb: 'So many people, so many minds...' Now, in conclusion, I tell you: 'So many people, so many haiga...'

Jim McDonald

Teaching Haiku to Junior School Children

As a Primary School teacher in South London I am obliged by the National Curriculum to teach haiku to children from year four (aged eight and nine) annually. It is a privilege and a challenge.

The debate about the age at which children should first encounter haiku is not one that I will cover here – although I will say that on a personal level I regret not having the opportunity to study haiku at all until I was seventeen.

First, a little background: The children that I taught this lesson to are all eight or nine years old, and as the lesson was in late April the majority were by then nine. They come from a broad range of backgrounds; the majority being of either Caribbean, West African or Indian heritage. The area of South London where they live is relatively underprivileged, but most of the children are lucky to come from supportive homes. Three of the twenty-six children speak a language other than English at home, and six are classified as having special educational needs (difficulties with learning in one or more areas of the curriculum). The school is in an extremely urban setting, bounded on one edge by tall office blocks, another by flats, and the other two by busy roads. There is no school field, and play takes place on a concrete playground. Three years ago a memorial garden was built in an unused corner for a late pupil, and this provides the only real greenery on the site. There is one large Horse chestnut tree, and a number of small other species dotted around.

The lessons in this essay took place over two days, the first in the morning and the second on the following afternoon. The learning objective for the first lesson, which the children were working towards, was to develop an understanding of what a haiku is. The second was to attempt to write some haiku of their own, outside.

At the start of the first lesson I asked the children to think about photographs. I asked them to consider how photographs 'freeze' one moment in time. I gave a range of examples in order to help them to understand the idea that an image can be captured and recorded – 'pause' on a video, digital photos, Polaroid pictures, and so on. The analogy of the digital camera, which many were familiar with, was particularly useful because of the throwaway nature of digital pictures – 'it's OK to get it wrong, because the trying is the fun thing and you can always delete it afterwards'.

I then showed the children Basho's 'old pond / a frog leaps / water's sound' haiku. We shared this and explained any misconceptions. I likened the image to an old-fashioned 'snapshot', but better because it was more than a picture. The sound is there too, and with a little imagination I told them that you can 'fill in the rest of the picture'. I suggested that because all our imaginations are different, the 'extra bits' that the brain fills in will be different, too. This was beautifully confirmed by a host of different images that the children offered; such as deep green water, the frog jumping off a Lily pad, and a side discussion of the ripple effect on the water. The activity was repeated with another haiku, 'on a barren branch / a raven has perched / autumn dusk'. Again, the range of images that were offered by the children was both surprising and encouraging. Many alluded to a sunset, some spent time describing the bird itself.

The next step was to provide the children with a booklet of modern haiku for them to take away and read quietly by themselves. I was careful to select a range of haiku that were un-demanding in terms of vocabulary but rich on powerful images. I was careful also to include a variety of sound and other sensory haiku, to illustrate the fact that sight is not the sole sensory input. Finding good haiku that were simple enough for younger children to understand is tricky, but I relied on poems that made reference to universal themes. There was little point including the beautiful haiku that have been written about moon-viewing and cherry blossom. I had to keep in mind that about half the children have never seen a cow close up.

The children enjoyed their booklets – containing about thirty haiku – immensely. They continued to talk about the 'story' that was going on in each one and chose three favourites each. It was evident at this stage that some of the children were beginning to develop a 'feel' for what constituted a haiku. This is remarkable considering that many adults find this difficult! As this was the central learning objective I was happy at this point to let the discussion continue for a while before drawing things to a conclusion.

The second lesson took place on a warm late spring afternoon with a clear blue sky. It was a welcome break from the stuffy classroom and the children approached their tasks enthusiastically.

I decided to try to add a bit of importance to their task by helping them to make little booklets in which to record their jottings. Then off we set, with the spirit of Basho watching over us, to record our sartori!

The results were extremely interesting. I was tempted to 'steer' the children towards places and situations that I thought might make good haiku, but largely resisted the temptation. The most I did was to stand the children under the largest tree, in full leaf, before they began. They were then free, and I followed them with replacement pencils. I have listed some of the most inspiring results below. Please bear in mind as you read that they were written by children who have grown up in a very urban environment, some of whom have yet to celebrate their ninth birthdays....

grass near a pond,
mud on ground
- the sun warming my face

a leaf fell out of the tree
gently the leaf
as can be

breeze going through my skin...
Birds sing
on a Sunny and calm day

wren sings
I see the teacher
I ignore him

a playground
long last
forgotten

birds singing
in the trees while
I sit and feel the breeze

long laughter
fills the ear
with joy

Friday afternoon
empty garden
plants growing

I see the light blue sky
the clouds are floating through
and the warm sun shines on my face

The session concluded back indoors with a haiku-sharing and a chance to edit work. I mentioned that there is great debate as to whether haiku should be altered after the event, or left as spontaneous records, and left the children to make their own decisions.

There are some interesting conclusions that can be drawn from the poems that the children produced. The greatest challenge they faced was resisting the desire to make their poems rhyme. The second problem was the fact that subject knowledge hindered them. They could all see trees and hear birdsong, but did not have the knowledge of specific species to draw on. Many also have an impoverished colour vocabulary, which is why the sky is blue and not azure. Considering this, I think the poems that were written are remarkable. Hopefully the fact that their initial experience of haiku writing was a pleasant one will bear fruit in years to come.

Mike Chasty

Aldous Huxley, Haiku and Zen

It has been seventy-five years since the publication of Aldous Huxley's *Brave New World*,[1] his visionary novel of dystopia. In it, far into the future of a world state, he saw an order of stability and organisation guaranteed by social engineering, perpetual indoctrination and the removal of literature from public consumption for, like science, art is incompatible with human happiness. [2] In addition, a general indifference to identity and a chemical-induced extinction of individual depression virtually guarantees society's unreflective monotony. But political events, scientific and technological advances occurred so rapidly and unforeseen in his lifetime that twenty-five years later Huxley wrote *Brave New World Revisited* (1958) The future of *Brave New World* was happening faster than he had imagined and gave him little optimism.

Something else was developing though by the mid 1950s, alongside and certainly more positive than the threat of atomic obliteration, the Cold War, the results of overpopulation, brainwashing and political propaganda through the newly invented medium of television. Simultaneously, haiku began to appear as a force within English language's literary consciousness.

As we learn through David Cobb's *One Hundred Blyths*,[3] the works of R.H. Blyth began to be regularly reviewed through British literary columns in the Fifties and Sixties. Highlighting just how much of the haiku and Zen essence pre-existed in Western poetry, Blyth succeeded in bringing this new Eastern approach fully and appreciatively to where perhaps it had been happening only in obscure fits and curious starts in the first half of the Twentieth Century. By 1951 E.E. Cummings had read Blyth, [4] as had J.D. Salinger, as had the Beats (most notably Kerouac). According to David Cobb's essay however, despite review success, Blyth's impact at that time was 'so eclectic and in some ways eminently British' that it was paradoxically resisted in Britain. Huxley, another 'eminently British'[5] author, also living abroad, adopted and incorporated Blyth's works with relative immediacy, ease and vigour.

It is in his classic study and generation-influencing *The Doors of Perception*, [6] recounting his initial experience with a dose of mescaline in the spring of 1953, that evidence of his awareness of Blyth and haiku first appears:

> 'Drooping in green parabolas from the hedge, the ivy fronds shone with a kind of glassy, jade-like radiance. A moment later a clump of Red Hot Pokers, in full bloom, had exploded into my field of vision. So passionately alive that they seemed to be standing on the very brink of utterance, the flowers strained upwards into the blue. Like the chair under the laths, they protested too much. I looked down at the leaves and discovered a cavernous intricacy of the most delicate green lights and shadows, pulsing with undecipherable mystery.
>
> Roses:
> The flowers are easy to paint,
> The leaves difficult.
>
> Shiki's haiku (which I quote in F. H. Blythe's translation) [7]expresses, by indirection, exactly what I then felt – the excessive, the too obvious glory of the flowers, as contrasted with the subtler miracle of their foliage'.[8]

That the introduction of the post-war modern reader to an experimental and cosmos-infused state of mind should coincide with this relatively new form of poetry, in hindsight, seems wonderfully appropriate and significant. It is as though haiku hung on the automatically opening doors of this new fulgent mental state of transcendence.

Unsurprisingly, the heady Sixties unfolded as they did with their florid escapades into new states of consciousness and experimentation, and haiku as a Western force was not only quoted but began to be created. As for Huxley, towards his latter years, his psychedelic forays were measured (he himself was aware that involvement with it was certainly nothing to be toyed with) while haiku remained in his own works a companion element to be drawn upon.

In 1959 he gave a series of lectures at the University of California, under the theme of *The Human Situation*. [9] In it we find, under the lecture titled *'More Nature in Art':*

> 'In Chinese and Japanese poetry and landscape painting we find images that are curiously prophetic of the Wordsworthian attitude towards nature; in that strange art form of Japan called the haiku, a tiny poem of seventeen syllables, we find it again and again expressed in an abbreviated and elusive way. Consider for example a poem by Bashō...'

An interview from 1961 also makes specific reference to Blyth:

> 'Did you read a book, which I think is a very good book, by this Englishman who has lived many years in Japan and taught there, Blyth, called *Zen In English Literature*[10] – a very good book. Pointing out how much there is in English literature, which is profoundly Zen-like. I mean Wordsworth is full of Zen and Whitman is full of Zen. Many people have this sort of attitude towards nature. I mean, the Japanese artistic representation of it both in landscape and in haiku is perhaps more refined than anything we did and more sort of elegant. But nevertheless, it is of the same order, it seems to me.'[11]

In poetry and in haiku, Huxley recognised that Zen or a Zen approach was a recurrent product of literature and part of the answer to the endless question and concerns of human existence. His past works, stretching back across his career to the early Twenties, are full of an actual and established awareness of Zen as well as indirect examples of it. The following are just two of many examples:

> 'A man misses something by not establishing a participative and living relationship with the non-human world of animals and plants, landscapes and stars and seasons. By failing to be, vicariously, the not-self, he fails to be completely himself. There can be no complete integration of the soul without humility towards things as well as a will to subdue them. Those who lack that humility are bad artists in life. *Do What You Will, 1929*[12]

> 'The mind must be open, unperturbed, empty of irrelevant things, quiet. There's no room for thoughts in a half-shut cluttered mind. And thoughts won't enter a noisy mind; they're shy, they remain in their obscure hiding places below the surface, where they can't be got at, so long as the mind is full and noisy. Most of us pass through life without knowing that they're there at all.' *Those Barren Leaves, 1925*[13]

This necessity of space and freedom for the mind to properly function would be echoed thirty years on in *Heaven and Hell,* [14] where, in discussing the Zen-inspired landscape artists of the Far East, he talks about the *'single feature ... absolutized by isolation'.* Perhaps unconsciously he hit upon this very Zen-like instant, even earlier, in his poetry book *Leda,* [15] from 1920, of which the stanzas of the poem 'Soles Occidere Et Redire Possunt' conclude with a striking resemblance to haiku, albeit a haiku that is possible after the initial strictness of nature as the predominant theme has been relaxed:

> Between the drawing of the blind
> And being aware of yet another day...

In commenting on the experience of Zen, again, from the 1961 interview, [16] he stated:

> 'After all, nobody has been more acutely aware of the landscapes of flowers, of birds than the Chinese artists. This does represent, Japanese artists too represent, a whole social attitude towards the external world – of seeing infinity in a grain of sand. I mean the whole Blake poem exactly sums up what they were after and what they succeeded in doing. I mean this is simultaneously outward and inward which seems to me to be the most desirable state you can possibly have ... this idea of a non-dogmatic, non-symbolic, I wouldn't call it religion, I just call it 'approach to the universe'. I mean, they are not worshipping anybody particularly but this is the way they want to respond to the universe with the maximum of sensibility with the greatest perception of the sort of mystery within the explained and understood world. I mean, again this is making the best of both worlds, to understand as much as you can, to label and classify but

at the same time, behind labels, to perceive the fathomless mystery of existence, which is the whole essence of Zen, it seems to me.'

Huxley was born in 1894 and died in 1963 – a life almost identically coeval with Blyth's (1898-1964). That he should become acquainted with haiku through Blyth and in turn, literary elder statesman of the intellect that he was, echo it further, proves the immediate effect and stature of haiku, not only on the emerging figures of the day but also in influencing the established literati.

Huxley still remains a prophetic and poetic polymath of astonishing reach and synthesis. In his career he was largely concerned with the condition of the planet and the state of society with all its beauty and joys, its inherent stresses and future perils for the individual's health. Meanwhile, he always recognised that everyone possesses unique sensibilities, intellects, psyches and stomachs. His concern was evermore imperative as he saw world population increase from less than two billion in the Twenties, to three billion in the Sixties and would, as in our current times, shift towards a move from six to nine billion. The issues he raises in his works have an unending relevancy, if not urgency.

It is interesting that the character of John the Savage in *Brave New World,* a native creature of freedom and feeling, who, by a strange symbolic quirk is influenced by a mouse-nibbled edition of Shakespeare, eventually commits suicide for he cannot cope in the structured, clinical, unquestioning and passionless environment that society has become and in which he is eventually hounded as a media-prize. Had he instead of Shakespeare, a copy of Huxley's classic, of Blyth's works or of Bashō, one wonders how that might have enabled him to negotiate and endure or to even personally influence society away from the prospective dangers of *Brave New World.*

1. *Brave New World,* Aldous Huxley, Penguin books. 1955
2. ibid, p 177
3. *One hundred Blyths,* David Cobb. *Rediscovering Basho,* Global Books, 1999,
4. *Dreams in the Mirror,* A Biography of E.E. Cummings, Live right, 1980

5. *One hundred Blyths,* David Cobb. *Rediscovering Basho,* Global Books, 1999, p89
6. *The Doors of Perception,* Aldous Huxley, Chatto and Windus, 1954
7. Sic. How often Blyth's name been misspelled?
8. *The Doors of Perception,* Aldous Huxley, chatto and Windis, 1954, p49
9. *The Human Situation,* Aldous Huxley, Chatto and Windus, 1978, p44
10. *Zen in English Literature,* R.H. Blyth, Hokuseido Press, 1942
11. *Speaking Personally,* Aldous Huxley, Interviews recorded on July 7 and 11 1961, P &C 2002 Artifact Music Ltd. Huxley also quotes Basho in *Literature & Science,* Aldous Huxley, Chatto and Windus, 1963, p21
12. *Do What You Will,* Aldous Huxley, Chatto and Windus, 1929, reprinted 1939 p166
13. *Those Barren Leaves,* Aldous Huxley, 1925, reprinted 1967 p294
14. *The Doors af Perseption and Heavan and hell,*Aldous Huxley, Chatto and Windus, 1959, pp137-8
15. *Leda,*Aldous Huxley, Chatto and Windus, 1920, p80
16. *Speaking Personally,* Aldous Huxley, Interviews recorded on July 7 & 11, 1961, P&C 2002 Artifact Music Ltd.

Stephen Henry Gill

Shinto in Haiku

ganjitsu o / tenchi wagō no / hajime kana

(Shiki)

New Year's Day:
This, the beginning
Of the sacred accord
Of Heaven and Earth.

The word *Shintō* means different things to different people; but to most Japanese haiku poets, above all it means the natural cycle of the year and its traditional observances – particularly those centred on the local shrine, whose roots often lie deep in mythology, and whose branches stretch out into the lives of its present parishioners. The local people energize its sacred spaces with their respectful bowing and clapping of hands in prayer. In contrast to the Buddhist temples with their heady incense, beautiful sculpture and sometimes lavish architectural embellishments, Shinto shrines are rather plain, sometimes even empty-feeling.

rusu no ma ni / aretaru kami no / ochiba kana

(Bashō)

Its god is away;
The shrine utterly ransacked
By fallen leaves.

Shrines are in essence 'frames' for us to enter to commune with the natural order of things, to ask favours and give thanks. Once you step through the sacred *torii* archway, you will often enter a world of aged trees, of moss and rocks, and perhaps of broad, blank areas of pebbles, gravel or earth. But these are not gardens of meditation. So, what *are* they, then?

ugoku ha mo / naku osoroshiki / natsu-kodachi

(Buson)

Not a single leaf stirs:
How numinous is
The summer grove!

Long, long ago, the local priest would represent and interpret the community to the gods, and *vice versa*. Offerings would be made in a sacred glade of the forest, at a spring-fed pool or at a rocky outcrop on a mountainside or island. Today, most such places have become shrines – *jinja* or *hokora* – where today a wooden worship hall or a simple roofed altar may now stand, and where anyone, Japanese or foreigner alike, may go to pray around the clock. In the distant past, there was no structure at all; a sacred place as nature had made it. Prayers were for the order, the natural cycle from which man benefited, to continue – the blessing of the natural gods ensured by the periodic devotion of the people, who felt they depended on it.

amagoi ya / ten ni hibike to / utsu taikō

(Shiki)

Prayers for rain –
As they echo up to heaven,
The pounding of a drum.

After a long period of partial integration with Buddhism (*shinbutsu shūgō*), this respectful, well-intentioned ancient faith was tainted by the forces of militarism slapped onto its adaptable self during the latter nineteenth and early twentieth centuries, when the state reformed the *jinja* system. Today, Shinto has largely returned to its folk culture roots, where shrines and sanctified nature remain a bastion of everyday haiku imagery. The shrine is linked to the agricultural cycle – particularly to that of rice and (in certain areas) silk production – and pious farmers, silk spinners, rice merchants and sake brewers will pay their respects here, and leave offerings for the gods. They will probably lend a hand at *matsuri*, festival times, too; as will many of the shrine's other worshippers.

kamidana no /hi wa okotaraji / kaiko doki

(Buson)

Silkworm-feeding season –
Though busy,
Still the farmers tend
The lights of their household shrines.

Try to forget the image of government ministers visiting the Yasukuni Shrine in Tokyo to pray for the souls of those fallen in past wars – at least for haiku's sake. That is not the grassroots Shinto of which I write. Traditionally, the local shrine has not addressed death or the afterlife. The Buddhist temple has that role. The *jinja* is about life – birth, growing up, marriage, celebration, music and dance offered to the *kami* - and the awesome, spiritual qualities of nature.

tsukiyomi no/ kage ya ōtomo /-daikagura

Shadows of the Moon God
Lie across the ground –
The Festival of Sacred Dance
Begins …

(Sōin)

And who are the *kami*, the enshrined gods? Firstly, there are the personified forces of nature – sun, moon, wind, rain, sea, mountain, river, spring, cereal spirits, tree spirits, rock spirits, sometimes 'represented' by the spirits of wild animals, too. And then there are the gods built out of semi-historical figures, who (like Britain's King Arthur), more than a millennium ago brought the Japanese people unity, technology, education and order, where there had supposedly been chaos and ignorance before. Of all these *kami* and their exploits, the ancient history books, such as the *Kojiki* and the *Nihon Shoki*, have much to say.

ganchō ya / kamiyo no koto mo/ omowaruru

New Year's Morn –
Thinking too of the things that happened
In the Age of the Gods.

(Moritake)

The world of mythology comes alive at the shrine, and the priest and his calendar of rites and celebrations is still today for many as much a part of the local community as the school or the shopping arcade. Too much has perhaps been made in the West of Zen Buddhism's influence on haiku, and not nearly enough, of Shinto's. Do you find any Zen in the poems here? Any latent philosophy? There is little or none in *kami* worship, and this imperviousness to 'ideas' *per se*, a sense of observance, of natural propriety and respect, is exactly where much classical haiku has come from.

te o uteba / kodama ni akuru /natsu no tsuki

Clapping hands together
In prayer at dawn:
With their echo,
The summer moon fading

(Bashō)

Ernest Berry

Judging Haiku

Despite haiku's rocketing popularity over the last decade – with countless promotions, competitions, on & off-line workshops; regional, national & international get-togethers, competitions and how-to books et al, the quality of entries does not appear to have improved much since I last judged this competition seven years ago:

Too many of the offerings disqualified themselves by breaches of basics and a large proportion of the remainder were of marginal quality. In my opinion, it is counter-productive to deny aspiring writers fair feed-back on the faulty premise that the truth may offend so I have tried to be as considerate as possible in this is respect - hopefully without discouraging anyone or overstepping the line between constructive and destructive criticism.

The setting-out and printing of entries was interestingly varied - from pencilled scribble to 48pt. fonts on fancy paper. Such attempts to IMPRESS are a waste of time and effort. Remember, judges are only swayed by what they read - not by "the jewelled finger pointing to the moon" [Basho] - a barely legible masterpiece will always beat brilliantly presented mediocrity.

Those who wonder why their baby didn't 'make it' may like to check the following essentials

Was it:
1. brief 2. believable 3. evocative 4. fresh 5. poetic 6. syntactic?

Did it:
1. scan 2. sing 3. expose. 4. juxtapose 5. ahaa! ?

Did it Avoid:
1. predictability 2. tautology 3. read-ons 4. similes 5. emotions 6.hackneys
7. adjectives 8.adverbs 9. metaphor 10. anthropomorphism
11. sentiment 12.cuteness 13. contrivance?

The commonest fault was ***trying too hard*** - usually showcased by adjectival diarrhoea and a surfeit of *in*'s, *and*'s, *a*'s, *are*'s & *the*'s. One incredible first line (referring to a cat) read: "*Sweet, warm, cream soft fur* " Blimey! Reminds me of Twain's classic reference to adjectives viz: " ~ if you see one, kill it ~ " To that I'd add my own axioms: "the keener the axe the cleaner the cut" - and: "all lit is too looong"

Haiku writers should bear in mind that 'spoon-feeding' the reader with every detail, - however ingenious, is counterproductive and only tends to blunt the axe of imagination. Refer Eric Amann's book *Wordless Poem*, plus another of my axioms: "haiku = delete" Haijin tight-rope between brevity, impact, poesy, lyricism and comprehensibility; so If we want our work to be appreciated we should avoid enigma, esoterics and anything which tend to confuse or look like shopping lists, sentences, headlines, epitaphs, epigrams, or telegrams. Nor do we want riddles; political, religious, romantic or emotional rants; or rehashes of tired haiku about sunsets, reflections, cherry blossoms, 'fall' leaves et al. OR: random snippets of prose which any untutored scissor could produce.

Consider the famous: "old pond/ a frog jumps in/ water sound" [Bashō], or - the lesser known but equally evocative "dusk/ up to my ears/ in birdsong" [John O'Connor], or: gunshot the length of the lake [Jim Kacian]. These three classics, which between them contain only one adjective, 2 definite articles and average only 8 syllables, could have been written by any [literate] toddler; so you see, complexity is no match for simplicity. I've noticed that most mainstream poets and literary brains - including many of our own haiku eggheads still can't get their heads around WRITING the stuff so you don't need to be a genius to master it. On the other hand, we do want poetry - something which grabs us by the shorts - where every word & syllable works toward an end product that SINGS! ... Discipline, constraint and the courage to delete could prove the difference between winning and losing.

No dissertation on haiku is complete without stressing brevity Even apart from haiku it could mean the difference between life and death: the fewer words we use to get a message across, the quicker it's comprehended and acted upon.

the quality of haiku is not strained
it droppeth like a gentle
plop from a
strain
e
r

Natalia L Rudychev

Co-creation: The Case of Haiku in the West

> Stating the feelings alone builds walls;
> stating the causes of the feelings builds paths.
>
> *William J Higginson, The Haiku Handbook* 1

It is amazing how eagerly westerners embraced haiku and how quickly it turned into an international phenomenon that has found its way into cultures all around the world. This reinforces T.S. Eliot's statement that 'what happens when a new work of art is created is something that happens simultaneously to all the works of art which preceded it'.2

First the Japanese haiku had to be recognized by western culture as a distinct phenomenon, and second it had to become an *other,* something beyond the scope of phenomena commonly accepted by a particular cultural community. Thirdly, western culture had to be ready for a cultural dialogue with that *other.* For as soon as a westerner writes a haiku he/she turns into a reader of the whole Japanese tradition (if ever so inattentive) that created the phenomenon of haiku. Moreover, by the act of writing this westerner changes (if ever so slightly) the whole preceding tradition of haiku practice as well as the future development of this practice. This mediation brings us closer to a deeper understanding of haiku because even within the realm of Japanese culture it is a co-creation, an equal effort both on the part of the writer and on the part of the reader. Basho said: 'the haiku that reveals seventy to eighty percent of its subject is good. Those that reveal fifty to sixty percent we never tire of. 3 Thus we can conclude that an excellent haiku leaves forty to fifty percent of its creative realm to the imagination of the reader, making him/her an active co-creator of the poem.

The western understanding of culture and poetry as intrinsically dialogical began acquiring its scientific status in the 19th century with the efforts of Ferdinand de Saussure. This process continued and gained strength through the works of Mikhail M. Bakhtin, Julia Kristeva, and Yurij Lotman. Martin

Heidegger was among the modern philosophers who put a particular stress on the importance of co-creation for a work of art. 'Not only the creation of the work is poetic, but equally poetic, though in its own way, is the preserving of the work; for a work is in actual effect a work only when we remove ourselves from our commonplace routine and move into what is disclosed by the work, so as to bring our own nature itself to take a stand in the truth of what is'.[4] Critical writings by T.S. Eliot and Ezra Pound on the theory of impersonality ('The emotion of art is impersonal. And the poet cannot reach this impersonality without surrendering himself wholly to the work to be done. And he is not likely to know what is to be done unless he lives in what is not merely the present, but the present moment of the past..') [5] provided a background for the Imagists' experiments with the genre of haiku.

When haiku appeared on the horizon of the general writing public, the latter was to a certain extent ready to engage in writing without emoting. The notion of co-creation and the idea that a certain freedom of interpretation was permitted to the reader were already floating on the cultural waves when R.H. Blyth wrote that 'haiku demand the free poetic life of the reader in parallel with that of a poet. This "freedom" is not that of wild irresponsibility and arbitrary interpretation, but that of the creation of a similar poetic experience to which the haiku points'.[6]

I am fully aware of the heated discussions concerning seasonal references in contemporary life. Space limitations of this essay do not allow me to go into subtle details of these debates. But in so far as this issue concerns the topic of co-creation I must mention that certain experiences of the natural world are deeply ingrained in the cultural milieu that tacitly surrounds us in our daily existence. Therefore a reference to the first snowfall or the last day of school can greatly contribute to the process of co-creation between the writer and the reader. 'The apogee of culture is what can be recognized in a person, but is not on display, ever'. [7] Haiku works when the author succeeds in presenting a thing or an event that left a profound impact on his/her soul in such a way that it makes this thing or even a part of a similar experience for the reader.

Even the brevity of haiku turns out to be a treasure in disguise. It is not enough to have the sensitivity of perception that allows you to experience a profound revelation in an everyday encounter; even a deep breath followed by the decision to put your emotions on the back seat does not count if you cannot properly express yourself You have to give away just enough to engage another person into a creative dialogue without invading his/her world with your emotions and preconceived notions. On this road to the right mode of expression confined to the limitations of several syllables we can greatly benefit from the Japanese practice of *shikata* ('way of doing things'). 'The challenge facing the Japanese was to know their own *honshin,* 'true' or 'right heart', then learn and follow the kata that would keep them in sync with society and the cosmos'. [8]

1 William J. Higginson, with Penny Harter, *The Haiku Handbook: How to Write, Share, and Teach Haiku,* (Tokyo: Kodansha 1985), p.5.
2 T.S. Eliot, 'Tradition and the Individual Talent', *The Critical Tradition,* (New York: St Martin's Press, 1989), p.467.
3 Kenneth Yasuda, *Japanese Haiku,* (Boston: Tuttle, 2001), p.7.
4 Martin Heidegger, 'The Origin of the Work of Art', *Poetry, Language, Thought,* (New York: Harper & Row, 1975), p. 74.
5 Eliot, op.cit., p.471.
6 R.H.Blyth, *Haiku,* Vol.I, (Tokyo: Hokuseido, 1962), p.xi.
7 Gian carlo Caiza, *Japan Style,* (New York: Phaidon Press,2007), p.66
8 Boyé Lafayette de Mente, *Kata* (Boston: Tuttle, 2003), p.3

Charles Christian

Moving on from 5-7-5 Existence

We've had a few essays in *Blithe Spirit* in recent issues from people reminding us of what does - or does not - constitute a 'proper' haiku and/or haibun. Thank you for this - but it does ignore the whole point of any form of creative writing, namely the 'creativity' bit: The bit that makes it original; the bit that to quote Ezra Pound "makes it new".

Bashō has been dead for over 300 years but this doesn't hold back the flow of haijin imitating his traditional 5-7-5 structure and subject matter. Just how many haiku does the world need about lazy frogs plopping off logs into lily ponds? This unthinking imitation displays the creativity of that other great Japanese gift to culture, namely karaoke. And what creative pleasure is there in being a writer of karaoke haiku - or karaokaihu?

Instead of focussing upon what some people think haiku poets should be doing, I'd like to move the debate on from questions of definition towards questions of practice and craft. In other words what are modern haiku poets actually doing? The short answer is they are doing (and have been doing for over 50 years now) far, far more than 5-7-5 and worrying about whether they've got their kireji, kigo, kidai and wabi sensibilities in the right order.

For simplicity, we can break down these developments into three different areas: (i) pushing beyond the traditional boundaries of haiku and senryu subject matter, (ii) taking the traditional haiku form as a jumping off point to explore new or experimental literary forms, and (iii) taking advantage of new digital technologies to reimagine or revisit traditional haiku forms.

Subject matter

Take subject matter ... For the last 20 years 'hacker culture' has been devising computing oriented haiku. True, some of these are just 17 syllable sentences run over three lines with a bit of cod oriental/fortune cookie mysticism thrown in for good measure - but there are others that possess all the literary qualities of classical haiku/senryu. Here's a well-known example (author unknown & in the public domain):

first snow, then silence -
this thousand dollar screen dies
so beautifully.

Then there are people taking haiku into the realms of science fiction (sci-faiku). I've already written about sci-faiku in *Blithe Spirit* on a previous occasion but I think the key point to stress here is that this subject matter is taken very seriously by sci-faiku authors - there is even a Science Fiction Poetry Association (www.sfpoetry.com) based in the US, with its own magazine and annual awards for the best SF poetry of the year. Here's an example of a sci-faiku of mine that was published in the US magazine a couple of years ago:

space time dilation –
when I return
the only face I know is mine

Swap out the part about space time dilation and substitute something about returning for a high school reunion and you have an equally valid conventional haiku about the unsettling experience of growing old and failing to recognise old friends and lovers because they have changed out of all recognition.

And we also have the phenomenon of subject matter being pushed into social and political commentary - remember the *Blithe Spirit* (December 2006, 16/4) responses to war?

white contrails against the blue –
tumbling bombs glitter
in the Beirut sun

As a challenge to BHS members, shouldn't we now be seeing some more haiku on the subject of the current recession?

Jumping off

Then there is the idea of treating (or subverting) the traditional haiku/haibun form as a jumping off point from which to explore new or experimental writing forms. The broad haibun-type approach to both non-fiction and fiction, started off by American West Coast renaissance/Beat Generation writers (such as Gary Snyder and Jack Kerouac - and Kerouac's been in his grave for 40 years now, so this is hardly something new) has now become a standard feature of modern prose writing and prose poetry. As, incidentally, has writing in the first person, present tense replaced other points-of-view in fiction and creative non¬fiction.

Sticking with the Beats, we even have Allen Ginsberg, inspired by the traditional Japanese haiku, inventing a form he calls the 'American Sentence' - one sentence of 17 syllables, end of story. The key here is the moment sharply observed, a brief 'aha!' of pleasure or recognition or awareness, which obviously echoes a traditional haiku. However, there was a difference. Ginsberg was a believer in the Pound dictum of 'condense, condense, condense'. For example, in his poetry he frequently omits the articles ("a," "an," "the" etc.). In addition, he felt the Japanese haiku form couldn't cut it as 17 syllables of English, and that divvying up into 5-7-5 syllable lines made the whole thing an exercise in counting, not feeling, and too arbitrary to be poetry. Ginsberg's solution, which first appears in his book Cosmopolitan Greetings, is his American Sentence, which makes for a rush of a poem - although today probably we'd describe them as micro prose poems. The website of the Allen Ginsberg Trust (www.allenginsberg.org) has a revolving sequence of American Sentences. Here are a couple:

> Put on my tie in a taxi, short of breath, rushing to meditate.
>
> Rainy night on Union Square, full moon. Want more poems? Wait till
> I'm dead.

The impact of new technology

There are the modern successors and alternatives to renga and renku, including renrepeats, tan-renga senryu, renbun, renkay and rengay, plus sequences for haibun and tanka. And, then there is the haiga form, where the old brush and ink technique is rapidly being replaced by digital haiga, using photography and/or computer graphics to create the image - in fact (putting on my hat as a publisher of a poetry and prose webzine) in the Western world there are now more haiga (and taiga = applying the haiga approach to tanka) being created digitally than by traditional methods. Check out the social networking site Facebook for plenty of examples of new digital haiga and even 'haiku films', These have their own Facebook group and are variously described as "a concentrated impressionist sketch..." and "short, laconic, meditative, therapeutic and inspiring... ".

Of course the big attraction of on-line publishing is that it is possible to publish colour graphics, such as haiga - whereas most print poetry magazines do not have the facility to even consider reproducing colour images. Indeed, you have to wonder whether one impact of technology is that certain poetic forms - such as haiga - will one day cease to appear in print and become totally a digital phenomenon.

Another technological development, now starting to make an impression on the cultural radar, is Twitter. For those of you unfamiliar with the technology, Twitter (http://twitter.com) is a 'micro-blogging' facility that allows users to post 140 character (including spaces) blogs about anything they fancy - and for other people to sign up to follow them - all free of charge. Rachel Green, who is a writer and digital haiga artist, is now using Twitter to post haiku to all her friends and contacts - typically she composes them first thing in a morning, while she is out walking her dogs, and then posts them on to Twitter (and also onto Facebook) direct from her mobile phone - thereby recapturing the whole immediacy of the haiku moment that traditional publishing methods inevitably lose. In fact I have seen the suggestion that Twitter messages - technically called 'tweets' - 'are the new haiga' in that crafting a compact message within the confines of 140 characters requires all the skills and discipline of creating a haiga.

No doubt traditionalists will dismiss all these developments as pseudo-haiku but this is ignoring the fact that any genre must continually evolve if it is not to become fossilised and a pastiche of itself. Perhaps, more importantly, they also gloss over the fact the people they now hold up as the paragons to be followed (or aped) were themselves the iconoclasts of their own age. For example, in his day Basho broke with tradition by reflecting his real emotions and environment, rather than sticking with the formulas of kigo.

My own view is that when it comes to creative writing of any kind - but particularly poetry in all its many genres - there is only one rule: and that is there are no rules.

Graham High

The Pun and Related Wordplay in Haiku
Part 1: Types and Techniques

The pun (also known as paronomasia) has for long been regarded as an English disease. It is no surprise therefore that English language writers have readily embraced the pun and related wordplay for use in haiku. This practice is sanctioned by its equally frequent occurrence in Japanese and while a consideration of the pun in Japanese haiku is not a part of this essay there follow a couple of examples by way of introduction.

First, a death poem of Chirin (died 1794)

In earth and sky no grain of dust – snow on the foothills.	*Ametsuchi ni* *chiri naki yuko no* *Fumoto kana*

Chiri naki means "without dust". The poem is a play on words using the poet's name: *Chirin naki* would mean "without Chirin" (Hoffman, 1986 p.151)

The 2nd from Hokushi, who was a sword sharpener and a pupil of Bashō

I write, erase, rewrite, erase again, and then a poppy blooms.	*Kaite mitari* *keshitari hate wa* *keshi no hana*

Hoffmann notes (1986, p190) "Hokushi's death poem is built around a pun. *Keshi* means *"to erase"* as well as "poppy", so the poem may be read, "I write, erase, rewrite, / erase again, and then / a flower erases."

The pun reinforces the poem's intended suggestion that nature in the end always overwhelms the creations of man. It will be noted that in the above examples the wordplay and double meanings are not used for humorous purposes, (they are both death poems) but instead enable both a compression and an opening out of meaning.

In most encyclopaedias and dictionaries the definition of the pun stresses its humorous potential. For example "a humorous use of words that have like sounds but different meanings" (Odhams), or, "A pun is a humorous figure of speech ..." (Chambers). Its use in haiku however exploits, in the main, other aspects of the pun. The following is a brief analysis of the purposes to which the pun and related wordplay has been put in English language haiku. In writing this article I looked at a variety of magazines, anthologies and individual collections but, for the sake of containment, have restricted my examples from just six journals. [1]

One thing to notice at the outset is that puns, in their widest definition, come in various forms. These include:

Homographic puns which exploit the difference between words that look identical (and usually sound identical) but have divergent meanings. In haiku terms this is the most common form of pun.

Homophonic puns which play on the difference in meaning of words which sound alike but have different spellings. This is perhaps the most familiar pun in common usage.

Double Sound, where words which are similar but not identical are intentionally confused.

The Discrete anti-contextual pun, One of the more subtle and open-ended of puns which refer to two different situations, or contexts, by using a word or phrase that may have two or more meanings, but only one of which makes sense in the context. All these appear, in varying instances, in modern western haiku. Examples of each are presented in the haiku that follow. [2]

---

1 Four US publications: Frogpond; Modern Haiku; Geppo; Haiku Headlines, and two UK journals: Blithe Spirit and Presence.

2 Other types of pun include: *The Antanaclasis,* a punning figure of speech in which the same word is repeated in a different sense; *the compound pun; the extended pun;* and the *multi-functional layered Ironic pun.* These forms of pun seem to have few, if any, opportunities for use in the small space of a haiku.

Following the tone of the Japanese death poems above here are two English language haiku that demonstrate that puns need not be exclusively concerned with wit and humour -

Graveyard stillness
shrouded
in the sound of traffic *Arwyn Evans (Blithe Spirit 9/2)*

a discrete use of pun that conflates the burial shroud with a more metaphorical covering that is made more intangible with the synaesthetic idea of being shrouded with sound. This Homographic pun operates as a pivot word with a line to itself between two images and opens up a variety of links and overtones.

graveside
my father and I
find common ground *Tom Painting (Frogpond XXVII. 2)*

A compound pun where 'common' contains the meaning of shared understanding as well as the connotation of basic, fundamental, the death that we must all come to. 'Ground' clearly refers to the earth and place of burial as well as the shared territory of understanding. The pun suggests in a subtle way a history of communications, misunderstandings and finally, the shared destinies of father and son.

In both these examples the use of pun very economically opens up extra avenues of understanding. Here is another successful use of pun -

Sagging in the middle
all his springs gone
old grey horse *Roberta Davies (Only a Few Seeds Left, Hub. 2000)*

The pun on 'springs' subtly conjures up the twin images of a derelict sunken sofa whose upholstery springs have collapsed, and of the old grey horse who has seen all the spring seasons he will ever see. (the link between sofa and horse contains another mortal spin when one considers that sofas were traditionally stuffed with horse hair). The fact that it is a homographic pun means that the mind doesn't have to make a substitution. This makes the pun, and the resonances coming from it, more subtle. It is sometimes an issue of doubt, with a homographic pun, whether a double meaning was even intended. If the additional layers of meaning that emanate from this kind of wordplay operate in a subliminal way this makes the haiku both more subtle and more powerful. The Davies haiku above is interesting in that the primary meaning is also a metaphor whiles the more direct and 'natural' image is the one that hits our awareness a fraction later. Many puns in haiku have this delayed action effect -

The muddy water,
A school of children
Swimming. *Natsume Soseki (translated by Soiku Shigematsu)*

This haiku appears to be an example of where the same pun, 'school', or some equivalent of it, has been able to be transferred from the Japanese to the English. In transferring the pun the translator may have sacrificed more evocative aspects of the poem. However, it still contains 'the shock of mild surprise' (Wordsworth).

Another homographic pun that works sequentially rather than immediately is represented by this haiku –

crisp blue morning –
spring in the air
and in the postman's feet *Cyril Childs (Blithe Spirit 10/3)*

Another 'spring' pun, like that of Roberta Davies, its second meaning becomes apparent as the haiku progresses with a slight delayed action. The pun is introduced in the second line but the surprise of the second meaning is only released in the third line. A similar 'slow burner' is –

my late dad's effects –
the startle when I find
his heavy belt hanabi (USA)

This wordplay has a delayed effect resting on the reader's realisation that 'effect', as well as meaning 'goods and possessions' left by the dead father, can also indicate 'to cause to happen' – the response upon finding the heavy belt. This then spans across to the associated word 'affects' where its meanings of 'to produce a change', to move the emotions' also cut in. Here then we have a double meaning and a punning use of two words sounding the same which all add extra dimensions to a seemingly straight-forward haiku. A comparable delayed action is achieved in the following –

In the compost box
absorbing yesterday's news
worms   bacteria *Richard Cluroe (Blithe Spirit 12/1)*

Though a rather lumbering pun (and this can be the effect of the slow-fuse strategy) this double-duty word definitely increases the effectiveness of the haiku and links the world of thought with the world of decay in a range of stimulating ways. 'Absorbing' is the key word of the haiku and acts as a hinge between the two applications.

This use of the homographic pun as a pivot, very often in the second line where the meanings tilt back and forth is a fairly common application of wordplay in the interests of economy, the pun word doing double duty.

yoga retreat
stretching
his budget *Gregory Hopkins (Modern Haiku, 37.1)*

Halloween
the ghost of something
on her mammogram *Pamela Miller Ness (Modern Haiku, 37.1)*

Alternatively the double-valance word can simply give a second connotation to the haiku as in the two meanings here of 'still' – 'enduringly' and 'without motion'

still
against the blue of sky
the massive oak *Janeth Ewald (Geppo XXXII:3)*

It becomes clear that puns and haiku share much common ground. "The qualities of haiku are brevity, concision and surprise" and are "suggestive of something not stated" (James Kirkup, 1992). Puns are used in haiku for their brevity and economy and to suggest another aspect or level of meaning. With the use of the kiregi, line breaks and pivot lines there are frequently at least two thoughts going on at once in haiku. The pun, at its best, with great economy can provide an unspoken link between the two images, or indicate a second application or nuance not immediately apparent.

full moon
barn owls face
every quarter *John Parsons (Blithe Spirit 19/1)*

The image of the owl's enduring vigil through the quarters of the moon also holds before our imagination all the moon's phases and the owl's ability to turn its head almost 360° to every quarter of the compass.

One of the conclusions that the process of sifting for examples of puns in haiku has thrown up is that, of all the types of pun available, it is the homographic pun, the least obtrusive on the page that predominates. Examples of the more familiar homophonic pun, where two words which sound alike have different spellings, are less commonly attempted. If keeping it subtle is difficult with the homographic pun it can even more hard with the homophonic variety.

  on the lawn in her
string bikini ... mosquitoes
  whining and dining *Gertrude Morris (Haiku Headlines #172)*

While this pun is obtrusive on the page it might be missed altogether when read aloud. The same pun is used as a double valence in this haiku too –

hot summer sun
the elderberry whine
of cicadas *Kay Grimnes (Geppo XXIV.4)*

The homophonic haiku-pun has more to deal with in terms of our prior associations of its use in other situations. The tale/tail pun is a familiar one and the following haiku just about gets away with its use by not making too much of it. Awareness of the pun adds little to the haiku itself, but can give us a small add-on flicker of pleasure as a little extra pay off.

hayless loft
horseless stall
end of tale *Jane R. Harwood (Haiku Headlines #166)*

In the homophonic pun, it is less easy to ignore the fact that some wordplay is taking place. Some writers however, hide their craft in very shrewd ways, even when using two puns close together -

first frost
sticking together
a bowl of sloes *David Cobb (A Bowl of Sloes,2000)*

Here the last line contains two puns, one homographic the other homophonic, which are entirely private and dependant on the reader knowing that the writer is also a slow spin bowler. If one picks up the reference then an extra nostalgic seasonal 'spin' is put on the approach of autumn by invoking the end of the cricket season. That this very personal, even wholly private, use of wordplay is not uncommon is seen in both the Chirin and Hokushi examples cited above. There is however another version of this poem in which the puns are more explicit.

the old spin bowler
fingers busy
with a bowl of sloes *(David Cobb (Blithe Spirit 9/3)*

Here the witty application of the pun is in the foreground and is more recognisable as a display of wordplay intended to surprise and amuse. Perhaps the haiku as a whole suffers by having a shorter life-span after the initial delight of recognition in the reader has died down. But the conflation of the two images, with their autumnal and nostalgic overtones, still remains.

Sometimes there is a hint of a pun but we are not quite sure of its application. Here is an example of a Discrete Anti-contextual pun also from David Cobb–

trundle of the train –
the musician settles
a score in his lap *David Cobb (A Bowl of Sloes, 2000)*

We all know the phrase 'to settle a score' and the same words in a different context give rise to reverberations which cannot be resolved. This open-endedness can in itself give the haiku continuing appeal despite the fact that the second meaning, if there is any, is totally elusive. Another example of an anti-contextual pun is:

A shower outside inside nothing flows
Marlene Mountain (Frogpond XXVIII.1)

Here our familiarity of the characterisation of our thoughts or of writing as 'flowing' immediately gives us the image of the frustrated writer on a rainy afternoon and also gives the 'outside inside' conjunction additional resonance.

The following is similar too –
Struggling
to make ends meets
the broken bridge *Leo Lavery (Blithe Spirit, 10/4)*

We might suspect some ramifications will spread out from the wordplay until we realise that the familiar connotation of making ends meet, the making do in a situation of poverty, doesn't really have anywhere to go. After a brief flicker of excitement the wordplay may disappoint and seem undirected, though a general impression of an under-cared-for society is left.

In haiku, as with all poetry, the rhythm and sound of the words can also add to the beauty and effectiveness of the lines. Accordingly the 'sound pun' can also find a use in haiku.

empty beer can
crickets
chip away the light *Michael Kriesel (Frogpond XXIX:2)*

'Chip' works as an onomatopoeic pun, the sound of which links the two images. This is an invented pun and therefore has more chance of being effective since it contains an original perception. Another made-up onomatopoeic pun, an example of the double sound pun, in the following haiku is simply cheesy and sentimental with its play on 'cheer up' –

blue Monday
the skylark's call
chirr-up chirr-up *Carolyn Hall (Study haiku 4132. (Geppo XXIV:3)*

Most often wordplay in haiku is at its most evocative when least explicit. In the next haiku the pun is almost hidden; the barely audible 'cracks' of spring thunder almost go unnoticed –

spring thunder
slight cracks in the
swollen tree buds *w.f. owen (Modern Haiku, 36.3)*

Using a word to include two of our senses, sound and vision, is an interesting and very haiku-suited employment of wordplay. Here is another example of how haiku poets sometimes like to use puns to bridge the senses –

lingering puddles
around budding willow trees
unseen spring peepers *Dana Rapisardi (Haiku Headlines 169)*

Both buds and birds are 'peepers' here, either peeping out at the ends of twigs or making a peeping noise. Since the birds at least are unseen perhaps they are peeping out on the writer too. It depends on how sympathetic we are to the haiku to decide how much the 'cute' cleverness of the pun may be being used to ginger up a rather commonplace and sentimental thought.

There may be pitfalls as well as benefits in wordplay. Sometimes the reader has the feeling that a pun is definitely intended but its meaning is not readily understood. Lack of clarity should not be mistaken for subtlety. Sometimes the pun, instead of creating an opening for wider possibilities, leaves a rather confused feeling of what is intended –

L'Apres-midi d'un faune
the brass section
empties their horns *Carolyn Hall (Frogpond XXVIII:2)*

A visual connection is made between the Satyr's horns and those of the orchestra but does it really sharpen the image or make a meaningful link?

Wordplay in haiku seems to be an acceptable device to add other levels and nuances in a verbally economic way. As with every verbal conceit, the writer has to be very sensitively alert to whether the wordplay is working or not. For a double meaning to really pay its way haiku writers need to be on the look out to find increasingly nuanced ways of using words to gain both compression and expansion of meaning.

winter solstice
the frozen lake
looks hard at the moon *Michele Harvey (Modern Haiku 37.1)*

The adjective/adverb options of 'looks hard' are exploited to increase the brittle and cold atmosphere. The active verb 'looks' puts the perceiver into the scene as he gazes, as the icy lake seems to be gazing, not only at the lake itself but also at the moon and the eye of its reflection. There is even a suggestion of the moon too looking down if we mis-read '*appears* hard *to* the moon', the moon and it's reflection in some way looking at each other.

From this brief review it would seem to be the case that effective use of wordplay and pun is by no means incompatible with haiku. The pun, as well as the haiku deals for the most part in concrete images, with succinctness, and with delivering its transformation in as few and precise words as possible. It is the catalyst for a change of view point, very often with a sense of surprise or revelation.

Having taken a brief look, in the first part of this essay, at the various types of punning wordplay and shown something of how they work within the haiku, I will look in part two at some of the pitfalls and temptations that might arise from having a penchant for wordplay.

Diana Webb

Tired Old Sunsets?

In recent issues of 'Blithe Spirit' it has been put forward that we do not want 'rehashes of tired haiku about sunsets, reflections, cherry blossom, falling leaves etc.' and the question asked 'just how many haiku does the world need about lazy frogs popping off logs into lily ponds?' A writer in *Frogpond* suggested in somewhat similar vein that many boring haiku are being written because people are not writing them from life but from memories of haiku that were hits long ago. I suggest that maybe we repeatedly write haiku about these things, not because we can't delete the message that focussing on them is part of an accepted recipe for successful haiku, but because phenomena like sunsets, petals, small creatures both still and moving, tinted leaves and reflections in water actually supply an image language for our inner selves eliciting 'some hint of movement in the soul of the writer' as mentioned as being desirable by David Cobb in his Hackett award report.

Also, perceived from moment to moment, they can exemplify 'that fantastic randomness' in nature which David Hockney so admires in many of the unfinished watercolours of Turner, the energy coming 'direct from the heart down the arm'. Every wave breaks on the shore in a slightly different way which can't be predicted and the waves of his brushstrokes perhaps echo that. I would say that for me every sunset is the first sunset, every kingfisher is the first kingfisher, and that it's not so much a question of haiku giving things repeatedly perceived a fresh lick of paint but more of steeping them from a deep well of intense inner colour with its infinite variety of shades every time we write a new haiku on a familiar subject. This could apply to experience of all the other senses too.

Colin Blundell

Where do you Stand?

In his editorial in *Blithe Spirit* 19/1 Mark Rutter pointed out that English language poets come to haiku along many different paths. Justifying his heterodox approach, he neatly covered the ground: 'For some the haiku is primarily a form of spiritual discipline, others come to haiku as a way of rejuvenating nature poetry. Still others are attracted to the brevity and down-to-earthness of the form, or by the way it invites the reader to participate in the unfolding of meaning. Some prize the haiku for its attention to the momentary, or for the Zen-inspired ethos of the ego-less look. For others, the haiku movement is a kind of avant-garde, forging a new poetic language by adopting aesthetic ideas from another culture, and for still others haiku is an alternative to poetry altogether...'

Where do you stand?

Though they might want to think about it occasionally, it's not so important that haiku-submitters answer this question but haiku-sifters are very much under scrutiny; it seems to me that editors of haiku journals need to be very clear about where they stand, presupposing, of course, that they are at all concerned about 'standards', or 'the future', or 'a judicious eclecticism' or even just 'getting it right for a single issue'. Currently, editors could, if they chose, find themselves under attack for maintaining a 'Shiki-orthodoxy' or for rejecting a 'Natsuishi-drive'.

Shiki-orthodoxy or the so-called Formulaic Approach

Introducing extracts from Jim Kacian's July 2008 paper (BS 19/2), Ken Jones dismally asserts that Shiki's *sketches from life tradition* 'is so deeply ingrained in poets, editors, reviewers and judges that it seems possible that English language haiku may have no literary future, and remain an eccentric, self-limiting byway on the poetry landscape...'

Jim Kacian laments the fact that the West's first contact with haiku occurred at a time when Shiki was engaged in retooling 'the moribund haiku into an objectivist art...' so that his model seemed to us to be the norm; Jim makes the rather extraordinary statement that Shiki 'jettisoned the ethos of 400 years of haiku...'

In presenting his Typology of Disjunction (BS 18/1-3), Richard Gilbert asserts that editors have demonstrated 'selective editorial sensibility' by favouring those haiku of a 'shasei' *sketch from life* nature, deeming 'haiku techniques involving metaphor, allusion, psychological interiority, surrealism' to be 'improper to English haiku form'. What Richard, by the way, seems to me to do very well is to present a way of looking at haiku as a form of universal literature rather than as an alien and 'eccentric, self-limiting byway' of a poem; in the same way as one might look at a 'proper poem' in order to figure out how it works linguistically so he provides us with a very useful taxonomy of types of 'disjunction' that appear in the haiku-form.

The great thing about a haiku is its incompleteness, its elliptical nature, incorporating elements of shock, surprise and absence; the way it contributes to what William Carlos Williams called 'the renovation of experience'. Haiku is an 'open text'; haiku that close things down for the reader are less acceptable than something like -

sash window
the broken cord
frozen in a gesture

Ken Jones

which leaves a kind of extraordinary tingling in the brain, does it not? It is 'a knot of language [that] holds its energy tight within it' (Jim Kacian) and positively defies unpicking. In trying to find a contrast to this, plucking a book from my haiku-shelf at random, I opened Robert Bebek's fine book *The Shapes of Emptiness* and came across:

from a hollow stump
a row of ants marching out
into the morning light

which, I take it, could be classed as a sketch from life – it just says it as it is, no more no less. You can feel the difference in the two haiku for yourself... What a relief! One wouldn't, I fancy, wish to be all knotted up, however splendidly, for too many pages, one after another! As Martin Lucas pointed out so eloquently in BS 15/2, there are haiku that appeal to some poetic sense or other for their simple clarity, 'taking us out of the agonising business of being human...' In BS 19/3, Diana Webb suggests that 'simple imagery' haiku about sunsets and frogs and reflections (and ants) are worthwhile because they 'supply an image language for our inner selves...' – they are not necessarily the result of formulaic writing: for her, 'every sunset is the first sunset'... I'm reminded of Fernando Pessoa's reference to the 'singularity of the ordinary' which is precious in itself.

Just to level up, Robert Bebek has:

> summer thunderstorm
> my neighbour is gazing
> at this same sky too

which for me, whilst not quite such a tight knot of language as Ken's haiku, fits David Cobb's reference to Kaneko Tōta's haiku-category of 'primary confirmation of existence' which comes close, I think, to Ken Jones' plea for 'existentially liberative' haiku.

As I understand it, what Richard Gilbert calls 'disjunction' is about the gap that opens up in a haiku which the reader has to fill with a kind of meaning; there's an irruption into consciousness (assuming there is such a thing) managed by some shift – of register, of semantics, linguistics or image-structure, a reversal of expectation that can sometimes leave the reader quietly gasping for breath.

But, as Mark Rutter points out in his review (BS 18/3) of Richard Gilbert's *Poems of Consciousness*, Richard is not after 'a complete revolution in haiku as much as for a new uncertainty about what a haiku is and should be'. About *shasei* stylism, Richard there says, 'This is not always a bad thing when trying to establish ground rules, definitions and guidelines... On the other hand, many published haiku are formulaic, lack authorial creativity [sic] and possess little sense of language creativity...' This last sentence would require a good deal of unpicking and exemplification.

Shiki Saved Haiku from Extinction

In BS 19/4, Fred Schofield refers to Janine Beichmann's great book on Shiki and points out that many in the West 'have followed and advocated a relatively simplistic and superficial interpretation of his poetic and literary achievement...' It's we who are at fault for making assumptions about the sketch from life thesis, for taking simple observation to be the norm. Janine Beichmann seems to be saying that, far from diverting the course of haiku, Shiki actually saved it from extinction: 'since becoming the sport of amateurs and ignoramuses, haiku have become more and more numerous, more and more banal...' Nothing changes! 'The purveyors of spam', as Ken Jones calls them, are seemingly ubiquitous. Perhaps we, serious amateurs, are the rescuers now! Beichmann comments that 'the haiku had degenerated to a popular amusement and was no longer a serious art... Shiki succeeded through realistic description in evoking a complexity of meaning that goes beyond literal realism...' We surely have to be grateful that our first contact with haiku was at a time when Shiki put the brakes on the 'shallowness and poverty' of formulaic haiku from the 15th to the 18th Century that he quotes in Blyth Volume 2 Chapter XXVI. The 'formulaic' has always been around...

Taste always changing, with the new dispensation, I suppose one of the haiku Shiki rejects by Teitoku would be highly regarded nowadays! –

> Like a snake
> the cloud swallows up
> the moon-frog

Apart from anything else, Shiki reinstated Buson. Blyth comments (Volume 1 p267): 'Buson cannot be excelled, though Shiki sometimes equals him, in pure yet meaningful objectivity. This kind of thing is difficult, because 100% objectivity is a mere photograph. Nature without humans is a body without a soul. But when a particular person's feelings are inserted into nature, it is spoiled. Nature must be faintly suffused with humanity to give us complete satisfaction...' He quotes Buson:

the water is deep;
a sharp sickle
cutting reeds

A haiku has been written by *somebody*; they may get themselves out of the way but they are still there somewhere or the other: who's cutting the reeds? What's the relationship between a sharp sickle and deep water? There's a resonance here beyond the 'simple image'.

Irruptions into Consciousness

What does go on in the spaces that the brevity of haiku creates? What 'irruptions into consciousness' take place? Let's have a look at three Shiki haiku.

wisteria plumes
sweep the earth and soon
the rains will fall

Is this just a *sketch from life*, saying nothing more than the obvious? I enter the spirit of the poem, as I always try to do, and visualise dangling bunches of 'wisteria plumes' that 'sweep the earth and soon' [I know – and feel – the stress of time passing] 'the rains will fall' [and I will soon feel quite different about comparable things that dangle and fall and sweep my space...] The squared brackets contain some indication of what happens inside me as I read this haiku – I am moved to a different place in time and space.

I think I understand the sense of what Jane Beichmann writes: 'Shiki imbued the haiku with a new psychological complexity and made it a poetic form that would survive into the modern period...' p73

getting a shave!
on a day when Ueno's bell
is blurred by haze

getting a shave [50 years since I had one, but I suppose that the ill Shiki feels that he's being pampered and made presentable, and then there's a shift of attention – synaesthetic compound of the visual and the auditory] the bell [a specific bell] blurred [or muffled] by spring haze [how the poet wishes he could go towards the sound to un-blur it as he might once have done...]

Blyth says that 'Shiki began with *shasei*, the theory of the delineation of nature, but he soon found that he had also to include the delineation of his own mind...'

open the shutter
I'll just have a look
at Ueno's snow!

The ailing Shiki is in a dark room pining for the outside world of Nature; 'open the shutter' [please! – we are addressed conversationally as though we were there – so we are intimately involved in the scene] 'I'll just have a look [just a quick one before you close it down again so I can rest but, oh, the strength of my desire...] 'at Ueno's snow' [which once I could have enjoyed to the full]...

Each of these poems seems to me to be 'existentially liberative' in that they have 'some kind of metaphorical resonance with the human condition... they strike a spark of insight, of compassion shared with the reader...' (Ken Jones' definition)

Each of these poems seems to me to put one under a 'poetic spell'. (Martin Lucas' phrase) It all depends what you mean by a 'poetic spell' – Tennyson's brand or Eliot's, for instance?

The Interior Landscape in Renga

In pursuing this retrospective exploration, I came across a really interesting idea in Blyth. He says, 'After the death of Bashō, haiku began to degenerate into triviality, from lack of new poetic experience on the part of the teachers of it...' But, he continues, betraying more about himself than anything else I feel, saying that Shiki was on the path to 'irreligion and unpoeticalness'. However, and here's the point, he attributes this to Shiki's divorce of haiku from renga: 'haiku were the isolated phrases and themes which renga underline' and build on; detached from a context, 'haiku found themselves beating their ineffectual wings in the void...'

Look at any renga in any copy of *Blithe Spirit* and what Blyth is saying here gives pause for thought. In renga, each participant is free – within the leader's parameters – to draw on interiority, psychological inclination, myth, memory, flights of fancy, surrealistic connections, random association, allusiveness – all the kind of subjective things which shasei-dominated editors might frown upon when they appear in isolated haiku; but they let them go in renga... [I let them go in renga... Prize them, even...]

What lessons can we learn from this? What poetic sensibility can be 'legitimately' transferred from participation in renga to the writing of haiku?

The Affective Connection

Plenty of research has shown that everything that impinges on our being has an affective tinge to it. We cannot make or read a sketch from nature, see a leaf or a tree or a sunset or the pulse of a wave on sand, without it holds some affective connection for us. But emotion is never a fixed point; there's an illusory fixity and we imagine it would be nice if it were real & permanent but it's just the case that it only lasts a split second: 'something moves at the centre of my phenomenal being... neither space nor time exist any longer, nor forms; it moves where it is...; I touch there the eternity of the instant...' (Hubert Benoit: *The Psychology of Zen*)

Benoit goes on: 'it is not a question of laboriously dwelling on it as though there were something to seize. There is nothing to seize. It is a question of noting, as in the winking of an eye, instantaneous and perfectly simple, that I am conscious of myself globally in that second (through an effort to observe how I am conscious of myself in that second). I succeed instantaneously or not at all... It is in my interest to make this gesture as often as possible but with suppleness and discretion...'

I am reminded of Sartre's pre-reflective and reflective cogito: something there is that impinges on awareness, hits the sense-mechanisms (to avoid the invented concept of 'consciousness'), initially unverbalised, uncluttered by prior associations. Only then, with intention, do we bring it into mental focus by 'thinking' – only by deliberately intending to do so.

In this context I began to think about a haiku I wrote this summer, having been on my own for several days and feeling uncharacteristically 'lonely'. It was only the precipitating event that made me feel thus; it was absolutely without words – the event itself – but I have to tell you, just so we know where we are, that there was the sound of a peacock amongst tall trees by a large hotel with a view of mountains and a distant sea. Now, forget I ever mentioned these items and simply imagine the scene for yourself: every time the words 'peacock' or 'tall trees' or 'landscape with sea & mountains' come into what you call your mind, dismiss them and go with the wordless sensation – whatever it might be for you; your construction of things will be just as accurate as mine was or is. We invent the world.

All this constituted a momentary 'gesture' in a billion-trillionth of the time it's taken to explain it. It was a noting of something moving inside my being, an other-than-conscious set of affective [pre-reflective] connections that sent me lightly into what I take to be my reflective cogito.

My haiku started off thus: ...the lonely cry [who's lonely? Not the peacock who has its mate...] of a peacock [there is a peacock noise falling from the trees behind me] echoing through trees [yes, there's an echo? from a high bank of tall trees...]... [I cross out 'the lonely' and go for the objective 'falling' – the sound is literally higher up than I am and so it falls...].

It may be that you get back to the idea that 'I' might be lonely (that you might be lonely if you had had my experience, as you have had, more or less, now...). But I'm not forcing the issue.

falling – the cry
of a peacock
echoing through trees

I've taken myself out of the poem (show not tell...) but I'm still there as the writer.

Benoit again: 'Suppose that in the darkness I seize an object and turn it round in my hand; I have thus an active perception of this object which gives me information concerning it. Let us suppose now that in the darkness an immense giant takes me in his hand, turns me round and presses me; I realise the existence of the giant, I find him more or less agreeable or disagreeable according to whether he caresses me or crushes me but that is all; I have obtained no information about the giant himself, and it is impossible for me to describe him...'

In the darkness of my central being I had some indications – peacock, trees, hotel, landscape with far-off sea – but no words – pre-reflective cogito. There is no such thing as consciousness – there is just a black hole or gap, as Sartre calls whatever passes for 'consciousness'. There is a happening in the darkness: I make a gesture and net what it is briefly; the poetic connections begin to coalesce in reflective cogito.

Beyond the bowsprit
the lift and dip
of a thin line of hills

Ken Jones

Beyond the bowsprit [oh god, I'm on a boat, going up and down? I don't do boats...] the lift and dip [just as I thought, going up and down and no let-up...] of a thin line of hills [but it's the hills that are moving, not me – I can't even rely on remembered advice that to overcome travel sickness you have to focus on something stable... Let me out!...]

Maeve O'Sullivan

Mindfulness, Haiku-poets and 'Regular' Poets

The following article is a selection of freely-associated thoughts by someone who writes haiku and poetry, and tries to practise mindfulness. James W. Hackett's well-regarded list of 18 tips for writing haiku starts with this one: 'The present is the touchstone of the haiku experience, so always be aware of this present moment.' Number 13 builds on that advice: 'Remember that lifefulness, not beauty, is the real quality of haiku.' So a haiku about a dying animal -or person -is just as worthwhile as one about a flower blossoming.

As haiku poet or aficionado, you probably knew that already. The question I hope to explore here is this: do 'regular' poets employ mindfulness to the same extent as writers of haiku and related forms? To the best of my knowledge, there haven't been any surveys of either group in relation to the practice of mindfulness, so I have no scientific base for my speculations. However, based on my personal friendships and acquaintanceships with fellow haijin, and my reading of the work of many others, it seems fair to deduce that a sizeable section of our community has some sort of spiritual practice, whether it's meditation/mindfulness, yoga, Reiki; Buddhist, Christian or Sufi or other prayers. I'm not sure if that is as true of 'regular' poets.

Of course you don't have to have such a practice to write haiku, but many say that it helps. For example, the Buddhist idea of impermanence, whether it's the changing of the seasons or the moods of our loved ones, underpins haiku that describe the passing of time or a range of other external or internal changes. Three of the four Great Masters of haiku were practising Buddhists, and this is reflected in their work, especially in their attention to detail and in that elusive quality of 'wabi-sabi' that permeates their work: Basho, the wanderer, reflects on the turning of the year in this haiku: 'year's end / all corners of this floating world / swept' (trans. Lucien Stryk). Another change of season is beautifully described by Issa here: 'once snows have melted / the village soon overflows / with friendly children' (trans. Sam Hamill), and he also wrote poignantly about the many losses in his own personal life.

Buson, also a master painter, gives us food for thought in this haiku: 'being alone / may also be pleasant / autumn dusk' (trans. Yuki Sawa and Edith Marcombe Shiffert). The bed-bound Shiki, widely regarded as the father of modern haiku, managed to admire -and paint -his surroundings despite the pain and lack of mobility caused by his tuberculosis: 'a morning glory's withered / before I can finish painting it' (trans. Students in the English Dept. of Kobe University).

A little later in the last century, the Zen monk Santoka immerses himself in a winter moment to give us 'peaceful, peaceful/chilly, chilly / snow, snow' (trans. Stephen Addiss). The women were no slouches at producing fine verses either: In the eighteenth century, Chiyojo shows us 'spring rain / all things on earth / becoming beautiful', and Enomoto Seifu reflects on the following: 'unchanging doll's faces -/ I've had no choice, except / to grow old' (both trans. Makoto Ueda)

My favourite definition of mindfulness is from teacher and author Rob Nairn: 'knowing what's happening while it's happening'. 'Being in the moment' is another way of saying it, and students are often urged to focus on their breathing to achieve that. Advice that many haijin and aspiring haijin are encouraged to take is to immerse themselves in the 'haiku moment', or in the 'frozen moment' as the Americans would have it; to let go of thoughts and experience sensations instead. Of course, for most of us, it's easier to aspire to this than to do it.

Aspiring regular poets, however, are not told to let go of their thoughts. Indeed it is from thoughts and ideas that a large part of poetry arises. It is, generally speaking, cerebral and conceptual in nature. That's not to say that most poets do not use their senses, take in their surroundings, or convert those sensations into verses. Of course they do, and that's what they have in common with haijin. Both sets of writers employ imagery, sounds and rhythms, along with the techniques of assonance and alliteration, and varying degrees of imagination. However, regular poets often *seek out* their poems whereas haiku tend *to find their writers.*

It might be more helpful to compare haiku and related forms, not to other types of poetry, but to other Japanese customs or rituals which require attention, precision and the achievement of a delicate balance: flower arranging, calligraphy, the tea ceremony or the cultivation of a miniature garden. Every flower, every teacup, every stroke and every stone has its rightful place, and so perhaps also with the placing of words -and punctuation - into a haiku.

Poets have freer rein when it comes to point of view, line and verse length, the use of similes and metaphors, and rhyming schemes. In short, there are fewer restrictions, especially for non-formalist poets who stick to freeform. Compare this excerpt from Wordsworth's famous poem: 'when all at once I saw a crowd / a host of golden daffodils' with the haiku by Sue Richards: 'under bare branches / -daffodil spears / another year', published in the *BS* issue of June 2011. The former uses explicit metaphor and end-rhyme, the latter some description and some reflection.

Of course one should not necessarily subscribe to any black-and-white duality, whether it's happiness v sadness, or haiku v poetry. As always, there is a lot of grey. There's wonderful 'regular' poetry written by Buddhists, including those gathered in the anthology *the heart as origami* (Rising Fire, 2005), and many other 'regular' poets -with or without spiritual practices -who show mindfulness in their work. In contrast, there are many 'regular' poets-of differing degrees of fame who dabble in the haiku form, playing with the syllabic aspect without showing much interest in its other criteria. They shall remain nameless!

There are those who straddle both worlds such as acclaimed poet Jane Hirschfield, who has translated tanka from Japanese, and multiform author Gabriel Rosenstock, who writes and translates poetry and haiku in several languages including Irish. Roberta Beary's 2007 collection of haiku, *The Unworn Necklace* (Snapshot Press), was selected as a William Carlos Williams Book Award finalist by the Poetry Society of America. Martin Lucas's essay *Haiku as Poetic Spell* (published in 'evolution', the 2010 Red Moon anthology edited by Jim Kacian et al), has caused quite a few ripples, and eloquently encourages haijin to inject more poeticism into their haiku.

Haiku takes on many different guises in the 21st century, as does poetry. And so it's up to each of us to find his or her own path in this regard. Keep reading. Keep writing. To quote a Tibetan maxim, 'it is necessary to understand that there is nothing to be done'.

Susan Lee Kerr

Awareness Gate: Towards Cultivating the State of Receptivity that allows Haiku to happen

Sometimes haiku just come, like manna from heaven. The current lively debate over *gendai,* or 'flying pope' -type, haiku focuses on a deliberate or even absurd creativity to produce haiku. My interest is in the haiku that just comes: a haiku arrives in the mind virtually fully formed, perhaps needing a bit of polishing later. When this happens I seem to be in a special state of receptivity. I have periods when many haiku arrive, and I have dry seasons. I take heart from the poet and highly regarded poetry editor and author Al Alvarez, now in his eighties, who in a talk a few years ago at the Troubadour poetry cafe said he perhaps should have written fewer poems, implying that only a few were truly good. So I feel okay, then, to have a low poetry production rate. Nevertheless I want to know if there is a way to have more of the fertile times, and this was the subject of my exploration and workshop at the BHS gathering in November 2011.

So how to cultivate a heightened - yet relaxed and unintentional - sensitivity to world and self that allows haiku to happen? One way for me is to read a quantity of haiku, an hour's quiet browse through *Blithe Spirit, Presence* or a haiku book, not as a quest, not in a critical mode, just for sheer enjoyment and response. I should do it more. A shift of environment, getting out into nature also helps. What else? I decided to seek indications from three kinds of practitioners of what I can only think to call the 'source state': artists, poets and meditators.

It seems to me that artists, that is, makers of visual art, have an advantage over poets (including haijin) in their use of materials. They can go from a wordless feeling, knowing or response, a wordless thought as it were, directly to paint, cloth, stone, clay, wire or whatever. They can bypass words whereas we haiku writers use words to convey the initially wordless response. Still, artists (and viewers and critics) experience the difference in art works that are 'inspired' or not, and ponder the source. An 'openness to the accidental seems a key ingredient of artistic inspiration,' says an editorial in the Royal Academy magazine.

Grayson Perry, who works in ceramics and many other media, describes his creative process as 'similar to that of a shaman or a witch doctor... '
I tell stories, give things meaning and make them a bit more significant. Like religion this is not a rational process, I use my intuition. Sometimes our very human desire for meaning can get in the way of having a good experience of the world. Some people call this irrational unconscious experience spirituality. I don't.

Haiku writer and artist John Parsons finds inspiration a will o' the wisp thing in both of his crafts:
It comes and goes, has to be persevered with... I have learnt to set visual preconceptions to one side by a kind of mental side-stepping. Writing haiku is in many ways very similar. It employs a stilling of the normal hubbub of thought, a standing aside to enable something deeper to speak.... Always surprising, always mysterious, always more to do with the feeling than the thought...

What produces this mysterious function? I found a clue from the master, Bashō:
In this mortal frame of mine ... there is something, and this something is called a wind-swept spirit, for lack of a better name, for it is much like a thin drapery that is torn and swept away at the slightest stir of the wind.

I love that 'wind-swept spirit', but I am not sure if the 'stir of the wind' is the ordinary world and mind sweeping away the receptive something, or if the 'thin drapery that is torn and swept away' is the response that results in poetry. It seems as tentative a thing as the state famously identified by John Keats: 'Negative Capability, that is, when a man [sic] is capable of being in uncertainties, mysteries, doubts, without any irritable reaching after fact & reason.' Negative Capability is an accurate description of a particular state of mind I think all creators can recognise: what is the mechanism of it and where did he get the terminology? A *Wikipedia* entry suggests it came from his time as a medical student:

In the same way that the negative pole receives [electric] current from the positive pole, the poet receives impulses from a world that is full of mystery and doubt, which cannot be explained but which the poet can translate into art.

This state was similarly described by Noragh Jones recently, and she uses negatives to get to the haiku-moment creative facility:

...in a state of 'Perhaps' -exploring the meaning of life through ... particular situations, and refusing to turn to the dubious certainties of any ... systems ... to know is not to understand, to think is not to solve problems, to be clever is not to be emotionally mature ... Now is that not a fine summary of the starting position for composing haiku?

How can we turn on this elusive state of mind? Some discussions in *Blithe Spirit* gave me more indications. A useful reverse angle comes from Mark Rutter when he comments that reading a successful haiku is 'to experience a 'cut' in consciousness, and irruption in everyday mind ... a transformation of experience.' This is similar to John Parsons' 'stilling of the normal hubbub of thought', referred to above. Duality of mind emerges as a theme from others, too. Jane Hirshfield says haiku 'unshackle the mind ... pointing toward both world and self.' Colin Blundell says 'Blyth on Shiki speaks of the delineation of nature ... and the delineation of his own mind ...' and puts all this together to ask our anguished question:

... haiku come 'from a momentary interior relationship between oneself and the not-self... 'But what is the nature of 'interior relationship'? Could it be said that there is no hook for what might be called 'real haiku'?

I looked to the methods of those who focus on the activity of mind and self without concern for an end product (poem, painting, sculpture etc.). Having heard long ago of the meditation methods of the 16th Century founder of the Jesuits, Ignatius of Loyola, I browsed various web sources under Ignation spirituality. I dodged around the God, Christ, Gospel, Bible, sin, mercy etc. elements to winkle out what might be of direct use to the haiku world. First of all, summarising and paraphrasing, here is an Ignation definition of a state of mind/being that even has the idea of creation as its end.

An emptying of self... it is not about finding, looking, but allowing oneself to be found. Creating an adequate space so as to arrive at an internal knowledge, a felt knowledge, a response of the heart. Creation is a now of gifts, with a human response being the link that allows the now to return. The human response is a free choice to allow creation to speak.

For our purposes I have transliterated to haiku practice St Ignatius's own starting methods for arrival at 'an adequate space'. It could be worthwhile to try anyone of the following methods, or all three in a progression.

(I) Getting calm while sitting or walking about considering a particular focus (a text or thought or intellectual fact -perhaps for haiku writers a sentence or phrase from *Blithe Spirit* or any other reading that caught your attention, maybe even a haiku).
(2) Sit with eyes closed and say or think the focus sentence one word at a time, considering each word.
(3) Quietly breathing, say/think one word of the focus between each breath; during the breath give attention to the meaning of the word.
Alas, I have not tried this yet. The followers of Ignatius have spiritual guides to take them through the process. Perhaps I need a haiku guide (or self-discipline) -perhaps that's what Maeve O'Sullivan's *Anam Cara* workshops do. If we had had time at the November gathering we could have tried this method.

In *Blithe Spirit 21/4* Maeve addresses aspects of the other practice I looked into: mindfulness. On the internet I found a definition that led right on to useful methods anyone could choose and try. Mindfulness means:

... in day-to-day life maintaining as much as possible a calm awareness of bodily functions, sensations (feelings), objects of consciousness (thoughts and perceptions), and consciousness itself. ... The mindfulness itself can take the form of nothing more than taking three successive breaths while remembering they are a conscious experience of body activity within mind...

This source says some training exercises aim to make mindfulness virtually continuous by using particular environmental cues. Examples of such cues are:

- the hourly chimes of clocks
- red lights at traffic junctions
- crossing the threshold of doors

Another source describes the simple (but hard!) method of just being still:

... Keep quiet and still and sounds or silence, and any other sensation, will appear in conscious awareness. We don't need to do anything to instigate hearing. It happens despite us. If we are quiet and still, nothing is blocking or interfering with the sounds of silence...

We haiku writers are looking for an artefact, a product in words on paper, arrived at through a certain state. Summing up the indications from artists, poets and seekers-of-inner-peace as to how to get to that state I pick out these words: openness, meaning gets in the way, good experience of the world, mental side-stepping, stilling of the normal hubbub of thought, without reaching after fact and reason, refusing to turn to certainties of any system, unshackle the mind, an adequate internal space, keeping quiet and still.

Indications are that a mental pre-focus allows a free-floating dual and defocused attention, a mode of not seeking but allowing. We seem to have an underused organ of perception whose functioning provides a person with a sort of absence in the present, and presence in being absent. As to the formation of actual words (the haiku), this has to come from groundwork in the craft of writing and a love of language: the thing that makes a person write poetry rather than paint pictures or compose music.

For the November gathering I set an exercise I have used in teaching creative writing which I call 'Awareness Gate'. It provides a single concrete word which the receiver keeps to him/herself as he/she walks about in the world: a mental pre-focus followed by openness, then some time to write, if any haiku arrived. Anybody who didn't write a haiku would come back and write a paragraph of impressions. Some of the words I suggested were: 'hands', the colour 'green', 'shine' or 'shininess', 'shadows' ...

In researching this subject I found Jane Hirshfield's observation on Bashō: his 'simple, deeply useful reminder: that if you see for yourself, hear for yourself and enter deeply enough this seeing and hearing, all things will speak with and through you .... In poetry as in life, he saw each moment as gate-latch.'
'Awareness gate', 'gate-latch', each moment ... after searching for the secret of hooking 'real haiku', an antidote arrived in my email inbox from another master:

stop pestering!
rice cakes are growing
on willow branches *Issa*

Sources

RA magazine Winter 2010, Editorial p 10
Grayson Perry, *The Tomb of the Unknown Craftsman,* The British Museum Press, London 2011. p 91
John Parsons, Haiku and its Relationship to my Visual Work BS 19.1 p 27- 29
Matsuo Basho, *Journal of a Travel-Worn Satchel* (tr. Nobuyuki Yuasa) from Jane Hirshfield's *The Heart of Haiku* , Amazon Kindle Single http://en.wikipedia.org/wiki/Negative_capability ace 20/11/11
Noragh Jones, The Flying Pope Mobile and Other Vehicles, BS 21.2 & 21.3
Mark Rutter, Review of *Poems of Consciousness* by Richard Gilbert BS 18.3 p 52
Jane Hirshfield, Seeing Through Words extract part 2 from *The Heart of Haiku,* Amazon Kindle Single, in BS 21.4
Colin Blundell, Where do you stand? BS 21.1 p 51
Colin Blundell, Editorial, BS 21.3 p 1
Ignation Way, various sources, starting at http://ignatianspirituality.com/
Mindfulness, http://en.wikipedia.org/wikilMindfulness ace 19/11/11
Adaptationpractice.tp://www.ap-staging.com/2011/09/focus-during-med*itation/* acc 19/11/11
Susan Lee Kerr, Creative Writing the Matrix: Exercises & Ideas for Creative Writing Teachers and http://teachingcreativewriting.blogspot.com
Jane Hirshfield, Op Cit BS 21.3 p 46-47
Daily Issa, http://cat.xula.edu/issa/ Issa, stop pestering, 1819

Kai Falkman

Tomas Tranströmer in Japan

At a haiku conference in Kyoto last November I had been asked to speak about haiku in Swedish but instead found myself fielding questions about Tomas Tranströmer. For some of the 300 delegates, Tranströmer's name had been familiar even before he was chosen as this year's Nobel Laureate in Literature, but for most, he arrived out of the blue with the Nobel Prize. Asked why Tranströmer's haiku were not mentioned in the Prize motivation, I referred to the Swedish Academy's presentation of Tranströmer's work tending progressively towards 'an increasingly smaller format and increasingly greater degree of concentration.' This general description applies to more than his haiku.

Later, in Tokyo, when I asked publisher Kyuro Oda what had persuaded him to publish Tranströmer's haiku in Japanese, he answered: "The visual language! When I saw Tranströmer's daring and innovative visual language in Eiko Duke's excellent translation, I was immediately entranced." Oda explained that haiku has gone through repeated renewals ever since Bashō's poetry revolution in the 17th century, when the first stanza, the hokku, in his linked-verse sequence became the independent haiku. Tranströmer's haiku imply a renewal that Japanese poetry must become familiar with. "Many of the old school will reject his unexpected metaphors, since metaphor is banned in haiku. But it is specifically the use of metaphor that is Tranströmer's strength!" According to Oda, Tranströmer uses an extraordinary visual language that belongs more to modern poetry than traditional haiku. This makes him thoroughly modern and potentially a model for Japanese haiku poets.

Oda stressed that a metaphor is also an image. It reinforces the initial image through extra energy. This opposes the conventional view that a metaphor diverts attention from the main point to a minor one, weakening the subject. Japan is currently debating the future of poetry and Oda believes that Tranströmer's work can contribute to the discussion.

Tomas Tranströmer's words are easily understood but his sentences are difficult, several conference attendees believed. An example is the last line in his best-known haiku:

The power lines stretched
across the kingdom of frost
north of all music. (trans. Robin Fulton)

Is the last line a hidden metaphor? Music notes are placed on lines reminiscent of power lines and serve the same purpose: the transmission of collected energy. Tranströmer's poems seem to be inspired by detailed observations leading to unusual associations, which, on reflection, can reveal a subtle realism. Professor Tadashi Kondo, one of the conference arrangers, wondered if the phrase "north of all music" was not an expression of the chill and silence that afflicted the poet after his brain haemorrhage, a silence he could not disclose because his ability to speak had been lost.

In Japanese haiku, winter is a symbol of nakedness. Nature's covering has wilted. Transferring this image to man, it can be seen that man can no longer hide his true nature under make-up and disguise. Is this an analogy Tranströmer wants to communicate? Such a gloomy picture, sighed one Japanese woman. No, countered Kondo, under nakedness, new creative strength is being gathered for the spring.

Hear the sough of rain.
I whisper a secret
so that I can get in. (trans. Anatoly Kudryavitsky)

This could be a Japanese woodcut, remarked the editor of one of Japan's 780 haiku journals: the vertical lines of the rain, the poet's horizontal whispering. This haiku image expresses a likeness rather than a simile. The lines cross each other without touching even though the poet attempts this with his secret. What does the rain care about secrets under the dense veil it covers the land with during the rain period?

A dragonfly pair
Fastened to each other
Went flickering past. (trans. Patty Crane)

'Isn't the entire haiku a hidden metaphor?' wondered an elderly woman in a kimono. Doesn't the fastened pair represent a couple linked happily by the years-fastened, not bound, and therefore easy to unfasten, if one should so wish...

Another method Tranströmer uses to construct unexpected images is anthropomorphism, the attribution of human characteristics to animals and nature. This, too, is alien to traditional haiku, but does appear in the works of Issa (1763-1827), known for his attachment to animals. Even Tranströmer can write a Syster snigel (Sister Snail) but of most interest are the images that demand re-reading and reflection:

A stag basks in the sun.
flies flit and sew the shadow
on the ground.
(trans. Anatoly Kudryavitsky)

The picture clears when you realize that the flies around the stag's body in the sun cast lively shadows on the ground. A housewife from Osaka praised how Tranströmer's haiku could change observation: "Although I see flies sewing - not mosquitoes... "

Trees are superior to man, writes Tranströmer, since they are higher and live longer; trees are individual and similar to humans. But they still belong to a higher group, the forest; a forest that forgives everything but forgets nothing. His testimony has a divine ring: only God can forgive everything, forgetting nothing. The Japanese will be astonished at this image, said Kondo. The country's forest-clad hills are untouched and blessed with temples, while the plains are secular and overpopulated. In Japanese haiku there is a spiritual dimension in all nature that should be apparent in the description of events without the addition of human attributes that diminish the essence of nature.

Tranströmer lends human characteristics even to objects: The letterbox shines quietly, what is written cannot be taken back. With this humorous remark, the letter-writer seems to realize the futility of regret, because the letter he entrusted the letterbox with cannot be recaptured. But he describes the situation not from his own rueful perspective but from the triumphant view of the letterbox. Tranströmer is using an 'opposites perspective': subject and object change places, forcing the brain to adopt' opposites vision'.

What is fascinating in Tranströmer is the surrealistic element, said the haiku editor. "Suddenly, he opens a door to a different world. From Manga, the Japanese recognize this unexpected leap into the unknown, but we do not dare use it in haiku." As an example, he mentions Tranströmers *Minnena ser mig* (The memories see me). "What is intended is probably not only memory in terms of associations or dreams but as a messenger from a parallel world. We Japanese have a great need of secret parallel worlds, since our physical world is so strictly regulated."

What do Tranströmers haiku and Japanese haiku have in common? One answer is the absence of the Ego. The Japanese often say that a haiku is too small to allow room for the poet. What is to be elucidated is the poet's inner image, not the poet himself. In his early poems, Tranströmer took pains to avoid the word 'I'. In a later phase, he introduced the Ego in the beginning of a poem, only to make it disappear later in the text. Fantastic to feel my poem growing / while I shrink. This analysis interests the Japanese, says Professor Kondo, since the transition from the personal to the impersonal in the creative process is fundamental in Japanese culture. In Tranströmer's later haiku, the Ego makes a return, at times disguised as 'he'. But as a rule, the images are presented as objective visual observations absent of Ego.

What Tranströmer's haiku and traditional Japanese haiku have in common is also the form: 17 syllables divided into three lines of 5, 7, and 5 syllables. Outside of Japan, this traditional form has increasingly ceded place to the freeform haiku. When the Swedish Haiku Society arranges haiku contests, the entries are usually equally divided between those using the 5-7-5 syllable form and looser styles, which however seldom exceed 17 syllables. The risk in counting syllables is that the poet becomes more concerned with the number of syllables than the haiku's poetic substance.

In Kyoto and Tokyo I was asked how Tranströmer discovered haiku. I had heard that he came across the first Swedish haiku book, containing translations of the four masters - Bashō, Buson, Issa and Shiki. The book was called *Haiku. Japansk miniatyrlyrik* (Haiku. Japanese miniature poetry) and the poems were interpreted by Jan Vintilescu. The same year that the book was published, 1959, Tranströmer wrote his first haiku. They were later published in a booklet entitled *Fëngelse* (Prison), comprising nine haiku snapshots from the youth correction centre where Tranströmer worked as a psychologist. Even back then, he demonstrated his sensitivity for the surprise effect in the image of the third line:

When the escapee was caught
his pockets were filled
with golden chanterelles.

In 1996 eleven of his haiku were published in his book *The Sorrow Gondola,* and eight years later, 45 haikus in *The Great Enigma.* The explanation most often given for Tranströmer's return to haiku after almost four decades is his stroke which no longer permits him to work on long texts. Even as schoolchildren, Japanese learn to describe situations using as few words as possible. Rejecting superfluity so that only key words remain becomes a game played with calligraphy characters that is greatly enjoyed by children. For Tranströmer, haiku is a creative jigsaw puzzle with pieces of personal experiences and memory notes set together to produce a new image of reality.

The only Japanese haiku poet Tranströmer refers to in his poems is Shiki. Professor Kondo believes that Tranströmer has more in common with Bashō than with Shiki. Bashō taught that to survive, a haiku must present a concrete image as well as a serious thought that is visually represented and only as an exception abstract. That is, the same demand for complexity that Tranströmer makes when saying that it is not enough to describe a situation with words in a poem; the image must be supplied with the energy of reflection. Tranströmer has also said that he wants to leave explanations of his poems to the reader. This deferral to the reader concurs with Bashō's advice: "Study the masters but do not seek to imitate them - rather, seek what they sought."

Fred Schofield

Wisdom of the Heart

'... deepest wisdom of the heart
That is beyond discriminative thought '
(tr. Rev. Master Jiyu-Kennett)

At the time of writing, this essay outlines a way which helps me to perceive important fundamentl qualiteies in haiku. For both reading and writing, our perception of these qualities is the primary function and without it any other considerations are a superficial game. It's at least as important to read haiku (especially the japanese masters) as it is to write it; otherwise how do we soak up the tremendous depth and breadth on offer, not to mention the authentic haiku spirit? We might end up not writing haiku at all. But I don't mean that we should imitate "proper" haiku poets. I think it was Paul Klee who compared art to a tree: it must have strong roots; the leaves don't look anthing like the roots but they wouldn't exist without them.

As writers, it seems many of us find that haiku in its purest form comes rarely. This is when we simply let go of everything - no trying, no thinking about it or even realising that we're doing (in fact, *not* doing) it. Our lives can be transformed by a haiku that speaks to us - mentally, emotionally, and in terms of energy, all at the same time or in various measures. Maybe it's one we read, maybe it just comes into our head from nowhere. This kind of experience is in tune with our truest being. Trying to conjure it, by any means, produces contrived results.

So, being haiku enthusiasts, what can we do the rest of the time, apart from reading? Well, maybe that pure thing we'd like to create is around more than we realise. Sometimes something comes which we think might be a haiku, or at least has some potential. We feel a need to work on it. Possibly this is when we start playing mental games with it or comparing it to other poems. I suggest what we really need to do here is not be in such a hurry to write but to get back to the original inspiration: enter the subject of the poem, and our life, more closely. This can only be done intuitively. The main thing is to ask ourselves, *'Are we getting nearer to the essence of this poetic experience?': 'Is our intellect serving our heart?'* We have to be quiet, and we need time to accept or reject what comes. Thsi may be for long or short periods over a number of days. It helps if we're playful: forgetting it, coming back - not getting too caught up in judging what we're doing, i.e. *discriminate* thought - more going by the feel of what fits, and giving the intuitive "wisdom of the heart" a chance. Of course, sometimes a haiku just doesn't work out, even when we think it's generated by a profound experience - accepting this is as much a part of being a haiku poet as is writing a successful poem.

If you have a bare patch, it seems to me you have one of two alternatives (maybe both): a) not to worry about it - you might need a rest; b) to go back to the masters'. The more we read them the more we begin to feel what their words are pointing to. Westerners occasionally come up with a masterful haiku and it's a joy to see them but what we can learn from the long Japanese tradition is inexhaustible. It always amazes me that there's such a thrill in discovering and rediscovering great Japanese haiku despite the barriers of time, culture and (sometimes bad) translation, The greatest haiku may have several layers of meaning, allusion and inference but they may also have an immediate appeal for us - a starting point. I find the best way into these (and any haiku) is to simply hold them (not too tightly) in the mind and notice what feelings they give rise to. The more I do this, the more rewarding it is and any research needed becomes a pleasure. Different people respond to different poems, especially on first reading, but here are some I savour:

A noon-day nap;
Pressing the feet on the wall
How cool!
Basho (tr. Blyth)

Borrowing my house
from insects
I slept
Issa (tr. Stryk)

summer grass...
the remains of so many
warriors' dreams
Bashō (tr. Coleman)

in the park
a man and his boomerang
all over the place
Brian Tasker

In the drizzling rain at Furue
The edge of the water
is lost.
Buson (tr. Blyth)

Scooping up the water,
Lifting it towards the moon,
Full of light.
Santoka (tr. Stevens)

Twilight mist-
horse remembers the gap
in the bridge
Issa (tr. Stryk)

sunset ...
little dark birds become part
of the tree
Bruce Ross

The long spring day,
My eyes are wearied
Gazing over the sea
Taigi (tr. Blyth)

all summer long
the river's edge just laps
against the steps
David Steele

Put the chair there—
where my knees
will touch the roses
Shiki (tr. Watson)

losing my way
is part of the journey
poppy flowers
Inahata Teiko (tr. Ueda)

Thsi essay has been about a procedure of writing haiku using material from our own life and attempting to eschew the emotions and the imagination. There are, of course, other approaches. Take these two well-known examples by Taigi and Buson:

Not a single stone
To throw at the dog:
The winter moon
(tr. Blyth)

A sudden chill -
in our room my dead wife's
comb, underfoot
(tr. Stryk)

Buson's was written while his wife was still alive. Perhaps he wrote it for someone else...
I might write these kinds of haiku when I feel experienced enough, or someone might beat me to it.

William M Ramsey

Haiku as Improvisational Play

How badly we need to look back on haiku's roots in haikai or sportive verse, in particular its spirit of group playfulness and improvisation. The reason is western haiku's long, pronounced reliance on conventional technical requirements, born of our need to acquire basic knowledge of a foreign art form. Syllable counts and seasonal reference – important in Japan, too – have come to us without the full social context in which haiku emerged. The result is a predictable dreariness, the scenic nature snapshot of gentle uplift, the precious observation, or the mechanically proficient phrasing for an uninspired juxtaposition. Having written loads of such verse, I find it necessary to recover a sense of haiku as social art, displacing a rule-bound focus in order to restore a sense of dramatic creative moment.

Emphatically, I find it useful to recall how haiku was born in a spirit of play, despite general notions that it is best suited for solitary nature snapshots or private contemplation of Zen profundities and mindfulness. Haiku's birthing ground in medieval Japan was haikai verse, meaning sportive, comic, or playfully unorthodox. In this respect it was a highly social verse. In a renga party, persons took turns improvising off each other, one person composing three lines, the next composing two lines of improvisational response, and so on in a succession of alternating three and two lines. What they were doing was co-writing a five-line tanka (a traditional lyrical form), making everything hang on an improvisational moment. This 'linked verse' had elaborate rules; however, whether the tone was poignantly serious or witty, the primary social expectation was on how well an improvisation could be achieved. Modern formalist coherence and overall unity were not the point. The group's interest was in creating an admirable artistic moment while others were waiting expectantly. Understanding this creative play helps one savor haiku's original performance value, which is to say its living, dramatic immediacy.

What we now call haiku was the first three lines of the renga and originally called its hokku. The first great haikai master Bashō (1644-1694) excelled at starting a renga gathering with an effective hokku. Knowing the special work that a starting verse must do, he eventually separated it from renga as something able to stand alone on its own intrinsic literary potential. What a leap of faith. Famously, he took the form to brilliant heights, but always the haiku moment that he created arose from agile creative wit. In sum, even when wholly serious a haiku demonstrated fertile play of the imagination, not a simplistic, mechanical proficiency.

Incidentally, in the next century, Senryu Karai (1718-1790) deployed a slight mutation of haiku, and his surname would become the form's name, a senryu. This is haiku lacking seasonal reference and which comments ironically and humorously on human behavior rather than the natural scene. As one can see, the original spirit of play was irrepressibly still intact in haikai arts.

As for Bashō, only a person of gifted talents could have made as much of the stand-alone hokku as he and others did. It was, in fact, a momentous move for the form's development. Once separated from renga, the hokku acquired a new and imposing burden. In addition to the original requirements for kicking off a social performance, hokku now had to become literarily 'complete', or independently and aesthetically 'realized' and 'finished' – short though it was. With extraordinary creative and verbal ability, Japanese haiku writers during the next three and a half centuries developed an arsenal of observational angles, rhetorical moves, and semantic tactics for literary exploitation of one *performance moment*. Their best efforts uniquely targeted the reader's involvement in *reception*, for they still had a strong sense of hokku's moment and function in linked verse's social situation. No wonder that a good haiku is a nuanced, compressed drama of perceptual shifts and powerful, unpredictable realizations.

In sum, besides the formal properties of haiku such as syllable counts and seasonal reference, how the reader's mind receives a haiku is much at the heart of haiku composing. That is why a merely mechanical pastiche of conventions often brings no wonder to perception.

One fascinating glimpse of Bashō at work in an improvisation is his writing of the old pond hokku:

old pond –
a frog leaps in
the sound of water

We know from those with him at the time that his first line came last. The initial composing was of lines 2-3 and then he struggled with how to cap or start the verse. Thus, an initial improvisation (the poem's ending) now hung entirely on the next improvisation – how to 'give rise to' or naturally introduce lines 2-3. First consider the two initially composed lines. Bashō's drama of perception is his deducing from the sound of water in a nearby estuarial pond that a frog has jumped into it. In short: noisy action implies water's existence and frog's. Standing on the porch of his little home, he cannot see the pond or the frog. Cleverly, a splashing sound indicates a preceding silence of still water, broken and thus felt by the frog's action. In that stillness lies a quietly charged spiritual depth.

What followed was Bashō's saying that he was now searching for an opening line. His haiku follower Kikaku suggested as apt nature description some yellow globe-flowers (often translated as 'yellow roses'). Nice and delicately beautiful as seasonal reference, but functionally just an elegant piece of scenic decoration – no special performance value there. Then came Bashō's key improvisation – the old, or ancient, pond that had been there all the while but which Bashō suddenly could value. The frog – a transient, mortal animal – leaps into the environmental source that pre-existed it, gave birth to it, and will long outlast it. All three lines imply water, this last improvisation intensifying rather than, like globe-flowers, diverting from the significance of water. This is a Zen moment of enlightened recognition: all the while that we transient mortals are caught up in the material realm there lies – always behind it though often not seen or felt – an ancient, timeless spiritual order. The shift of consciousness dramatized here is a paradigm of Bashō's spiritual transformation and altered perspective following his Buddhist training. Likewise, one can walk past a swimming pool for weeks and ignore it. Leaping into it, however, suddenly one is immersed in a wholly different reality – one's world dramatically is not what it was, and one's former, dry world is not familiar but strangely less substantial. Thus, perception of things as illusion opens one to the divine.

You might argue that this is such sublime, serious verse it can hardly illustrate haikai's original sportive playfulness. Yet, its improvisational shift is born of a hokku craft that grounds living performance in social immediacy and effectiveness. The full verse acts performatively on the reader in this way: *frog's ephemeral action evokes awareness of a pond/eternal order that always resides unseen behind illusion*. The first-time reader will glide right past the import of that old pond; then, after lines 2-3 do their work, one doubles back to line one and feels Bashō's low-key but dramatic call into richer awareness. Moreover, even though this hokku was not the starting verse for a renga party, it would fulfill such a group's expectations. The opening verse might indirectly praise the social host by suggesting the surrounding scene is both appealing and conducive to a writing occasion. The waiting others not only recognize the tactful praise of a host's residence, they are now creatively inspired to contribute their insightful thoughts, in the suggestive key of the leader's opening.

I will digress briefly to contrast a haiku performance with a Western form existing since classical Roman times, the epigram. This, being a witty statement, cleverly favors closure over openness. A fully formulated idea is pre-assembled by the poet and then transferred to the reader who applauds the finished concept. In contrast, haiku operates closer to the pre-verbal level, before grammar, as an impression just rising from sensory apprehension into cognition – *toward* ideation but still in unfinished openness. In epigram, ideation is first chiseled into perfection by the poet and delivered as a snappy statement, which is to say something already 'done'. In haiku, as the words end the reader is still readjusting to reordered perception. As the respected haiku magazine editor Bob Spiess often said, statement and explicitly finished ideation rarely work in haiku.

To say that haiku is an improvisational performing art, I am not saying it is easy or that one can experience success by virtue of some playfully catchy approach. I cannot count my personal number of failures, and to be honest I repeatedly fall into the trap of straining for a clever effect that I can't pull off naturally. I see numerous other haiku writers doing that, while genuinely admiring their urge to experiment. But I confess some impatience when seeing one particular clever effect borrowed by countless others into a trend of look-alikes that do not improve on the original mechanically clever and insincere effect. I doubt the remedy for this is to embrace a mythic-poetic ideal of 'the haiku path' – by which one hugs a pine trunk to become sublimely one with the pine. It is to keep on writing, to seek improvisation, and to perform moments.

I take the haiku to be a moment of performed consciousness, much as Richard Gilbert explores in *Poems of Consciousness*. His taxonomy of the tradition's rhetorical tactics is an impressively productive cognitive poetics. Here, I have explored haiku's roots in its original, social performative context to elucidate things about the 'haiku moment'. Surely one challenge is to render a moment that bears convincing value, a daunting improvisational moment. Persons not familiar with haiku at first see little in it and judge it trivial; yet, what moment of consciousness lacks any potential human value whatsoever? For haiku writers, the small space of a moment is precisely where one begins to stake out matters of significance. Indeed if it's your consciousness, then life even at the scale of one moment is precious. Thus, to echo William Carlos Williams, so much depends on a moment. Compare a haiku to a momentary kiss. Into that press of the lips may pour a swirl of yearning, hope, despair, and astonished excitation. Like that, a haiku moment performed well can be deeply charged.

Sanford Goldstein

The Eye of Tanka

Perhaps I sometimes take tanka for granted, but when I lost my tanka notebook with about 3000 poems in it at Minneapolis Airport in 2011, I felt devastated. I realized once again how important tanka is to me. That summer when I visited my daughter in Ohio, we spent time each morning at McDonald's over a cup of coffee and a roll or something else. I would 'spill' twenty-five tanka a day for more than a month and a half. On my return to Japan by way of Minneapolis, I had my daughter's phone number at the back of my tanka notebook, and I put it on a small counter below the phone. The call did not go through, and only after catching my plane did I realize I had left my 3000 tanka behind. I realized, anew, how precious tanka is to me.

I have been on my tanka road for more than fifty years, so my eye has steadily been on tanka. That means of course that I write about myself, the thoughts and feelings I have, the people I meet, the images in front of me, the family or relatives or few life-long friends. The possibilities are immense.

Tanka is perfectly adaptable in our culture or in other cultures in spite of its Japanese origin. My latest and probably last book on tanka is entitled *Four Decades on My Tanka Road*, (2007 Modern English Tanka Press):

My Acknowledgment:

again, Hamlet,
you haul me to your heart,
to your precious mouth,
and I feel even tanka
can scale the spectacular

My Epigraph:

forty years have passed
and still my ear remains
a soft carpet
on which others
dance their blues

The road was not an easy one, for when I began in 1962 to write tanka, all my poems were sent back with rejection slips. Haiku was the dominant form. The world of Japanese poetry was haiku, haiku, haiku, though Japanese in the

American concentration camps in the West were writing tanka in English. It was in Canada that my first tanka were published. To wait ten years before a tanka is accepted requires a devotion and patience many writers have had.

The outlets for tanka have grown since the first tanka journal was published. I am not a good historian in the use of dates, so let me move on to other difficulties; they involve the choices by editors who may have a particular interest they want to exploit. *Atlas Poetica* comes to mind with its emphasis on place. My tanka have appeared there. In its first issue, Spring 2008, the editor, M. Kei, accepted a tanka string entitled 'holy ground: a contrapuntal tanka string' (my own term 'string' to be defined later) of 44 tanka, of which here are two:

always I felt, Voltaire,
your telling me to keep that small plot
intact was right,
and still, why is it even a Bashō bush
is choked with China's yellow sand?

a Fitzgerald
disenchantment
these days,
and not once did I berserk Paris,
not once did I cast woes into wine

For those poets who want a journal with a broader perspective, I suggest *Gusts*, but only three poems can be submitted. The editor does not choose the poems – a committee of several members does. The tanka they read do not bear the poet's name. It always surprises me if I am lucky enough to have all three chosen as in Fall/Winter 2005 of which I will reprint two, the first one from the section called 'More Mars and Venus' and the second from the section called 'Tanka People':

of late
the backlash
of nature,
and even the moon and stars
seem deficient

lonely
the way that woman
in the cancer ward
brushes and brushes
her teeth before dawn

Sometimes a particular journal will have a special section on haibun or even haiku. One editor that fascinates me is Michael McClintock with his 'The Tanka Café' that appears in each issue of *Ribbons*. McClintock is a well-known tanka poet whose 'Tanka Café' is quite a challenge. Only one poem can be submitted. McClintock gives the one theme for the forty or so poems he chooses. But if you are selected for the best poem in the series, you must choose the best three tanka for the next issue of the café and give a comment on each. The twenty-five dollar award is one of the few places where a tanka poet can earn some rare dollars. For *Ribbons*, Autumn 2008, Volume 4, Number 3, my entry was selected. The theme McClintock gave was 'transience'. My tanka was chosen as one of the forty or so:

only a moment
and the famous Stanford poet
cast down my ten haiku
fifty-two years later and still
the ephemeral sting holds on

The poet was Yvor Winters. He told me that at twenty-one he was writing better haiku than I was – at that time I was thirty or thirty-one.
Other tanka journals among my favorites are *Blithe Spirit* (England), *Kokako* (New Zealand), *Red Lights* (USA), and *Eucalypt* (Australia).

But it is time to move on to the construction of tanka itself. I consider all my tanka to be Takubokuian. My Japanese colleague at Niigata University was my hero, my adopted father in Japan, the precious Japanese who translated with me (I call myself a co-translator) Takuboku's *Sad Toys*, which Purdue University published in 1977. Later, in 1985, Charles E. Tuttle published *Sad Toys* and Takuboku's *Romaji Diary*. The introduction Professor Shinoda and I wrote for this book contains the following statement from an article entitled 'Poems to Eat', printed in the Tokyo Mainichi newspaper which serialized it from November 30 to December 7, 1909: 'Poetry must not be what is usually called poetry. It must be an exact report, an honest diary, of the changes in a man's emotional life...' I have called myself Takubokian for decades.

In another essay called 'Various Kinds of Tanka' (December 20, 1910), Takuboku wrote, as quoted in our introduction (p31): 'As for the content [of tanka], we should sing about anything, disregarding the arbitrary restrictions which dictate that some subjects are not fit and will not make one. If only we do these things, tanka will not die as long as man holds dear the momentary impressions which flash across his mind, disappearing a moment later during his busy life...'

A great deal has been said about the syllables in tanka. At one point I became a minimalist tanka poet. Once I was strongly criticized in our translation of Akiko Yosano's *Tangled Hair* for having one line with the word 'I'. Sometimes I tried the long ago tradition of tanka as 5-7-5-7-7 syllables and found it was easy to count syllables. Sometimes writers are advocating tanka with 20 syllables to be equal to the 31. But what I found most helpful has been the sudden appearance of short-long-short-long-long as the equivalent of 5 (short) 7 (long) 5 (short) 7 (long) 7 (long). In the early days I made my tanka either minimalist or free, but now I feel short, long, short, long, long is just right. When I read a poem that breaks this pattern, I feel it is weak. This pattern is a recent one, so many of my early poems do not follow it.

The tanka itself is a dramatic vehicle – that is, the first three lines give a problem or area of interest and the last two make some statement related to that problem, preferably indirectly. Three recent poems of mine in *Gusts* (Spring/Summer 2012, pp.11, 17, 20) reveal my belief in the system I have just cited:

an editor
writes as if perturbed about
just turning thirty-two,
Wordsworth comes to mind saying
'to be young was very heaven'

begin
to feel I am parading
on the wrong path
I ought to muse more each day,
reread books loved decades ago

at the exhibit
women crowd around necklaces,
rings, pins, earrings –
my friend's watercolors
hang in their own shadows

One of the traditions of tanka is the tanka sequence and another the tanka string, the latter term being my own invention. In 1989, Purdue University published Professor Shinoda's and my co-translation of Mokichi Saito's *Red Lights*, which contains 38 sequences by Saito. In our introduction, we define sequence. It is a series of poems focusing on one problem and is arranged by having a beginning, middle, and conclusion. Each new tanka has a transition to the preceding one, but I believe I can say that even the last sequence leaps to the beginning to show connection. I have seen sequences that do not follow this pattern, so I always wonder if they are truly sequences.

But later I found that poems could be joined as a tanka string (my own term as I have indicated). It makes me feel good that 'tanka string' has been used by some poets, though most ignore it. What is different about a tanka string is that it does not have a chronological order, that is, a beginning, middle, and end in a tight logical pattern, but each tanka focuses on the selected major topic. Each tanka has to have a transition to the one before it, but there is no conclusion. It is more open and can be interpreted as the reader sees fit, but by knowing it is a string, the reader is given some direction. Poems are listed and the transition follows, but the subjects are more diverse, the poems more open even with the major topic.

Sometimes I see something marked 'sequence', but often I feel it is not a sequence but a string. One by Kei, the editor of *Atlas Poetica*, called his series a sequence, but with no conclusion, it could not, to me, be a sequence. Kei was a good sport and never reprimanded me.

for Sean, a sequence

you'd think
as old as I am,
this youth desiring me
would delight, but –
performance anxiety

dawn on
another continent
still this young man
keeps me company
tonight

his relatives don't like him,
so he tells them
that he's sleeping with
a famous male poet
twice his age

Persian carpet,
my denim leg over
your bare one,
my book resting
against your back

there is nothing
quite so delightful
as someone
eager to learn
all my vices

It occurs to me now that if Kei had stopped after the fourth tanka, the poems would have been a sequence. In tanka four we see the boredom of the older more experienced man. The younger man has undressed, but the partner is bored, preferring a book to sex. Though I do now know where this series of five poems was published, again I thank Kei for finding it for me – and I still think he is a good sport.

Mark Rutter

Bashō's Narrow Road to Poetry

Bashō's aesthetic philosophy is often taken to be an anti-poetic one. Famous and often quoted statements of Bashō', such as 'if you would learn of the pine go to the pine', are interpreted as anti-poetic and anti-literary. In fact an English-language convention has arisen around such quotations, a convention in which a supposed truth-to-experience is valued above, and opposed to, the self-consciously poetic. Basho is presented as a proto-empiricist, and his complex amalgam of Shintoism, Daoism, Confucianism and Buddhism is naturalised for a contemporary western readership as a variant on minimal realism.

Yet Bashō's writings don't present a single view of what a haiku is, nor do they lay down a set of consistent poetic rules. The plain and ordinary are frequently praised, as has often been noted. What has been largely ignored is the strain of imagery and thinking in Bashōs travel journals and haibun which presents the poetic as a realm in its own right: 'From of old many who abandoned the world and entered these mountains fled into Chinese poetry, took refuge in Japanese verse... '[1]

Bashō's long and hazardous walks were in part journeys into the deep north of poetry itself. Even more surprisingly, Bashō turns out to be far from hostile to the imagination and the imagined:

... one thread runs through the artistic Ways. And this aesthetic spirit is to follow the Creative, to be a companion to the turning of the four seasons. Nothing one sees is not a flower, nothing one imagines is not the moon. If what is seen is not a flower, one is like a barbarian; if what is imagined is not a flower, one is like a beast. Depart from the barbarian, break away from the beast, follow the Creative, return to the Creative.[2]

This passage weaves ambiguously between the familiar notion that the haiku poet should be 'a companion to the turning of the four seasons' to a much less familiar exhortation to not only see but to imagine, and to follow the 'Creative' in doing so. Landis Barnhill explains Bashō's use of the term 'the Creative' (or 'zōka') as referring to 'the world's unceasing and spontaneous disposition to give rise to beautiful and skilful transformations throughout the natural world', and goes on to say that 'true art is a participation in nature's own creativity'; 3 In seeing and imagining, and in writing poems, we take part in the larger creative processes of the cosmos. Far from being opposed to the real or 'experiential' the poetic and the imaginary are in harmony with the creative flux of existence.

Nor does Bashō present words as a barrier to, or distraction from, direct experience. Encounters on the road are 'seeds for words' and words in turn are 'a way to become intimate with winds and clouds'. [4] Rather than a puritan insistence upon 'wordlessness', Bashō presents a fluid, metamorphic relation between language and the world, one in which poetic composition paradoxically brings us closer to the non-human realm. It is entirely consistent then that Bashō would reject the argument that poetry should be 'artless':

From long ago, people who took up the brush have embellished the flower of writing's beauty while the fruit of its meaning grew weak. Or they dwelled on the fruit and forgot the art. But with Sodō's writing, we can love the flower and also feast on the fruit. 5

Words are not best thought of as transparencies through which we see a truth. We take pleasure in the words themselves, in their skilful arrangement in the poem, and the poem's meaning is linked to its aesthetic qualities in the same way that the flower is necessary for there to be a fruit. Unlike Bashō, the more extremist proponents of 'shasei' or even 'fact-based' haiku would have us dwell on the fruit' and forget the art'. Recently re-reading Basho's travel journals after a break of some years, I was struck by how unexpectedly unfamiliar the territory was. For instance, against all expectations Basho uses simile:

eye-brow brushes
come to mind:
safflower blossoms

'Come to mind' is a substitute for 'like'. - this is really a simile slightly disguised. The most famous travel journal of them all, *The Narrow Road,* ends with a simile-haiku:

like a clam from its shell,
setting off for Futami Bay:
departing fall

It is wrong to assume, as many contemporary English-language haiku poets do, that metaphors and similes are an egotistic decoration imposed upon perception by the poet. The simile draws attention both to the limits of language and demonstrates language at its most creative. Every simile and metaphor is an attempt to express something for which we have no already available name. The metaphorical is the forge of new words - it shares in that Creative which manifests in the myriad forms of nature, and which Bashō celebrates.

The recent emergence of 'gendai' haiku in Japan and modernist haiku in the west has often been taken as an aberration in a poetic form otherwise dedicated to a scrupulous (some would say naive) realism. But the above passages from Bashō's 'Journal of Bleached Bones' suggest that an emphasis on the aesthetic and the imaginary is a neglected aspect of our founding poet's legacy. The work of haiku poets like Ban'ya Natsuishi and Scott Metz can be seen as being grounded in and growing out of this rarely discussed strain of thought in Bashō's work. In trying to walk in Bashō's footsteps we may find that he was able to travel in several different directions at once.

1 Matsuo Basho, 'Journal of Bleached Bones in a Field, *Bashō's Journey: The Literary' Prose of Matsuo Bashō,* edited and translated by David Landis Barnhill, (2005), p.17.
2 Matsuo Bashō, 'Knapsack Notebook', ibid. P.29.
3 David Landis Barnhill, endnotes to 'Knapsack Notebook', ibid. p. 151.
4 Bashō, 'Knapsack Notebook', ibid. p. 30.
5 Bashō, 'Postscript to "Comments on the Bagworm"', ibid. p. 105.

Klaus-Dieter Wirth

Haiku at the Crossroads?

The following article is the result of a critical reading of Haiku 21 – An Anthology of Contemporary English-Language Haiku edited by Lee Gurga & Scott Metz, Lincoln, Illinois, Modern Haiku Press 2011, 205 pp., perfect softbound, ISBN 0-9741894-5-6, US $20 + postage www.modernhaiku.org

Texts for the anthology were taken from the first decade of the new millennium. The result was to me a bit of a shock! It made me take stock of what I myself have learnt from experience during roughly 25 years of active participation in the international haiku scene. Thinking back over all those fierce arguments about the traditional 5-7-5 syllable pattern, the influence of Zen, the rejection of the 'I', the acceptance of desk haiku, the discrimination of literary devices (personification, comparison, metaphor), or the problematic nature of more or less mere description, so-what-haiku, observations, or just a three-part sentence, I come to the conclusion that things have changed much for the better, not least thanks to the easier interchange of ideas made possible by the rapid evolution of the Internet. We have witnessed an emancipation that helped a lot to widen our view well and truly beyond our nosetips. A fact that is quite characteristic of what has happened for instance in particular in German haiku life. Well then, this is definitely the positive side of the coin!

The other side, however, has turned out to be, in my opinion, extremely worrying. I do not even want to mention so-called spam haiku; its strength and lasting influence can simply not be argued away. One hopes that the normal reader will be able to identify nonsensical or quite witty everyday garbage hitting out at topical events in politics and society. Oddly enough, its outpourings are nowadays easily recognisable by its strict compliance with the set syllable count!

What are the sources of danger then?

In *Haiku 21* I am irritated by apparent willful disregard of the division into three lines, i.e. not only by changing the way of writing according to the Japanese model in just one line, but also by playing with numerous extravagant variants that are in opposition to any normal recognition of the genre. There seems to be a careless handling of tradition, presumably arising from the eager wish to appear to be different. The following examples, not at all chosen to especially show this, may serve as a testimony.

Considering the contents five main precarious items may be pointed out:

* the strained upgrading of banalities
* the prediliction for minimalism
* the exaggerated striving after originality
* taking refuge in the montage of surrealistic images
* the juxtaposition of phenomena that can hardly be connected

First, increasingly unjustified importance is attached to just crude realities making readers think that they are lacking common sense, a mark of undisguised contempt.

out of nowhere isn't — *Marlene Mountain*

a delay in large leaves — *Philip Rowland*

A road crosses a road another road does not. — *Michelle Tennison*

Second, there is an ominous trend towards excessive brevity - based, perhaps, on the belief that the shorter the result the better the quality. Yet a telegram style will never be suited to meet any poetical requirements.

sept-
ember — *Carolyn Hall*

The initial lower case letter of 'September' might still be regarded as some queer conceit. However, what are we expected to think of the separated 'sept'? In comparison with other word compositions such as 'septet' or 'septuplet', it may be understood as an allusion to the number 'seven' or as an allusion to disease as in '(a)sept(ic)'; and is that 'ember' (generally met with in the plural) just a burnt down piece of wood or coal or perhaps a hint at that famous 'Indian summer' in autumn? May everybody make up their own mind! Anyway the result is surely of little significance.

Hungover ignorable
Jerusalem cactus
pissing   the cats

Richard Gilbert

horizon
why and
why not

Lather Rajiv

Third, we have to deal with a penchant for contrived originality. A characteristic of haiku is the search for the extraordinary, but within the ordinary! Extreme expressions such as these two 'poems' contain do not at all fit the spirit of haiku as we have understood it. As soon as even native speakers are forced to consult the dictionary, the case is likely to be more of a definite example of the author putting on that famous jeweled ring in order to focus our view just on itself, diverting us from the essential. The desire for individual admiration is most probably also revealed in obvious attempts to showcase formal extravagances. Such pomposity has nothing to do with the spirit of haiku!

body: wash fill empty repeat   *S. B. Friedman*

the rumble of earthworms
seeding the clouds

Eve Luckring

breathes
on his
fire
that
little

ani
mal

john martone

Fourth, another quirk is resorting to plain surrealist contents, most clearly initiated by the 'Flying Popes' of the Japanese Gendai Haiku movement, only too eagerly taken up by those restless representatives of the new world order who leap on every new fashion. I do not at all deny that every now and then an example may crop up to justify its existence, yet only in a small niche – never as a trendsetter in the market itself!

spring mud
I find a comb
left by a nymph

Fay Aoyagi

somewhere
fireflies are
eating rhinos

Scott Metz

inside the mushroom
the canary builds its nest
of guns and ammo *Greg Dykes*

Fifth, maybe a less alarming manifestation, though rather predominant is the too arbitrary, thus mostly incomprehensible, use of direct juxtaposition. No doubt, at first glance this method satisfies the need of the caesura, so typical of the haiku, quite perfectly. But as soon as you have the feeling that you cannot do without the help of three psychologists to figure out some abstruse mental acrobatics, any enthusiasm for the genre will rapidly die down and turn to annoyance: no reader wants to realize that he is being made a fool of.

the numbness
of scar tissue
forsythia *Peggy Willis Lyles*

sun on the horizon
who first
picked up a stone *paul m.*

vermillion maples
a man at the bus stop
could be Odin *Ebba Story*

As things stand it has to be feared that the dagger is already drawn to stab our beloved haiku in its prime. A dangerous development in two respects: newcomers will only see the present state of affairs, and as English has become the basic language for international exchange the fatal effect will be multiplied. Looking for example at the German, Dutch, French, Spanish, Italian or Balkan haiku it has not been infected so far but for how long? So we ought to be quite watchful and take particular care of the welfare of our precious gem!

Dick Pettit

Renga- Change and Continuity

"Fashion has changed four or five times in the last 50 years" said Nijö Yashimoto (1320-88). There were at least four distinct changes of manner in the century which included Matsunega Teitoku (1571-1653, the Teimon school), Nishiyama Söin (1605–82, the Danrin school) and Bashō (1644-94). Yet many types of topic and most of the styles of linking appear in both the 100-verse hyakuin of the Muromachi era (1336-1598), and the 36-verse kasen of the Edo (1603-1867). So, with whatever changes and disputes, writers of all periods would recognise the renga of other ages as the real thing – though perhaps with contemporary exceptions.

A renga has three aspects, corresponding to body, mind and spirit: the topics of each verse; the links between verses; and the za – the communal or artistic feeling of the players, manifesting itself in the flow and consistency of the whole.

The topics of the medieval renga are limited, though there was room for originality, and the treatment is mainly melancholic-poetic. The linkage varied from close to distant, but was, within limits, predictable. However, the movement over lengthy sequences can have beautiful and touching modulations, as in the first eight verses of *Three Poets at Minase* (Sögi, Shöhaku, Söchö, 1488). 1

Snow on top   haze on the slopes below   a mountain at dusk
waters flow, far off: a plum-scented village
The wind off the river   stirs a clump of willows   in Spring colours
the clear sound of a punt,   poled along in the dawn
Night-fog lingers   yet still the moon is there   hid in the sky
the fields are covered with frost   as Autumn comes to an end
Insects cry out   the heart also mourns   as grasses wither
on a visit: I reach the fence   a path has been cleared

Each verse has possible positives and negatives. In this sequence vv 2-4 & 8 are mainly positive, vv 6 & 7 negative and vv1 & 5 balanced. The whole renga has similar runs, waverings and course corrections: so that, considering also the topics – not all pastoral, but close in feeling to vv1-8 - it's fair to say next to nothing happens.

Reeds Broken under Snow (Shinkei, Sögi & 8 others, 1468), being partly a meditation on the civil war, and muchly an attempt by the others to raise Shinkei out of his forebodings and depression, is more dramatic; even though the progressions and range of scenes are similar. Here are vv 91–100. 2

A tree - felling gale scatters the autumn clouds all over the sky
lonesome too the wild goose flying in the shadows of dusk
I am not alone in weeping such tears so I console myself
the world is full of misery from the changing forms of desire
Open your eyes! the six paths of illusion are clear before you
toil as one may at poetry it's essence can't be grasped
Across the bay the marvellous Isle of Jewels is shrouded in mist
[the Isle, a pilgrimage spot, actual as well as figurative]
we sense the rustle of spring as breeze moves though the pine trees
The heart is at ease [only/alone] among the blossoms this glimmering dusk
the glory of our days will echo for ages to come

Probably four-fifths of this hyakuin is lamentation: so the last three verses seem to be whistling in the dark. I suspect some irony in vv 98-100, but there's a contrary translation in *Heart's Flower* (Esperanza Ramirez-Christensen) from which extraordinarily fine and sustained work this version is adapted.

Both extracts link by word, phrase, heart, simultaneous and consecutive happenings, echo, allusion, and scent. There are no obvious *parallels*, but the linkage in Reeds Broken uSnow 94-98 is partly the 'debate' type of opposed statements.

Such close linking and gradual movement is unusual in haikai, even in the slow introductory vv 1-6 *jo*. But here is the beginning of *The Tub of Ashes (Bonchö, Bashö, Yasui & Kyorai, 1690).* 3

drops of water from the bucket of ashes*, stop. Now: crickets
having to save on oil asleep in the Autumn evening
fresh green mats newly arranged in the moonlight
happily setting out ten wine cups
the New Year Feast** all you could desire for wealth & happiness
thin snowflakes are falling to the notes of the nightingale**
(7,8) the rider 's pulled forward arms too weak to hold the spring stallion
on the peak of Mount Maya clouds clash and linger

* water is leached through ashes for lye, used in cleaning & making soap

** the sense of this verse is clear, but the exact meaning obscure.

*** *uguisu*

Verses 1-6 move from indoors to out, and Autumn to Spring; but otherwise are a composite scene, with more only partly translatable links. By contrast, the first verses (vv7&8) of the *ha* are suddenly dramatic, a jump forward mimicked by the break in the linkage. Much simple modes of linking are the norm in the school around Nagoya, encouraged by Bashö on visits in 1683-4 and three years later. These renga, such as *The Cockle Gatherer, (here vv 1-14* collected in *Arano (1690),* have clear and lively scenes with often narrative and picturesque links. (vv 1-14) 4

Far out on the shallows stakes of cockle gatherers among the waves
a flat spring calm the saké boat can't get in
nor the ferry out the baggage is quickly unloaded to stop the night
these centipedes bite they burn incense to keep them off
a moonlit night carefully studying the whiteness of clouds
so cold they cover the feet with their straw rain-cloaks
in this strange place I hear the rustling of reeds from where I know not
another dray horse passes loaded with cotton waste
beside the road trying to make a living the village sorcerer
the man looks old enough to retire and live at ease
when will he stop building new go-downs all over the place?
dressed in white cotton for the Yudomo pilgrimage
how cool he is having spread out his mat on the river bank
ready for fun with someone rolling around in the moonlight

The *jo* is about events, simultaneous or what came next, in the little port, though vv 5&6 could be elsewhere. 7&8 take things into the open and then come a series of *transformations*, a witty and thrilling type of link: the sorcerer becomes the pre-pensioner, who is then the merchant/businessman, who is the pilgrim, then the student with thoughts on fun.

In *L'orge Oubliée,* the 2nd& 3rd verses are also transformations. But the person(s) can only be guessed at. Instead there is an action *shading the eyes,* for all three: the geese, the sun, and the hikers: 5

the storm forgotten   no waiting for the blossom   the geese are off
hands shade the eyes   as sun touches the peak
climbing boots   stumble along the paths   spring is here

Another type of haikai linking is bantering conversation shown here in *Le Saké Nouveau, vv1-3.* 6

not worth drinking   there's a lack of fortification   in new wine
jolly nippy this autumn   but I don't care for hot baths
while he sleeps   moonlight through the window   on his scattered books

The *waki* prefers wine to hot baths to keep him warm; the *daisun* mocks this wimp. The flyting can become edgy as in *Une Nuit à Fukagawa (vv1-6 & vv33-6)* though Bashö and Etsujin were friends and collaborators at the time . Bashö signals the mode of linking with an apparently disjunct, insulting (?) v3. 7

listening in silence   to the cries of the geese in flight   spooky   [E]
times like this in the moonlight   you're forced back on the saké   [B]
puce pants!* Who could fancy a flower   with such an ugly name?   [B]
Why indeed do we argue   this fine Autumn evening?   [E]
the capacity   of the calabash**   was over a thousand litres   [E]
gone with the wind   that's these businessmen for you   [B]***

*   *puce pants* was also a name for starched and uncomfortable breeches.
**   The *Calabash*, title of another collection, is an in-joke, not clear now.

*** Etsujin had set up a dyeworks in Nagoya.

It seems in the following verses that from here on Bashö sets up a little challenge, testing out Etsujin's resolution and mettle now he has followed Bashō & poetry to Edo. 7

Very striking!   The herbalist's porch   with its new tiles   [E]
the child pampered and spoilt   dies without a hope   [B]
much envied   he goes gaily to the sermon   at cherry blossom time   [E]
eating snails from the fields   makes your mouth smell   [B]

Obscure. Maybe the herbalist fails to save the sick child, whose uncaring father goes piously to the sermon, where it's noted that his breath smells. Also Bashō is shooting down Etsujin›s fine verses; possibly the whole renga.

There is little of this kind of sequence in the canonical Winter, Summer and Autumn kasen in *The Monkey's Straw Raincoat* (1691). For example, the Summer kasen starts with a hokku both realistic and transcendent:

all over the town   many smells and stinks   the summer moon

and then has many clearly linked *person* scenes swinging from farce to deprivation. There is much transformation, and at the beginning of vv 27–34, *parallel* links: Maybe the first verse implies that there was nothing worth following on from in v26: 8

a mouse trap   tipped on its side   catches nothing
the lid so warped   it no longer fits the chest
a short stay   at one hermitage   then off again
a joy to be still alive   my [poem] is in the anthology
so many   ways of loving   I have known every one
in this fleeting world   all end as Komachi*
just sipping gruel   why is it that   the tears gush out?
how empty the floorboards   when the man's away from home

*Omo no Komachi, (9th C.), beauty & poetess, thought to have died in poverty.

After *The Monkey's Straw Raincoat* Bashö developed a lighter style, signalled already in its 1690 Spring kasen (12 participants): vv 1-6 [9]

grasses sprout, plum blossoms,   and yam-froth soup   at the Mariko inn
this Spring morning   a new umbrella
lark song flies up   fresh dirt in the paddies   it's that time
dumplings for Horse Day   Thank you, sir.
sitting in the corner she holds her toothache cheek twilight & the moon up
the upstairs guest is gone   Autumn

The verses have a zippedy-doo-da feel, almost guying themselves. This style makes unpredictable and lightly connected links: sometimes none, except for the improvised tone; and the scenes are often inconsequential (kitchen sink?), only occasionally reverting in topic to those of the earlier renga. Some of the verses seem oblique comment on what has gone before. It is also true that here as elsewhere there may be hidden puns, word & phrase echoes, sound patterns and, as Dr Johnson said of Shakespeare's comedies:"... allusions which now only obscure the pages they once illuminated."

This is shown further in *Fragrance of Plums,* 1694, *vv18-24:* [10]

jostled at the gate in the queue   for the Mibu mystery plays
the east wind spreads   a stifling smell of manure   all over
he just sits around   arthritis of the elbow, he says
the master across the street   is back, and telling   us all about Edo
we need our millstones   but I let his wife use them
bells ring   from every direction   for the jüya services
high above the pawlonia tree   the moon is clear
I closed the gate   and went to bed, wordless   for the fun of it
he changed the straw mats   with the money he found in the street

Some of Bashö's previous followers, such as Etsujin and Kikaka were unhappy with the new style – arbitrary and idiosyncratic, thin links and flimsy scenes - though it is a development from what went before; and has counterparts in modern renga. Nevertheless, the Monkey's Raincoat style, which mixes pathos and wit, the everyday and the beautiful, indirect links with obvious, seems to me the best model. [11]

1 Minase : assembled and adapted from Nobuyuki Yuasa: *The Narrow Road* , p 13, Penguin 1966 .
Earl Miner: *Japanese Linked Poetry,* p 189, Princeton U.P. 1979.
Steven D Carter : *Traditional Japanese Poetry*, p 307, Stanford U.P. 1979.

2 Adapted from Esperanza Ramirez-Christensen *Heart's Flower,* pp 363-7, Stanford U.P. 1994

3 Adapted from Miner

4 Leonora Mayhew *Monkey's Raincoat ,Autumn Cricket* Tuttle, 1985.

5 translated from *Le Ramasseur de Coques* in René Sieffert in *Friches* (Jap - *Arano*, Waste, *or* Fallow Land) Verdier Poches 1992-3.

6 (L'orge Oubliée)

7 (Le Saké Nouveau)

8 (Une Nuit à Fukagawa)

9 Numerous translations of *Summer Moon / Monkey's Raincoat* consulted:
Miner, Mayhew, Carter, John Carley & Eiko Yamaguchi(net publication)
Maeda Cana : *Monkey's Raincoat,* Grossman 1973.
Bill Wyatt, *Monkey's Raincoat* , Hub Editions(?) 19(?).

10 *Grasses & Plums* has various titles in Miner & Odagiri :

11 *Monkey's Straw Raincoat,* Princeton U.P. 1981, & Mayhew, Cana, Wyatt.
Slightly adapted from *At a Fragrance of Plums* in Hiroaki Sato : *From the Country of 8 Islands, p 305,* Doubleday 1981.

Michael Fessler

A Tanka Primer

The selections that follow are meant to provide an introduction to the history of the tanka. In most cases I have relied on the translations of leading Japan scholars past and present, but I have also translated a few of the poems myself. The selections are arranged chronologically, extending from the time of the eighth-century *Manyoshu* to the present. The commentaries accompanying the tanka are intended to enhance appreciation, not to pre-empt interpretation. Occasionally I have supplied details that are not strictly literary-textual but which locate the poems and afford insights into the elusive question of tanka-ness itself.

Preliminary Notes

Uta is the general term for tanka or waka, and it is usually translated as "song" or "poem." An example would be the collection of tanka by Masaoka Shiki, titled, *Take no Sato Uta* (Tanka from a Bamboo Village). The kanji for *uta* is read as *ka* in combined forms.

The word *tanka* means "short song." In the 8th century *Manyoshu* there are over 4,000 tanka. Some of these are stand-alone poems. Others are affixed to a *choka* ("long song") as coda or envoy. The *Manyoshu* is a product of the Asuka and Nara periods, and is associated with the court and its activities in the ancient capital of Nara, though not confined to them. The poems are by various hands: princes, soldiers, fishermen, border guards, etc. The language of the *Manyoshu*, called *Manyogana*, is not comprehensible today to any but scholars (and they have their differences.) Some of the adjectives in English commonly used to describe the poetry of the Manyoshu are: open, simple, direct, heartfelt and primitive. In Japanese the word, *masuraoburi* (manly, virile) is often applied. *Waka* became the term *du jour* for the tanka during the Heian Period. The word, waka, means "Japan song." The change in terminology reflects growing national pride and respect for indigenous writing (*id est*, less reliance on Chinese literary models). The two great waka anthologies are the imperial *Kokinwakashu* (Ancient and Modern Waka Collection) and the *Shin Kokinwakashu* (New Ancient and Modern Waka Collection). Whereas the principal locus, or nerve-center for the *Manyoshu* was Nara, the medieval waka was based in Heian, the present Kyoto. The waka of the imperial anthologies are courtly and elegant. Many were the result of *uta awase* (poetry contests). There were twenty imperial anthologies in all but the two above are considered benchmarks.

Over time the classical waka fell into something of a derivative state due to infighting among rival schools and a preoccupation with technical issues. By late Meiji, various younger poets felt that the genre itself, irrespective of quality, could not hold its own against Western literature. One of the poets calling for reform was Yosano Tekkan who founded the magazine *Myojo* (Morning Star) to promote more individualistic tanka poetry. His wife Yosano Akiko contributed intense (and shocking for the time) love poems to the journal. Ishikawa Takuboku was also a contributor. Masaoka Shiki (1867-1902), founder of the Negishi school, had perhaps a more lasting impact as a reformer. His poetic platform of *shasei* (realistic depiction) and *masuraoburi* (a return to the values of the Manyoshu) was highly influential and his ideas have extended even into our own time. The term tanka gradually came to supplant the appellation, waka. Tanka became the new and improved version of waka, so to speak. Saito Mokichi continued the tradition of Manyo poetics in the important tanka journal *Araragi*, and throughout the twentieth century there were attempts to expand and revitalize the tanka even further. Poets produced proletarian tanka, surreal tanka, social-reform tanka, and other varieties of the genre; they also experimented with syllabicity, emphatic spacing, and lineation.

In Japan at present there are tanka columns in the major newspapers. Tanka are transmitted via cell phone, and there are internet *utakai*. There has also been a resurgence in the study of tanka in primary and secondary schools. The card game, *Hyakunin Isshu*, based on the anthology edited by Fujiwara no Teika, is still played during the New Year season. Every January the Emperor and Empress present their own poems to the Japanese nation in a ceremony known as the *Uta Kai Hajime*. In all of the above cases (short poem, courtly poem, modern poem, internet poem, and imperial poem), the form of the tanka-waka has remained the same: 5-7-5-7-7 sound units. Carmen Blacker, the British Japanologue (1924-2009), referred to this prosodic scheme as having a magical quality and being related to the genius of the Japanese language itself.

A Note on Method

I first peruse secondary sources (volumes of tanka in English) and choose examples that appeal to me or illustrate a point. I then compare the English version against the *romaji* (transliteration into roman letters) and the *kana-kanji* of the original. If I feel the translation measures up, I retain it. If I feel it does not, or that the poem could sustain a new look, I re-translate it. I then discuss the translation, whichever it is, plus the original, with Japanese colleagues and associates. I ask a host of questions relating to grammar, meaning, feeling, quality, etc. The process is harmonious and fruitful, and I have learned loads from such talks. (A colleague sang one of the tanka for me.) These discussions, conjoined with my readings, contribute to the views I advance in the commentaries.

But now to the tanka themselves . . .

In the Garden Palace, in the Curved Pond, the roaming water-birds long for men's eyes and do not dive.	Shima no miya magari no ike no hanachi tori hito me ni koite ike ni kadukazu
(Tr. Ian Hideo Levy)	(Kakinomoto Hitomaro, *Manyoshu* 170)

Hitomaro, the author of the tanka above and a person of whom we know virtually nothing, is generally viewed as the greatest poet of the *Manyoshu.* The above poem of his, superbly translated by Ian Hideo Levy, is the coda (*hanga*) to a longer poem about the death of a prince. The tone of both the *choka* (long song) and *tanka* (short song) is elegiac. What is striking are the final two lines, which have a haunting quality. Rather than avert their gaze, the water-birds long to make eye contact with humans; rather than dive, they remain on the surface of the pond (*ike*). In other words, the birds are thought to be affected by the prince's death. As in many great elegies, both east and west, nature mourns along with humanity. The *k* sounds in the Japanese (*koite, ike, kadukazu*) punctuate the poem. There is something simple but deep about Hitamaro's tanka. Levy's translation is a little artwork in itself.

On this night that is cold	Awa yuki no
With the light snow	Niwa ni furi-shiki-
That has fallen and spread over the garden	-Samuki yo wo
Unpillowed by any hand-pillow	Ta-makura makazu
Am I to sleep alone?	Hitori ka mo nemu?
(tr. Arthur Waley)	(Yakamochi, *Manyoshu*)

Yakamochi (d. 785) was a senior counsellor of state and his poetry is known for its subtlety. He was one of the compilers of the Manyoshu and is ranked among the 36 Immortal Poets. His tanka above has for its setting a cold winter night (*samuki yo*). The garden (*niwa*), a locus of growth, is fallow and under a layer of light snow (*awa yuki*). The speaker is sleeping alone: *Hitori kamo nemu*. The line (old Japanese) expresses uncertainty and is plaintive. He has no one to give him comfort (to pillow his head). The poem breaks 3/2. The first three lines describe the external world and the final two the internal world, which is one of loneliness. As with all good poems, Yakamochi's waka is *situated*; it has location. (In lesser works we don't always know where we are.) Arthur Waley (1889-1966) who translated this tanka was one of the last century's great Orientalists. He was also a member of the Bloomsbury set.

	Tsurugi tachi
I dreamed I held	mi ni tori sou to
A sword against my flesh.	Ime ni mitsu
What does it mean?	Nani no satoshi zo mo
It means I shall see you soon.	Kimi ni awamu tame
(tr. Kenneth Rexroth)	(Lady Kasa)

Not too much is known about Lady Kasa but she had twenty-nine waka in the *Manyoshu*, all centering on the topic of love and all directed at the same man.

That is, Otomo no Yakamochi, the author of the preceding poem translated by Arthur Waley. Lady Kasa's waka here is a *Traumdeutung* before its time. She imagines (*mitsu*, sees) in a dream (*ime,* now *yume*) that she has put a sword (*tsurugi*) to her person (*mi ni*), and she interprets this as a portent that her lover will be coming presently (*kimi ni awamu tame*). Her feelings are "edgy" if nothing else. (Other waka by her support this point.) Rexroth's translation, in four lines rather than the customary five, ably brings across the turbulent nature of the Lady's passion.

Note: Kenneth Rexroth (1905-1982) was one of the leading figures in the San Francisco Renaissance of the 1950s and an important promoter of tanka. This translation and *romaji* text were published in *100 Poems from the Japanese*.

This night of no moon	Hito ni awamu
there is no way to meet him.	Tsuki no naki yo wa
I rise in longing--	omoiokite
My breast pounds, a leaping flame,	Mune hashiri hi ni
My heart is consumed in fire.	kokoro yakeori
(tr. Donald Keene)	(Ono no Komachi, *Kokinshu*)

Ono no Komachi is one of the most iconic figures in Japanese history and literature. She was a talented poet, reputed to be beautiful, and known for her passionate nature. She appears as a character in several No dramas. This tanka is from the *Kokin waka shu*, the famous Heian anthology edited by Ki no Tsurayuki. The poem is nicely translated by Donald Keene. The setting is a dark moonless night (*tsuki no naki yo*). Komachi cannot meet with her lover (*hito ni awamu*), and she becomes overwrought. Pounding breast (*mune hashiri*), heart on fire and charred with emotion (*hi ni kokoro yakeori*), etc.

I wondered if the emotion wasn't excessive and I put the question to a few Japanese acquaintances. One response was that the display of passion was something new at the time of writing. Komachi was breaking the mould by expressing herself so overtly. Thomas McAuley of Sheffield University has written that Komachi's waka "is judged to be the most direct expression of a woman's desire in the entire canon of classical poetry."

If only when we heard
that old age was coming
One could bolt the door
Answer, 'Not at home.'
And refuse to meet him.

(tr. Arthur Waley)

Oi raku-no
komu to shiri-seba
kado sashite
'Nashi,' to kotayete
Awazara-mashi wo!

(Anonymous, *Kokinshu*)

Anonymous san had a sense of humor, but there is a ruefulness to his poem as well. The light tone is cut by the conditionality of the phrase, "if only" (*shiri-seba*). If only we could bolt the door (*kado sashite*) and say "not home" or remain silent and not reply (*nashi, nai*, nothing) - but we can't. Both Arthur Waley and Donald Keene have translated this waka, and their versions are practically identical. The candid tone of the poem is refreshing, especially in that it occurs among the many lachrymose love poems that populate the *Kokinshu* (wet sleeves, gossip, romantic contretemps).

Note: Arthur Waley and Donald Keene are great names in the field of Japanese literary scholarship. Though some of Waley's scholarship has been superseded, he remains a model of the brilliant autodidact. (He once remarked that he would rather be dead than be a Cambridge don.) Keene is still writing and has recently published a biography of Masaoka Shiki.

He said of himself at the outset of his career that he wanted to be "half Waley." That is, that while Waley was expert in both Chinese and Japanese literature, he, Keene, was going to focus on only the latter. Keene is a master of the anecdote, and I would highly recommend his autobiography, *Chronicles of My Life*.

Now that they have aged--
these grasses under the trees
at Oaraki Woods--
no horses come to eat them,
no reapers come to cut them.

(tr. Helen Craig McCullough)

oaraki no
mori no shita kusa
oinureba
koma mo susamezu
karu hito mo nashi

(*Kokinshu*, #892, Anonymous)

The waka above, *oaraki no*, is a poem from the *Kokinshu* in which the anonymous poet muses on the natural setting at Oaraki. The tone is melancholy. The verb, *oinureba* is variously translated as withered, aged, tinged with age. Because the grass (*kusa*) is no longer flourishing, the area is a lonely and unfrequented one: no ponies (*koma*) graze, no reapers (*karu hito*) labor. The parallel punch at the end is very effective: *koma mo, hito mo*. McCullough's translation of the *Kokinshu*, which I have dutifully worked through, is quite good all around.

Note: Bill Higginson discussed McCullough's translation in conjunction with his own and one by Edward Seidensticker in the journal *Five Lines Down* (1995). "Oaraki no" is alluded to in *Genji Monogatari* where it said to have been transcribed on the hand-fan of the aged courtesan, Naishi. Seidensticker's two volume translation of the *Genji Monogatari* was published in 1976.

On this spring night, the floating bridge of my dreams has broken away: and lifting off a far peak-- a cloudbank trails into the sky.	Haru no yo no yume no ukihashi todae shite mine ni wakaruru yokogumo no sora
(tr. Steven D. Carter)	(Fujiwara no Teika)

Fujiwara no Taika is one of Japan's greatest waka poets, and *haru no yo no*, which appears in the *Shin Kokinshu*, is probably his most famous poem. The waka divides 3/2, the *kami no ku*, or upper part, about the spring dream (*yume*), and the *shimo no ku*, or lower part, about the lifting of the cloudbank (*yokogumo*). Scholars differ as to the interpretation, but it seems clear that Teika intended a connection, if not a correspondence, between the waking from the dream of the floating bridge ('*ukihashi*') and the clouds separating (*wakaruru*) from the mountain. *uki* is the same kanji that occurs in *uki-yo-e* (picture of the floating world), the term for the Japanese woodblock prints. (The *yo* is a different *yo*.) The use of the character *uki* arguably hints at a Buddhist connection. The floating world, *ukiyo*, is said to be impermanent, like a dream of reality, whereas enlightenment is permanent and irreversible. (*ukiyo* is sometimes used as a dismissive term, though the locution is old-fashioned.)

In any case, Teika's poem works on a primary level without requiring us to drift into metaphysics, at least not straightaway. Steven Carter, the scholar and haiku poet, has translated the poem deftly and poetically. The translation comes from his book, *Waiting for the Wind*.

Though a swift stream be	se o hayami
By a rock met and restrained	iwa ni sekaruru
In impetuous flow,	Takigawa no
Yet, divided, it speeds on,	warate mo sue ni
And at last unites again.	awan to zo omou
(tr. Clay MacCauley)	(Emperor Sutoku)

Emperor Sutoku's waka is from the *Ogura Hyakunin Isshu*. The translation was made by Clay MacCauley and dates from 1917. A boulder (*iwa*) obstructs the fast (*hayami*) flowing stream (*se*), dividing it (*warate*) in two. When the water has passed the boulder, the stream comes together again on the other side. "Unites" is a good rendering of *awan.* The Japanese is a little more tentative, however. "*omou*" would indicate "hope/think." That is, one hopes what has been sundered will reunite. The emperor Sutoku was exiled late in his reign, so presumably the image relates to his own situation. MacCauley (1843-1925) of whom I know little (a photograph, a few biographical details from the internet) was a missionary and a professor at Senshin Gakuin in Tokyo. Among his publications was *An Introductory Course in Japanese*. His translation, though somewhat dated, possesses a certain charm. It is in 57577 syllables.

Even a person free of passion	kokoro naki
would be moved	mi ni mo aware wa
to sadness	shirarekeri
autumn evening	shigi tatsu sawa no
in a marsh where snipes fly up	aki no yugure
(tr. Burton Watson)	(Saigyo)

Saigyo, the famous medieval wandering monk (and one of Basho's heroes), was the author of this waka which was included in the *Shinkokinshu*. The important phrase in the poem is *kokoro naki*, which Watson translates aptly, "free of passion." Literally, it means no heart or lacking heart. It refers to a person who has subdued his passions (conquered his feelings). Saigyo's point is that even such a person would be affected by the fluttering of the snipes (*shigi*) on an autumn evening (*aki no yugure*). Keene has also translated the poem and he uses the singular, "snipe." I have visited the area in Oiso, not far from Tokyo, where the incident in the poem is reputed to have taken place. It is low-lying and toward evening a bit soggy and damp. R. H. Blyth lived in Oiso and one of his daughters still resides there

Note: Burton Watson has translated many texts from the Chinese and Japanese. He has written an autobiography, brief and in essay form, titled *The Rainbow World*, which I have read and would highly recommend.

Awakened by the wind
that rattles the rice leaves
Of this mountain village--
I hear the call of the deer
in the dead of the night

(tr. Michael Fessler)

Yamazato no
Inaba no kaze ni
Ne-zame-shite
Yo fukaku shika no
Koye wo kiku kana

(Minamoto no Morotada)

Minamoto no Morotada (12th c.) served as an officer in the Imperial Guard, and his waka was included in the *Shin Kokinshu.* The setting of the poem is a mountain village (*yamazato*); the time is the deep of night (*yo fukaku*); the event is the speaker's waking from sleep (*nezame shite*); the denouement is the sound of the deer's cry (*shika no koye*). The belling of the stag is an autumn *kigo* and evokes the feeling of loneliness (desire for a mate.) The waka has the traditional 3/2 divide. The final two lines contain a plethora of *k* sounds. There are seven of them! The best I could do was two *d* sounds. (I was tempted to use *descry* for *kiku*, which would have extended it to *three*, but "descry" pertains more to vision than auditory effects.) I have used Waley's text from *The Uta*. Notice the slightly dated transliteration of *koye* for the now standard *koe*.

Our lives,
This way or that,
Pass just the same.
Whether in a palace or a hovel
We cannot live forever.

(tr. Susan Matisoff)

Yo no naka wa
Tote mo kakute mo
Onaji koto
Miya mo waraya mo
Hate shi nakereba

(Semimaru, *SKKS*)

The waka above is attributed to the legendary blind poet and musician, Semimaru. The first line, *yo no naka wa*, which turns up fairly often in waka and which Matisoff has translated as, "Our lives," means "in the midst of this world." The *mo-mo* construction (both/and) occurs twice and, according to Matisoff, would have been considered infelicitous in courtly circles. Nonetheless, the waka has a nice resonance to it. Waley, who also translated the poem, rendered the final line as, "Come to nothing in the end." I think I would put it: "There is a limit to the span of life." Semimaru played the biwa, or Japanese lute. He was the subject of Noh and kabuki dramas and a play by Chikamatsu. Matisoff's translation comes from her book, *The Legend of Semimaru*, which contains much information and is enjoyable reading. She is a professor at UC Berkeley.

Hail strikes
the warrior's wrist guard
as he straightens his arrows,
on the bamboo field of Nasu.

(tr. Janine Beichman)

Mono no fu no
yanami tsukurou
kote no ue ni
arare tabashiru
nasu no shinohara

(Sanetomo, *Kinkaishu*)

Minamoto Sanetomo, the third Kamakura shogun, wrote this waka, and it comes from a 17th century supplement to the *Kinkai waka shu* (the Golden Pagoda Tree Waka Collection). I first encountered the poem in Beichman's useful *Masaoka Shiki His Life and Works*. A warrior (*mono no fu*) is adjusting his arrows (*yanami tsukurou*) during a hail storm (*arare*) on a bamboo field (*shi no hara*). It is a manly outdoors scene. Shiki felt that Sanetomo's poem possessed the Manyo spirit, one that he believed was superior to the so-called "feminine" sensibility exhibited in the *Kokinshu*. Sanetomo has been referred to as a military man or "soldier-poet." That's certainly the image derived from some of his poems. On the other hand, he was dominated by his mother (albeit, a tough woman, aka, the *ama shogun*), he was an alcoholic (Eisei the monk tried unsuccessfully to convert him to tea-drinking), and he was assassinated by a relative in front of a gingko tree at the foot of the Hachimangu Shrine in Kamakura.

In my begging bowl
violets dandelions
all mixed together
my offering to the buddhas
of the Three Worlds

(tr. Michael Fessler)

Hachi no ko ni
sumire tampopo
kokimazete
miyo no hotoke ni
tatematsuritena

(Ryokan)

Ryokan (1757-1831) who wrote this waka was a Zen monk known for his eccentrically simple life style. He was referred to affectionately as *Taigu* (Big Fool). The speaker in the poem, presumably Ryokan himself, has gathered in his begging bowl (*hachi no ko*) violets and dandelions (*sumire tampopo*), and they are unsorted (*kokimazete*). "Slim pickin's" perhaps. In the final two lines, however, he declares that these flowers will serve as his religious offering. He refers to them without using any type of connective: *sumire tampopo*. That is, "violets dandelions." This gives the line a feeling of childlike simplicity. The epithet "Three Worlds" (*miyo*, or *sanze*) refers, according to Burton Watson, to "Desire, Form, Formlessness."

It is a pleasure
When, without receiving help,
I can understand
The meaning of a volume
Reputed most difficult

(tr. Donald Keene)

Tanoshimi wa
Yo ni tokigataku
Suru kaki no
Kokoro wo hitori
Satorieshi toki

(Tachibana Akemi)

This waka by Tachibana Akemi (1812-1868) is from a series (*Doku-Raku Gin*, or self- pleasures) in which all of the poems begin with the same phrase *tanoshimi wa* (it is a pleasure). The delights enumerated (one in each waka) are such things as using a writing-brush skilfully, completing a poem, viewing blossoms, having a delicious piece of fish for dinner, finding a character like oneself in a book, encountering someone who is patriotic. In the waka above it's the satisfaction of understanding by oneself (*hitori satorieshi*) the heart of the matter (*kokoro*) of a difficult (*yo ni tokigataku*; the world can't figure it out) piece of writing (*kaki24.3*). It's that QED feeling. The kanji *toki* (when) is actually the last word in the Japanese text. For me it is a pleasure to read about Tachibana's pleasure. He was not well known during his lifetime. It was Shiki who drew attention to his work. Keene has translated the poem in an unforced 5-7-5-7-7 format.

Lynne Rees

Haiku Uncut

Take a look through any haiku journal or anthology and the majority of haiku will be constructed from a fragment preceding a phrase, or vice versa. They might be composed over the usual three lines or along a single line. The *kire,* the cut or caesura, may be explicit in the form of punctuation, or suggested by line break, or by phrasal construction, as in this fine monostich example from 'Blithe Spirit' 24.2 where the natural breath pause after *rock-and-roll* is obvious when read aloud:

rock-and-roll she outdid me that summer

Frances Angela

The American haijin, Jane Reichhold, was instrumental in articulating and disseminating this structure, both online and in her accessible and informative handbook, *Writing and Enjoying Haiku, A Hands-on Guide* (Kodansha International 2002). 1 American haiku poet, Michael Dylan Welch, also includes the following advice in one of his essays 2 *Giving your poem two fragmentary parts is also one of the most important things to do in haiku.* And that advice can result in haiku like this deceptively simple and effective one, from the same issue of Blithe Spirit:

a cup of tea
he thanks me for the things
I wish I'd never said

Naomi Madelin

But what of the less common 'uncut haiku'? Haiku that appear to be 'all of one thing': Haiku that read fluently from beginning to end with no punctuation, or explicit or implied pauses. Are they as successful and effective as their fragmented siblings? How do they work on us? What choices have their creators made? Take Jack Kerouac's well known:

In my medicine cabinet / the winter fly / Has died of old age 3

There's no *kire.* No phrasal construction within the lines. We have a simple declarative sentence extended over three lines. Kerouac wrote this in the 1950s, decades before the fragment and phrase structure had been so firmly adopted. But does it still work as a haiku today? It does for me because there's enough juxtaposition of image and idea within the haiku to pull me, intellectually and emotionally, in a number of ways.

There's the irony of something dying in a medicine cabinet. There's the moment where the human experience mirrors a no less insignificant experience in the insect world. There's the suggestion that death comes to us all despite our attempts to keep it at bay. And there's the precision of 'my' cabinet, making the moment personal, juxtaposed with 'winter' which contains and symbolises the universal experiences of ageing and death.

The haiku, unusually, also communicates the passing of time: for the fly to die of old age suggests that it has been there a while, perhaps during the passage of winter into spring. And the passage of time is also felt in the following uncut haiku by Ken Jones:

These hills
have nothing to say
and go on saying it

This complete sentence, combined with the personification of the hills, risk aphorism or, if you have some knowledge of Ken Jones' background, the philosophical whiff of Zen. But what rescues the haiku from those pitfalls, for me, is the use of colloquial language in the final line. We talk about people 'going on' about things, about being on their soap-boxes, so the haiku comes alive as a natural part of our daily lives. The personification is diluted and convincing too if we have ever walked in silent hills and felt the business of our own minds drop away in their presence.

Is this haiku imbued with *mu*, the allegedly inexpressible mood that we try to express as 'no-mind'? Perhaps it contains *ma* as well: the space for us to enter and to complete it in our own minds.

I have used the following haiku by Nick Avis in several writing workshops:

> *deep inside the faded wood a scarlet maple*

This isn't a sentence, due to the absence of a verb, but it still reads continuously from beginning to end. Read it aloud and notice the pattern of stressed/ unstressed syllable repeated six times, or trochaic hexameter:

> deep in/side the/ faded/ wood a/ scarlet/ maple/

The trochee is a fairly common metre in children's rhymes which makes the line subconsciously comforting. But the haiku's full effect is completed by the juxtaposition of lack of colour (*faded*) and colour (*scarlet*) and its opening words: *deep inside.* They read like a secret: an invitation to discover what is hidden from view.

My penultimate uncut haiku is by the late Martin Lucas:

somewhere
between
Giggleswick and Wigglesworth
I am uninspired

Again, this is a complete sentence, arranged over four lines, but like the best free verse poetry it has an effect on us even before we begin to read it. The form is 'all over the place': it sprawls and hesitates, reflects the subject matter of a haiku poet hunting for inspiration in the landscape. And like the best comic writing it utilises specific techniques to entertain: playful language – the inarguably funny sounds in the names of two North Yorkshire villages – and the unexpected direction of the final line.

Roberta Beary's haiku is a simmered reduction of seven words and ten syllables:

hating *him*
between *bites*
of unripe plums [4]

The absence of any pause between the lines allows for the concentration of emotion to be communicated, to be felt when we read it: from the breathiness of aspirated h, the punch of b and p and the sharpness of t. Anger, frustration, tension: they're all contained in those sounds and their repetition.

I am also persuaded by her decision to balance the present continuous tense with the plural of plums. The hate doesn't end with the eating of one plum: it continues through the eating of several, perhaps many.

There is no overt juxtaposition here, an element we have come to expect in haiku, but unpick the language a little more. Consider the eating of fruit, in particular a woman eating fruit, and we can't help but think of the biblical myth of Eve blamed for humankind's downfall in the Garden of Eden and all its associated ideas. Old Testament v 21st century: perhaps we're not that far apart.

The uncut haiku asks us, as poets, to pay close attention to our craft: to the shape on the page, to rhythm and sound, and to the language choices we make in relation to what the haiku is about, what we want it to achieve and to avoid. And while there is still so much more that remains to be said within the confines of prescribed form, whether that is fragment and phrase or the more traditional 5/7/5 syllable count, departing from a recognised path to explore another offers its own rewards for the reader and for the continuing critical haiku debate.

1 http://www.ahapoetry.com/Bare%20Bones/BBless5.html
2 http://www.graceguts.com/essays/haiku-checklist
3 This and subsequent 'uncut haiku' examples all taken from *Haiku in English, The First Hundred Years*, eds. Jim Kacian, Philip Rowland & Allan Burns, WW Norton & Co, New York & London 2013.
4 From *The Unworn Necklace* (Snapshot Press 2007 & 2011)